THE
DOG
IS
US

AND OTHER OBSERVATIONS

MARCELLE
CLEMENTS

PENGUIN BOOKS

PENGUIN BOOKS
Viking Penguin Inc., 40 West 23rd Street,
New York, New York 10010, U.S.A.
Penguin Books Ltd, Harmondsworth,
Middlesex, England
Penguin Books Australia Ltd, Ringwood,
Victoria, Australia
Penguin Books Canada Limited, 2801 John Street,
Markham, Ontario, Canada L3R 1B4
Penguin Books (N.Z.) Ltd, 182–190 Wairau Road,
Auckland 10, New Zealand

First published in the United States of America by
Viking Penguin Inc. 1985
Published in Penguin Books 1987

The following essays first appeared, in different form, in periodicals: "The Dog
Is Us" and "A Soldier's Life" in *Rolling Stone*; "Terminal Cool" and "The
Risks of Rock: Sting" as "Alas Poor Sting" in *Esquire*; "Why I Hate
to Go Below Fourteenth Street" as "With Malice Towards Everything
Below Fourteenth Street" in *The Village Voice*; "Technofear,
Technolust, Technoambivalence" and "They Can't Take That Away from
Me" in *Revue*; "The Night They Stared into the Gazpacho" in *Vanity
Fair*; "What Happens to Pretty Girls" as "The Model Game" in
Mademoiselle; and "Klaus Kinski" in *Playboy*.

The "Ladies Nights" series and "A Rendezvous with Sloth" first
appeared in *The Daily News*. Copyright 1981 New York Daily News
Inc. Reprinted by permission.

Extract from " 'Helpless Feeling' Rate Goes Down," *USA Today*.
Copyright 1984 USA Today. Reprinted with permission.

LIBRARY OF CONGRESS CATALOGING IN PUBLICATION DATA
Clements, Marcelle.
The dog is us and other observations.
I. Title.
[AC8.C5557 1987]   081   86-15136
ISBN 0 14 00.8445 2

Printed in the United States of America by
R. R. Donnelley & Sons Company, Harrisonburg, Virginia
Design by David Connolly
Set in Primer and Gill Sans

Contents

The author would especially like to acknowledge the collaboration of Gerald Howard, senior editor at Viking Penguin, who conceived of and edited this collection; to express her affectionate gratitude to Amanda Urban of International Creative Management; and to offer special thanks to Alan Weitz for special help.

INTRODUCTION

ALL the people I've ever loved have been exiles. Exiles from somewhere or something they came from and could never return to, or from some place on the map or in the mind they yearned for and never got to at all.

Exile is a state both painful and cheerful. Homesickness is painful, but freedom is cheerful: sometimes it's sad not to belong anywhere, but it's liberating too. In the end, exile becomes the place where you belong, and you can come to feel it's not such a bad home.

I am an expatriate myself, though, as I say, the map is only one aspect of exile. But I am glad that I have two citizenships, and that I have two passports, which I consider a minimum. My parents often had more than two, under various names, though at one point in his life my father had none at all, which was most inconvenient at the time since France was then occupied and Jews were being rounded up along with other riffraff.

My parents were expatriates in Paris when I was born, soon after the war. The community I knew as a child comprised people who were, so to speak, compound exiles. Born in Eastern Europe, many had been exiled from one Western European country after another until they came to France, and they had then spent the war years in exile, either in hiding or in the camps, and so none of these people ever felt safe, or at home, again. For years, in many of the houses I knew, a suitcase was kept, fully packed, in a spare room.

I really don't know what it means to Americans when they hear that two-thirds of Europe's Jews died. "Two-thirds" is such an innocuous expression. But I knew many of the shadows of the two-thirds. I was intimately acquainted with their aura, with their names, their personalities, their quirks, and, from salvaged but already yellowing photographs, their faces and their wardrobes. All the rooms of my childhood were crowded with the shadows of those who would have been my grandparents, aunts and uncles, cousins. In my own room, there was always present the shadow of my brother, whose bed I slept in, whose books I read, and whose name I had been given. The shadows hovered behind the chairs of the survivors at the dinner table, who still ate and drank and laughed. But, always, there was talk of the war. These people were obsessed by the war. To this day, it is impossible to have dinner with French Jews of a certain generation and not hear, at some point, a sentence that starts with the words "During the war..." I hate when they do that. I hate all conversations about that war. I hate all the gut-twisting tales of horror as well as the anecdotes of close calls, cunning, triumph. I try not to think about that war, and in fact this is the first time I've ever written anything about it. I wish they'd stop talking about it.

I know why they do it, though. It's because, like me in these pages, they cannot explain themselves without it.

Well, enough of that. The point is that there was a peculiar mixture, in that place and time, of melancholy and cheer. Exile from the places and the people they had loved made some people, like my mother, sad for the rest of their lives. Others, like my father, acquired a ferociously tenacious sense of humor. Their children would be, as I am, particularly confused as to whether life is sad or funny.

There are plenty of people who have this same confusion: you needn't have two passports or be born to expatriate survivors. I know people who have lived in the same place all their lives who don't really belong there, and who are confused as to whether this is sad or funny. And I know plenty of people who have gone from one place to another of their own free will, and never found what they were looking for. Many of them don't even know what they are looking for, or have no words for what they seek, or try to forget that they are seeking anything at all. This quest is an old theme, but it seems to me that it is worthwhile to explore it in this country at this time. The people I'm speaking of are an increasingly alienated minority. I know their alienation because they are my friends, and they are the people I like to write about.

I don't really ever feel comfortable, or safe, with the others. The others frighten me, because I know that among them are those who are capable of callousness, of cruelty, and some-times of atrocity to defend what they believe they belong to, or what belongs to them, and those who will commit any act, no matter how ruthless, to be sure to stay on the winning side. I prefer the other side, though it only occasionally wins. In my writing, what I like to do best is to try to convey pictures from this other side, although I often do so indirectly. In this book, I address the subject directly in the first and last pieces, but all the other pieces probably tell the same story, each in its own way. Generally speaking, I try not to be depressing about it. In fact, I don't find the subject of alienation depress-ing in and of itself. At least, it's a form of struggle against the status quo, and therefore, in my view, ultimately an expression of hope.

Homelessness is a great advantage for a writer, as is the always packed suitcase, as a metaphor. And I think that bi-culturalism is an advantage too, because it magnifies the jour-nalist's inherent dualism: the distance of the "I" of the narrator from the "them," "him," "her," "it" of the subject. But then I like to contradict that dualism, even to contradict my dualistic self, and sometimes to speak of "we" or "us," against another "them."

I'm not sure whether I'm explaining or justifying the kind of semi-alien approach I use to my subjects. To be frank, it's the only writing I know how to do. My first professional jour-nalism was written for *The Paris Metro,* an English-language biweekly published in France by a crew that you could characterize as either cosmopolitan or motley, and which I still miss for its enthusiasm, tolerance, and eclectic ingenuity. This was in the mid-seventies, and I had just moved back to Paris. In part because I had spent my adolescence and early twenties in the United States, in part because I wrote in a foreign language (and therefore thought mode) and for an expatriate publication, I cast a semi-alien glance on my native country.

So when I returned to New York in the late seventies and began writing about American subjects, it was in the same spirit. This semi-alien spirit allows me to be in (at least) two places at once in my mind, which is the only way I am comfortable. Or, rather, comfortably uncomfortable.

Biculturalism, though, causes some problems too: malapropisms or, I sometimes fear, misunderstandings of character. Sometimes I wonder if I can really understand Americans, without knowing the texture of their childhood. I try to bone up. I've dutifully watched reruns of old TV shows and read the Anglo-Saxon children's books. But I know it's too late. I'll never perceive these images the way my American friends did when they were children.

Of course, I knew a bit about America when I was a child. Like children everywhere in the world, I knew, for example, of American cowboys and Indians. After all, I'd read *Le Dernier des Mohicans,* by James Fenimore Cooper, and I also knew a song that began:

Il y avait un homme qui s'appelait Davy
Il est né dans le Tennessee.

The refrain was:

Davy, Davy Crockett,
L'homme qui n'a jamais peur.

But it was really a very vague idea I had of this country, and I know that, despite all my research, I will never catch up. I keep trying, though. I'm always curious, for that reason, about my American friends' childhoods. The differences are often comically drastic. In the fifties, their mothers wore pedal pushers, Orlon, a lot of beige, they tell me; I often saw my mother in black-and-white taffeta, burgundy moiré. They had mechanical or electric toys; I had a wooden hoop, with a stick. I was taught to curtsy when introduced to an adult; they merely said "Hi." My treats were glazed chestnuts, cubes of sugar dipped in coffee or brandy; they had Twinkies and Devil Dogs. For fun, I read the novels of Balzac; they watched "Ozzie and Harriet." I wore tormentingly itchy woolen stockings; they had bobby sox. When I had a cold, I was subjected to mustard plasters and cupping glasses; they only had to endure Vick's VapoRub. I dressed up as an eighteenth-century countess for Mardi Gras; at home, they knotted towels around their necks and pretended to be Superman. You see, I've learned quite a lot. But there's always a new bit of information that comes up. It's only a few weeks ago, for example, that I heard that all the men my age, now in their mid-thirties, wore, as boys, coonskin caps.

"Coonskin caps!" I exclaimed to a friend. "But that's so undignified. A little French boy would have considered it to be a mortifying punishment to have to wear a coonskin cap."

"You don't get it," he said. "Everybody had one. You *had* to have a coonskin cap."

"I guess it must have something to do with David Crockett," I said.

"Not *David*," explained my friend. "Davy. Davy Crockett."

I was annoyed at myself. I should have remembered that, from the song. Anyway, I added the coonskin cap to my data bank. I feel it's a revealing detail.

People often ask me if I think in French or in English. "Both," I answer. "It depends on whom I'm talking to." Occasionally, someone will ask me what language I dream in. I dream in both as well, but my dreams are linguistically confused sometimes: Americans are speaking French, and vice versa. This typifies my greatest worry about myself as an observer: that maybe there are some details I get wrong, because I view them in an incorrect mode.

But, as a rule, it doesn't bother me very much that I'll never be completely American, or that I can never be completely French any more either. In fact, when I'm in a good mood, I like it. Sometimes I even feel I do have a place I belong to, a home that exists somewhere in the interstices of the exchanges I have with people I love, or in my fantasies, or in my memory.

Just this morning, sitting on my living-room couch, I went home to Sunday morning in Paris in the fifties, when my father and I would stroll together to the market. My hand in his, I walked, as I thought, daintily, because he had pronounced it unladylike to skip. We ambled for a while along the market street, admiring the tidy rows of fruits and vegetables waiting to be placed on hanging scales balanced by lead gram and kilogram weights by the peddlers, who wore, in fall and winter, fingerless gloves, until it was time to go and my father selected a nosegay of violets to bring home to my mother, which I was permitted to carry on the way back. In the autumn, the sky was that luminescent gray-blue, like the sky of no other place or time; the street smelled of bread and Gauloises and dark coffee, like no other city's street. This is home to me, and I went back there just this morning, though I know that the street market is now long gone, and there are no more violets, and my father is dead, and someone must have long ago discarded that apartment's pink silks and deep green velvets among which my mother waited for us to return. My big sister was practicing the piano while her fiancé listened. My sister would often laugh when she made a mistake. In those days, my sister sometimes laughed so hard she'd cover her face with her hands, and her laughter was so irresistible that the man who was soon to be her husband would start laughing with her. All this time later, I remember his rather difficult laugh; only now, though, it occurs to me that it may have been his first in years. Then my sister would uncover her face, and wipe her tears off with her fingertips.

I remember too how my mother smiled when my father told her she was beautiful, a thousand times more beautiful than the violets. That particular smile of my mother's, my mother's real smile, was rare and precious, and I can still see it lingering then on her very red lips; she wore her hair pulled back by small combs embedded with tiny pearls, and had on black-and-white taffeta, or burgundy moiré, or a white linen dress with little cherries, bright red like drops of blood, embroidered near the neckline.

My father would leave the room to wash his hands, and return fragrant of a soap the name of which I have forgotten and which I have not smelled in twenty-five years. "Children!" he would thunder to all of us at large, startling my sister from her piano playing and me from my reverie. "To the table!" Though, of course, he spoke in French. *"J'ai une faim de diable!"* he would declare. In English, you'd literally translate that as: "I have the hunger of a devil!" But, no, I guess it doesn't work in English.

PART ONE

PICTURES FROM THE OTHER SIDE

THE RISE OF THE MUTANT ELITE

ERE, in my opinion, was the most irritating newspaper item of the year, this sad year of 1984:

"HELPLESS FEELING" RATE
GOES DOWN

Special for USA TODAY

The number of us who feel alienated and powerless has declined from an all-time high of 62 percent last year to 55 percent this year, a new Louis Harris Survey reports.

In the last year, the number who agree that:

■ "The rich get richer and the poor get poorer" has gone from 79 percent to 74.

■ "What you think doesn't count much anymore" has declined from 62 percent to 57.

■ "The people running the country don't really care what happens to you" has dropped from 57 percent to 48.

Frankly, I'm devastated that only slightly more than half of us still have the "helpless feeling." I guess that lately I've come to be pretty defensive on this subject. I mean, I think there are still quite a few people who feel the way I do, who have a predilection for the helpless feeling, but, as this poll all too clearly demonstrates, our numbers are dwindling. Maybe I should just resign myself: there's so much goading to be Positive in the culture that the ranks of the alienated will continue to be sadly diminished, day by day.

It's no secret that the message of our time is: "You too can be young, rich, powerful, thin, and beautiful." In this decade, the message has really reached its infuriating zenith. I don't know about you, but I'm really sick of having the message yelled at me. "Let it reveal the splendor of you..." coos a recent perfume commercial at full volume. Everybody knows the Hidden Persuaders have come out of hiding, but—are there no limits?! I wish the President would stop purveying the message: it makes my blood pressure rise to hear him peddle it in his best stage voice. I wish I never had to see another self-actualized blond starlet lob the message into the airwaves from a talk-show armchair: "I accomplished a lot in my career," one of these twenty-two-year-old pathetic specimens with nothing to show for her life but a cleavage will declare, "when I learned to be Positive about myself."

I was thinking about this last night, while I was watching television, maybe because whenever I watch television I get the helpless feeling, or at least worry about getting it.

But, of course, if you turn on a TV set at all these days, you generally get what you deserve. Last night I saw a spot for a show, the nature of which I didn't quite understand except that it seemed to have something to do with diet and exercise, hosted by a man named Richard Simmons. In the excerpt from his program, this strange person, this Richard Simmons, dressed in bunnylike exercise togs, was maniacally exhorting a group of overweight women to engage in various aerobic maneuvers. While the poor women struggled to touch their feet, he leaped up and down and shouted encouragement: "Do it for me!" The high point of the spot came at the end. On a cue from this maniacal bunny, the women, still painfully bending over or creakily stretching up, yelled, all together: "I CAN DO IT TOO!"

This was patently untrue. These women *cannot* do it. They shouldn't even be *trying* to do it. They will *never* do it. Some-

body should tell them that. Somebody should tell them that
what they are being indoctrinated to hope for is not that they
will lose a few pounds, but that they too can be Young, Rich,
Powerful, Thin, and Beautiful, and that this is what they're
yelling about when they yell "I can do it too!" Somebody should
tell them that instead of being on television shouting their
pitiful paean in unison to a nationwide audience, they should
be dieting and exercising with a modicum of dignity in the
privacy of their own neighborhoods, or even sitting at home
eating chocolates and reading Erich Von Daniken. I mean,
anything except making this spectacle of themselves. But
then, I find the spectacle heartbreaking, and maybe this is
my problem. I know, of course, that the spectacle is meant
to be not heartbreaking but inspirational. (It's also meant to
satisfy sadistic voyeuristic needs, but that's in addition.) The
spectacle invites the viewer to share these women's determination to be Positive.

I don't know why I'm picking on these poor women as an
example. I guess they're so transparent they make an easy
target. But at least they're powerless. The Positive attitudes
that really frighten me are in the board rooms, in Washington
and in Hollywood.

Mind you, it's "Positive" I object to; I wouldn't mind "positive." I don't mind positive or determined or hopeful or romantic or idealistic. "Positive" is not hopeful but hopeless, not
romantic but cheaply sentimental, and not idealistic at all.
For me "Positive" is tragically cynical.

So that's why the decline of the helpless-feeling rate makes
me pessimistic about the future. Maybe soon *everyone* will
be Positive. *Everyone* will be shouting together: I CAN DO IT
TOO! This, I have to say, is tragic. This is devastating. This is
terrifying. This is, no kidding, the end of the humanist tradition.

All indications are that the momentum of the Positive message is now unrelenting. Witness the decline, according to
the Louis Harris poll, in the number of us who feel "alienated
and powerless" from 62 percent last year to a mere 55 percent
this year. What's more, these statistics paint a Positively rosy

picture. After all, if you think of that 55-percent figure in terms of the American population, you get, I think, more than 110 million people. Now, forty million of those people, I figure, have the helpless feeling simply because they are living in abysmal poverty in the richest nation on earth. In fact, since that's the "official" poverty line, you'd probably be safe if you doubled the number. Then you'd have to calculate all the people who were having such a bad attack of the helpless feeling that they didn't answer the phone or the doorbell when the Louis Harris people called. Plus you'd have to figure in all the people who have no phone or doorbell, who have, as matter of fact, no home for the Louis Harris people to call on.

My arithmetic may be unsound, since there'd be overlap among the groups, but, anyway, you get the idea: that leaves very few of us who have the helpless feeling for emotional, aesthetic, philosophical, or disinterested political reasons. And if the percentage keeps going down at this rate, we may be witnessing an inexorable trend, the final result of which will be that almost *no one* will have the helpless feeling.

Granted this is the land of the pioneer spirit, of Ralph Waldo Emerson, of Werner Erhard, but how did things get so out of hand?

In truth, it seems to me that in the chaos of our society, *everybody* should have the helpless feeling. To begin with, there are the same old practical and metaphysical problems that have been giving people the helpless feeling for millennia anyway. When you add the current dilemmas of our culture, of our technologies, of our seemingly unsoluble social problems, you come to the conclusion that the basic old human organism just wasn't designed for this sort of thing, you know? So what happens then is that nature, as always, takes its course: there occur mutations in the species, and the fittest survive. This Mutant Elite does *whatever* is necessary to survive. Mutant Elites are Positive. Their motto is "Go for it!" Their battle cry is "So sue me!"

Other favorite clichés of theirs are "Stay on top of the situation" and "I'm OK, you're OK." (Mutant Elites love a cliché: it saves them thinking time, so they can devote themselves completely to scheming as to the best ways to "Go for it.") It's useless to tell them you are *not* OK, not in the least OK in the world they are creating; they'll only declare, "So sue me," or, depending on their personal style, start chatting to you about bootstraps and so forth, and informing you that you should be "Positive" and "Go for it!"

In a way, I prefer the straight-ahead "So sue me" style to the bootstrap-chat style. At least it's direct. The "Go for it" mentality is often articulated in a deceptively maudlin idiom, expressed with chest high and eyes lifted to great rhetorical horizons, but it is in truth the policy of ruthlessness. And even when they attempt to camouflage themselves with a projection of facile sentimentality, the Mutant Elite cannot hide their pride in the knowledge that they are in fact hard-boiled men and tough women. They do not have the "helpless feeling": they are too busy acquiring power and money.

"But," you may say, "what else is new? There have always been power- and money-hungry brutes, sleazy hustlers, unscrupulous misers."

Well, yes. But they weren't *admired*.

"Think of John D. Rockefeller," you might say, ignoring me. "Think of Sammy Glick. Think of P. T. 'There's a sucker born every minute' Barnum."

Well, yes. But that kind of behavior wasn't the *norm*.

"There have always been ruthless company men," you might say. "Think of the fifties."

Well, yes. But think of the sixties.

"So they won. So sue me!" you'll then say if you are a Mutant Elite. If you are not a Mutant Elite, you will by now be suffering from a severe attack of the helpless feeling.

The most prominent Mutant Elites are probably in Washington and in Hollywood, but we know that they are everywhere, in every field. There are welfare caseworkers, orchestra conductors, even zoologists who are Mutant Elites. There are sports stars who are Mutant Elites, hospital administrators, plenty of local-government officials, and lots of hairdressers. Even the professions once officially designated as "humanistic" have been invaded: there are now plenty of scientists who are Mutant Elites, and doctors, and, God knows, dentists. There are academics who are Mutant Elites, museum curators, and clergymen and rabbis who are Mutant Elites.

They are everywhere, and the rest of us have no choice but to cohabit their world, and sit around having the helpless feeling.

I am not a Mutant Elite. I am a fuck-up. My friends are fuck-ups too. They could call themselves humanists (in fact, the last of the humanists, if you're thinking about this when you're in a particularly gloomy mood), but most of these people are too insecure to call themselves anything so grandiose as a humanist. So what you'll hear in the course of a telephone conversation is not the plea, "I'm a dinosaur; I'm among the last of a dying breed and I don't know how to function in this new world," but the wail, "I'm such a fuck-up. Why can't I get it together?"

We don't tend to run in packs, like Mutant Elites, but many of us do try to stay in contact with one another, in order to attenuate the severity of the degree to which we suffer from the helpless feeling. So there are places where we tend to congregate, usually dismissed by Mutant Elites as little eccentric communities that have long been left behind, downbeat enclaves for fuck-ups. (It's a contemptible state, in the view of a Mutant Elite, to be "downbeat," that is, not to be "upbeat." Mutant Elites *loathe* anything downbeat, unless there is a buck to be made from it or, better yet, a megabuck.) I live in a place where there is still a fuck-up enclave—New York—though these days my friends and I worry a lot that we're being pushed out of even this niche. It's become evident that the Mutant Elite population density is rising here too.

"Women from Texas," one of my friends complains. "These women come here from Texas. They leave all their roots behind in Big Bend, Texas, so they have nothing else to do but pursue their careers with the most unrelenting ambition. They're terrific hustlers and they have incredible energy. Someone like me, who's much more talented but lazier, doesn't have a chance. There's no room for the lazy any more. It's a crime."

It's true there's no room for laziness any more. But it works the other way around too: being compulsive about the quality of your work is equally absurd, according to Mutant Elite criteria. "Will it play in Peoria?" is the crucial query, whether they are talking about cereal packaging, politics, or art. In fact, art has become the purview of the Mutant Elites to such an extent that I don't even want to talk about it. It'll make me feel too depressed to continue. Let's face it, I'd sound too Negative.

Another remark Mutant Elites are always uttering to one another is: "Let's talk bottom line." I don't just mean among business associates. Husbands and wives, *lovers* talk to one another this way.

Here's an anecdote that people dined out on in Los Angeles a couple of years ago. A Hollywood executive and his wife-to-be were in the process of negotiating a marriage contract. She was pregnant at the time; that's why he was marrying her. He wanted to stipulate in the contract that if she had a miscarriage or if their marriage ended before a period of one (1) year was over, whichever first occurred, his obligations to support her financially would terminate. She refused these terms. Their lawyers spent weeks negotiating, as the wedding date drew near. Naturally, a big Power Wedding had been planned: canopies, canapés, etc. The day before the wedding, the Hollywood executive's lawyer called and said: "She won't go for it." The executive then shouted into the phone: "The DEAL is OFF!"; and then slammed down the receiver and resumed taking his meeting.

I think this story is true: I heard it from someone who heard it from someone who was in the executive's office at the time. If it isn't true, it might as well be, since it's the sort of tale with which Hollywood raconteurs regale one another every day of the week.

I could give you other examples. But I bet you know many of these tales, no matter what field you're in. You know who they are. (Or who you are...) They know who they are. And they have no qualms about it either. "What's the deal here?" they're always asking.

The "deal" is now a metaphor for every relationship. It's the entrepreneurial spirit gone berserk. But people forming alliances, whether in "love," or in "friendship" for the sake of convenience and financial considerations, that is, in order to survive, is not the exclusive purview of people in the entertainment business. In New York City, for example, there are plenty of people with broken-down marriages who stay together because of the housing shortage. They too have a "deal." They too are thinking "bottom line." Not the least telling of the clichés being flung about these days is the ubiquitous "negotiation." In fact, all over the country people have come to find it natural to speak of "negotiating" personal problems. In our culture, a declaration that one is willing to "negotiate" a solution to problems in a relationship is considered to be a sign of mental health. A *relationship!* What ever happened to the love affair? Nonnegotiable, I guess.

Some might say these clichés are insignificant, merely banal. But I think there's something to the notion that an epoch's buzzwords are its emblems and, like its arts and its fashions, the clues to the texture of its reality. So it's interesting to note that Mutant Elites also are fond of using the expressions "You gotta pay your dues," "Never mind the details," "a piece of the pie," and "cashing in." Some are known to terminate telephone conversation with the words "Love ya, baby, gotta run."

Mutant Elites admire greed and are amused by cruelty. In the music business, for example, where there are many, many Mutant Elites, this recycled joke made the rounds not too long ago:

Question: What are the three biggest lies in rock 'n' roll?

Answer: The check is in the mail; I'll fix it in the mix; and I promise, I won't come in your mouth.

Some of the less overtly coarse, more sophisticated Mutant Elites may talk a smoother game, but that's the basic idea: moral parameters are a big joke.

They think it's cute to call someone by the name of some killer fish. If you attend a Mutant Elite dinner party, you will hear anecdotes in which various persons are affectionately referred to as sharks, piranhas, or, the recent favorite, barracudas. "He's such a barracuda," a Mutant Elite will say, with grudging admiration, of a colleague.

They use a lot of jock talk too. Mutant Elites consider it praise to say that someone "plays hardball." After all, that's the guy who'll wind up with the corner office. And they love lawyer talk. All of the Watergate phrases, for example, have passed into the Mutant Elite vernacular. They love to talk about "stonewalling" and "letting someone twist slowly, slowly in the wind."

In all interactions between Mutant Elites and fuck-ups, the latter are sad and silly putty in the formers' hands. Both Mutant Elites and fuck-ups know this, which turns the fuck-up into an anxious wreck and gives the Mutant Elite a pleasurable sensation of staying "on top of the situation." But, despite the ego-soothing benefits of experiencing this quasi-erotic sensation, Mutant Elites hate to have to deal with a fuck-up. They have complete contempt for fuck-ups and their time-wasting helpless feeling. The only reason a Mutant Elite will deal with a fuck-up at all is either that he is obligated to by law, or that he needs a skill the fuck-up has, or that the fuck-up has a contact the Mutant Elite wants (which then turns the fuck-up himself into a contact).

If you are wondering why a fuck-up will deal with a Mutant Elite, you should know that this is a question fuck-ups often ask themselves and one another. "I can't take these people any more," one fuck-up will lament to another. "Why should I have to deal with this?" My guess is that, as a rule, fuck-ups deal with Mutant Elites either because they are obligated to by law or because they persist in believing that they will discover some loophole in the Mutant Elite machine that will enable them to survive in a humane way in the world of the Mutant Elites without becoming one of them. In fact, once in a while a fuck-up will succeed in accomplishing this, which gives all other fuck-ups hope for a while and the urge to Keep Going (to "Keep Going" is the fuck-up's prayer, not to be confused with the odious "Go for it!") until they remember what the odds are against this achievement and sink back into a fit of the helpless feeling.

Mutant Elites know this. And, as a result, they are always telling fuck-ups not to worry. As soon as a Mutant Elite says "Don't worry," a fuck-up with any brains at all goes into an immediate fight-or-flight reaction.

"Don't worry!" a Mutant Elite will croon in his most soothing voice, at which point the fuck-up starts to feel adrenaline splashing wildly from one neuroreceptor site to another. "We're not going to let you twist slowly, slowly in the wind." By now the fuck-up knows he will be picking hemp out of his teeth for years.

Every fuck-up knows he or she must tread his way with fear and stealth in the world of the Mutant Elite, especially when the fuck-up has a skill or a contact the Mutant Elite wants. The fuck-up always recognizes this situation, because that is when a Mutant Elite will adopt the oleaginous crooning style that is the unmistakable clue to imminent disaster for the fuck-up. Of course, Mutant Elites have clichés for the oleaginous mode: they call it "massaging" or "stroking."

But few fuck-ups are so stupid that they don't know when they are being stroked. Stroking makes a fuck-up's anxiety level rise exponentially, because he knows that at the end of the negotiation, the Mutant Elite will be on top of the situation, and the fuck-up will be, naturally, on the bottom, lying in the gutter as usual. A fuck-up therefore quickly becomes *hysterically* worried in the course of these encounters.

My friends and I spend a lot of time worrying together about such things. In fact, worrying together takes up a large segment of our nights out. Whereas Mutant Elites will spend an entire evening discussing Steven Spielberg's grosses. As a result, it is now dolefully unfashionable to spend an evening with your pals pleasantly torturing yourselves over ethical issues, the kind of stuff that's been used for centuries to keep people busy on winter nights. Some die-hards still waste hours talking about politics or art. However, they feel pretty guilty about this. In their hearts, they know they should be talking about show business or real estate.

I get a good deal of consolation out of dolefully unfashionable fuck-up conversations. They give me the sense that at least we stick together. In fact, we mourn when one from our ranks defects to the other side. The tip-off to an impending defection is some version of the phrase "It's not so bad to be commercial" (translation: "Will it play in Peoria?"), uttered in an unambivalent tone. We all know it's not so bad to be commercial, but a bona-fide fuck-up will always stay ambivalent and worried as to what his priorities are. In truth, it's partly because of this ambivalence that defectors are mourned. For example, I have to admit that some of this mourning takes the form of whining and complaining at the amount of cash the defectors have. And, sometimes, fame, though, as a rule, fuck-ups are too embarrassed to refer to fame: they much prefer to speak of "recognition."

At any rate, we have team spirit. Mutant Elites have no team spirit whatsoever. Mutant Elites have absolutely no pity when one of their own makes a slip. If there is anything a Mutant Elite has more contempt for than a regular fuck-up, it is what they call a "wash-out," or a "has-been," that is, someone who used to be a Mutant Elite but has had a single failure. Most has-beens do not have the helpless feeling, however, because they know that with a single success they can claw their way once more into the Mutant Elite fold. Then they are no longer has-beens; they are said to have made a "comeback."

Writers are always being told by Mutant Elites not to worry. Writers, by and large, are fuck-ups. They are often also babies, and that would be beside the point except that, several times, I have heard Mutant Elites remark that "writers are such babies." They actually complain about this *in my presence!* These people are really shameless.

There is, of course, an increasing number of Mutant Elite writers, but I am relieved to report that most writers are still fuck-ups. That's why writers get agents. Agents are Mutant Elites, except for a handful who are fuck-ups and don't even despise writers for being babies, but who have learned to put on a great show. They can talk Mutant Elite language with the best of them, and in fact sometimes get into it to such an extent that they even forget themselves when they're talking

to writers and start using phrases that strike terror and confusion in a fuck-up's heart, like "bottom line," "the property,"
"hard/soft deals," and, worst of all, "Don't worry."

Many of my friends are not at all resigned to being helpless
fuck-ups. As I pointed out, there is powerful pressure in the
culture to be Positive. So there are numerous renegades who
don't want to be taken for fuck-ups; at the very least they
want to *appear* to be Mutant Elites. In between fits of the
helpless feeling, these people nourish ambitious plans to hoist
themselves out of their plight. I think these perennial would-
be defectors fall into two categories.

The first is those who by sly and relentless industry, sheer
overwhelming talent, or simply serendipity have managed to
succeed in acquiring the position and appearance of Mutant
Elites. Some of them even have full-time office jobs and a
hefty amount of Mutant Elite perquisites, like Money and
Power. But the proof that they are still fuck-ups and not Mutant Elites is the proportion of insomniac hours that they
spend *worrying* that they have become Mutant Elites. Whatever insomniac time is left over, they spend worrying about
various other moral considerations. As I hope I've made clear
by now, spending any time at all, insomniac or otherwise,
worrying about moral considerations is a sure tip-off to a fuck-
up. What's more, these people feel terribly guilty about whatever Mutant Elite perks they have managed to acquire and
don't even realize how glad and grateful other fuck-ups are
that they have a "contact" in the Mutant Elite world who will
be sympathetic to notions that a bona-fide Mutant Elite
wouldn't consider for a second. You can always spot one of
these fake Mutant Elites, because they are willing to empathize with a fuck-up's worries, concerns, and hopes, *even
when it is against their best interest!!!* Thereby, of course,
breaking the first and most important rule of the Mutant Elite
code.

The second category is those who have had it with being
fuck-ups and truly wish to turn themselves into Mutant Elites.
They will proclaim this to anyone who will listen and start
babbling in Mutant Elite language about "Going for it" and

so forth. But they don't have a chance. Because, deep down, they still feel like fuck-ups. True Mutant Elites never feel like fuck-ups. Never. At worst, they complain that they "blew the deal." But blowing deals doesn't make them feel like fuck-ups; it only gives them an irresistible urge to "recoup." True Mutant Elites not only never feel like fuck-ups, they also blame anything that doesn't quite go their way on other people's being fuck-ups, and perpetually express their contempt and irritation or, at best, condescension for these deadbeats.

"You're afraid of success," a Hollywood M.E. once had the gall to say to me. The funny thing is, this guy was trying to be helpful. Not that we were friends or anything. Mutant Elites don't have friends; though they sometimes have confidants or associates, mostly they stick with contacts.

Of course I'm afraid of success, you jerk. Success, in your terms, is something terrifying to me. Success is something I think about, analyze, try to explicate to myself. Success is something I *worry* about. Indeed, all of my friends who have any success spend a huge proportion of their insomniac hours tormenting themselves about having it, how they have to pay for it, whether they deserve it, and in fact spend a good deal of time listening to their psychotherapists explain to them that they don't have a "sense of entitlement." Mutant Elites don't have to worry about having a sense of entitlement. If they worry about anything, it is about how to get another buck out of a fuck-up, or a megabuck, or, in the spirit of art for art's sake, how to prevent another Mutant Elite from getting *his* megabuck, which they feel absolutely entitled to do, just for fun.

Ostensibly successful fuck-ups will often, in private, complain that they are "inauthentic," "not legitimate," and worry that they will be found out any moment. Or, worse, not be found out, which makes them feel ever guiltier about whether or not they are "legitimate." Whereas Mutant Elites declare, "I deserve everything I get." And what's amazing is that they mean it. But there was no point explaining any of this stuff to this Hollywood person. And, indeed, why should I? I mean, he wins: I have the helpless feeling; he doesn't. And not only does he not have the helpless feeling, but he has the cash to boot. I guess my problem is that I wish I had both. I still haven't figured out how to do it, though, so, by Mutant Elite standards, I personally have very little cash. And what's worse, I keep it all in checking.

Anyway, what's the point of trying to explain anything at all to someone who wakes up in a good mood because he's screwed someone else out of a deal the day before. Indeed, what would his degree of condescension have been if he knew that the kind of thing that puts me in a good mood is reading the chapter entitled "The Nature of Matter" in Bertrand Russell's book *The Problems of Philosophy*. In this chapter Russell speculates for pages and pages about what proof there is that, when you see a table, there really is a table; he finally concludes that if you think you see the table, there *is* a table. This is the sort of thing that will reinvigorate a fuck-up for as long as an entire day.

Do you think a Mutant Elite ever wonders whether a table is real? Of course not. If he sees a table, he puts down a line of coke and snorts it. Or uses it to reconcile his checkbook. Or something. I have to admit I don't know much about their personal habits, but if there is a certainty in this world, it is that these people do not waste a second of their time thinking about whether the table is real or whether anything is real or unreal. Fuck-ups are always saying things like "This is unreal" about subjects running the gamut from the prospect of nuclear war and the to's and fro's of U.S. troops to the quality of consumer goods or consumer culture. For Mutant Elites, thinking that any of this is unreal is as preposterous and time-wasting as thinking about whether or not the table is real.

In fact, it may be a misnomer to call what Mutant Elites do "thinking." They don't think, they scheme. They don't have ideas, they have plans. They don't have passions, they have hang-ups.

Sometimes I think: "*All* this is unreal. All this is the nightmare incarnation of some weird science-fiction concept." Indeed, *Brave New World* was published back in 1932. And, as Aldous Huxley declared some twenty-five years later in *Brave*

New World Revisited, "The most distressing thing that can happen to a prophet is to be proved wrong. The next most distressing thing is to be proved right."

We've been warned about the perils of modernity for the last century and a half. But we didn't listen, or we listened but were helpless to alter the course of events. Now a lot of people are writing commentaries on the chaos of our culture and on the disintegration, diffusion, or dispersion of the old values and structures. Some of these commentaries are optimistic about what the new structures will be; others are terrifying. Some remind the reader of the flames in which Rome perished; others speak of a brave new postindustrial order. I can never decide which I agree with.

"But," as I recently remarked to a friend, "it doesn't matter what I decide. Hardly anyone listens to these commentators anyway, because no one who writes a book that can't be made into a screenplay has any credibility these days."

"That's a cheap shot," he said.

"Why?" I queried somewhat belligerently. We were halfway through dinner. I'd had a bit to drink and was feeling rather rowdy.

"Irony is a cheap shot. It's just evasion. In fact," he said, "I read somewhere that irony is to the twentieth century what sentimentality was to the nineteenth."

"Where did you read that?" I asked.

"I forgot," he said. (Typical fuck-up answer. Mutant Elites are always ready with facts, names, and dates when they want to win an argument, even if they have to make them up.) "But it's true," he insisted.

"But what else is there," I demanded, "besides irony?"

"Passion," he said. "Do you think people in Nicaragua are ironic?"

"But we're not talking about Nicaragua. This is America in the 1980s. What do you want?"

"Hope," he said. (He'd had a bit to drink too.) "Hope with a moral underpinning. Irony is no help if you want to get any legislation passed. Republicans are impervious to irony anyway."

Basically, my friend is right, I mean about wanting hope, and it cheered me up to be reminded of it. But I don't know that I agree with him that irony is no help. Sometimes it's the only weapon you have against even your own impending cynicism, at those moments when your mind really becomes the devil's playground, and when you start feeling, along with 57 percent of the people living in this country, that "What you think doesn't count." (Well, maybe it's not so bad: it's true we're down from almost two-thirds last year but, thank God, we're still a majority!) But you need all the irony you can muster when you start feeling that, as Kafka remarked, there's an infinite amount of hope, but not for us.

But, then, why quote Kafka? What are the odds of anyone's considering turning *The Penal Colony* into a screenplay? Actually, that suddenly strikes me as an interesting idea. Well, there you are: a typical fuck-up's project. This is the kind of project a filmmaker fuck-up—there are a few around—could stay obsessed with for a good ten, twenty years of his life. You can imagine what effluvia of derision would emanate from the cocktail parties of Beverly Hills at the very idea of such a project.

You may be wondering why I'm coming down so hard on Hollywood. It's true that the most dangerous Mutant Elites are neither in Los Angeles nor in New York. But as a writer I get to hear more gossip about the inner workings of Hollywood than I do about corporate America or Washington.

Of course, frankly, I'd have a lot to say about the invasion of the print media by the Mutant Elite. To tell you the truth, my friends and I are not so loftily detached from our environment (or solemn, for that matter) that we spend all our time talking about art and politics. As a matter of fact, in addition to other normal human conversations that include the usual scurrilous gossip and so forth, my journalist friends and I also spend many a dinner hour whining and complaining about the rise of the Mutant Elite in our field, and waste our time expressing impotent rage that so many of these people have power over us. Naturally, we don't call them Mutant Elites. We call them by various titles too scatological to repeat here. My journalist friends and I are always commenting on the decline of non–Mutant Elite journalism, and perpetually declaring to one another, "That's it! I'm through!," just before we accept one more assignment.

Sometimes I seriously consider this option. In fact, sometimes I sit around and think, "Why write at all? Why do anything all? What's the point?" Sitting around thinking there's no point is a typical fuck-up activity. Well, maybe I shouldn't restrict it to sitting. My favorite posture for this activity is sitting on the side of the bed with my head in my hands, but I know there are people who do it lying down, standing, or even walking around. But I think most people sit. The reason I know it's typical is that I sometimes worry that I'm the only one who sits around feeling this way, so recently I asked several of my friends if this ever happens to them and how often.

"Do you know that feeling when you're sitting around thinking, 'My life has no point'?" I asked various people.

"Yes?" they all said.

"How often do you have it?"

"Whenever I think," said one of my friends. "I have to keep busy all the time. As soon as I stop, that's all I think about."

"If things are going all right, I can go for as long as a week without thinking about it," says another. "But if something goes wrong at work or at home, I can spend as much as six or seven hours a day feeling that way."

"I know what you mean, but the problem doesn't present itself in that way to me," says another. "I have a 'How am I going to get out of this?' kind of feeling. Like: 'What is it going to take for me to somehow get through this shit?'"

"Of my waking hours? Sleep doesn't count?" queried a man. "I guess at least ten percent of the time. But even the rest of the time, I know life has no point. I mean, *of course* life has no point. That doesn't mean it doesn't have a point. Do you know what I mean?"

"Any time I think about whether my life has a point, I come to the conclusion that it doesn't," says a woman. "But, depending on what mood I'm in, I either think, 'Oh, who cares?'

or 'This is terrible.' It partly depends on how powerless I'm feeling. Yesterday I saw this bum on the street, and it was really cold yesterday, you know, and he looked like he was getting hypothermia. It was right outside my house, so when I got upstairs I called the police and I said, 'There's a bum lying on the street and I think he's in bad shape.' And the cop on the phone said there wasn't anything they could do about it, they had no cars left. So I said, 'But I think he's going to die!' And the cop said, 'Well, it happens every day.'"

"A lot of times, I think about it, and if I really start drifting into my psyche, it seems to me that there is no point," says a man. "But I know that there are little things that you can get involved in, that do give you pleasure and are wonderful, even though a lot of them don't really count for much in the big scheme. I think you can string some of these things along to make up a point. It's true, sometimes I think about the way things are, or even just about the universe and infinity, and I get this chill. But, I know this sounds corny, but if you think about helping someone, or about politics and that your actions can make a difference, then it seems as though there is even an argument for an activist life, and that makes you feel as if there's meaning in your life."

"I guess it comes in waves," says one of my other friends. "These days I feel that way most of the time. You know, our trouble, the trouble of people who have privilege, is that we're too introspective, because we aren't faced with problems of survival, like hunting for food and shelter and so forth. Besides, we spend too much time inside. William James, who was a very sensitive, privileged person, spent his whole life trying to figure this stuff out, and in the end he said, Get a job outside, something that's not too abusive, but in which you use your body and you're outdoors. Then you'll go to sleep at night." My friend sighed. "Maybe what I should do is get a job in marine biology or something."

"Marine biology?" I repeated incredulously. William James or not, this was really absurd. This is someone who hasn't been out of the city in so long he wouldn't recognize a fish if

he saw one unless it was in the form of trout amandine or a
real-estate barracuda.

"Sure," waxed my friend, growing enthusiastic. "Or think
of Jane Goodall. She has the perfect job. I could be out in the
bush studying chimpanzees or something."

Fuck-ups are always having fantasies of being elsewhere.
They're always talking about moving to Paris, to Rome, or
back to nature. The day after the election this year was particularly bad. "That's it. I can't stand it any more," said one
of my friends. "I'm either going to fight back or leave." He's
considering Penang, he told me, "or somewhere else in Ma-
laysia. Or maybe Singapore."

In the meantime, though, they continue looking for loopholes in the Mutant Elite world. If they find precious few
loopholes, they continue looking for the point. They do this
in secret, you understand. This sitting around with your head
in your hands is one of the best-kept, most unpublicized secrets in our Positive culture. These people talked to me about
it because they're my friends, and the consolation of friendship is one of the great loopholes, as are solidarity and compassion among those who sometimes have feelings of
helplessness. They know very well that there are many who
would only have contempt for them for having or expressing
these feelings, or would ridicule them, or take advantage of
them. They know all too well that there is nowadays a con-
certed pretense that these feelings don't exist or don't matter,
and that it's not Positive to wonder what the point of it all
might be. They told me only because I asked them.

I have my own solution to the "what's the point" quandary,
or rather, I've adopted someone else's. It somewhat resembles
Bertrand Russell's theory about the table, but it was thought
of much earlier and wrapped in more convoluted rhetoric by,
of all people, Pascal. In fact, this notion is usually referred to,
by whatever deadbeats there are left around who still read
this stuff, as "Pascal's Wager." Roughly translated from Part
II, Section III, of his *Pensées,* there's a passage that reads, "If
man turns away from himself in order not to contemplate the

misery of his condition, this misery is no less real: he must die." Now, this sort of lugubrious thinking naturally led theologians of that time to speculations about the usefulness of faith. Pascal's Wager is that you might as well have faith: if it turns out you're right, you're in business, you get a piece of the eternal pie; if you're wrong, there is no eternity anyway, and you haven't lost a thing.

Of course, I'm wondering not about the existence of God but about the existence of a point. We all know these are related queries, though. So Pascal's Wager is extremely useful to think about when you are having a fit of the helpless feeling. Even if there is no point, you might as well go on the assumption that there is one. And, you know, Keep Going. See also Existentialism—the same general idea and one of the great philosophical modes by and for fuck-ups who are having a hard time dealing with the helpless feeling and wasting a lot of hours trying to figure out whether there is even a point to dealing with it. Existentialism also has the merit (strictly for fuck-ups) of still being despised, after all these years, by many Mutant Elites of the born-again variety, who continue to refer to it, with an expression of disgust, as "secular humanism." But Pascal is quicker reading.

Then, once I've come to the conclusion to Keep Going, I start to feel much better about everything. Sometimes in these strange states I even get optimistic. For example, I tell myself that maybe there are a lot of fuck-ups who *lied* to the Louis Harris people. Maybe, like the women who yelled "I CAN DO IT TOO!" to the bunny, there are plenty of people who are merely engaging in wishful thinking. They too are miserable, and feel helpless and alienated; they just don't want to admit it. Then sometimes I get really *wildly* optimistic and start thinking that if you put all these helpless people together, there may at some point occur an event that will galvanize them to rise against the Mutant Elite and to defeat them.

I know that's unlikely, though. Let's face it, I tell myself when my mood swings back to a more realistic pessimism, the fuck-ups don't have a chance against the Mutant Elites. That's why they're fuck-ups in the first place. And lately, things seem worse and worse. Politically, for example, it's really doleful these days. I mean, not only did Reagan (who, as old as he is, is a prince among Mutant Elites) win this year's election by a landslide, but, even worse, the number of persons who think that "The people running the country don't really care what happens to you" has dropped from 57 percent to 48. Not even a majority. I guess there's no stake in it, and that's why there are so many defections to the Mutant Elite faction: those who have any choice in the matter are forced to do what is necessary to survive.

So then I get depressed again. They'll win, I tell myself. Their number will grow, and with it their ruthlessness and their power. They will inherit the earth. And then I think our fucked-up, sad, and lovely world will end not in flames, but frozen in the cold glint of our atrophied emotional responses.

But then sometimes I think I'm wrong about the Mutant Elite. After all, the adherence (or at least lip service to adherence) to humanist ideals hasn't produced such a great world. And it's not until recently that people openly started saying, "So sue me." It's not the overt, unashamed "So sue me" crowd that created the problems of modern times. It's the others. Whether they were hypocritical opportunists or sincere and well intended but incompetent, it's so-called humanists that got us into all this mess in the first place. So maybe when the Mutant Elite inherit the earth they will make it a better place. Maybe their children will create their own values, their own morals, their own beauty; not ours, but better suited to the future.

At least I try to tell myself that. But, frankly, just thinking about it gives me, you know, the helpless feeling.

On the other hand, I sometimes tell myself, nature is, as even Bertrand Russell would admit, mysterious. Some mutants pop up, hang around the universe for a while, and then disappear, because it turns out they aren't the fittest to survive after all. Then, some other mutation occurs....

THE DOG IS US

TRYING to recall the spirit of a certain epoch is often like describing a dream: it's easy to chronicle the events, but almost impossible to characterize the motivations. Yet every once in a while one runs into a telling artifact. Rewind to the past. There's a photograph of Allen Ginsberg taken in 1965 at a demonstration to legalize marijuana. He's standing outside the Women's House of Detention in New York during a snowstorm. There is snow on his hair and beard and his glasses, and he has on what appear to be earmuffs, but no gloves. He's wearing a fur-collared overcoat and a vaguely eupeptic expression. He's sort of waving (at the photographer? at America?) with one hand. With the other hand he holds a crudely felt-tipped lettered sign that says "POT IS A REALITY KICK."

Many of us who started smoking marijuana around that year agreed with Ginsberg, and in any event, the sign reminds one of the preoccupations of the time: Both "reality" and "kicks" were major concerns. And in search of new interpretations of either the former or the latter, thousands of us—eventually millions—turned on.

Fast-forward to the present. About 15 percent of all Americans are estimated to be marijuana smokers, and fifty-six million have tried it at least once. These figures have been published so often that it's easy to get the impression that marijuana smoking is one of the more secure sixties legacies.

Wrong. The trouble is that the statistics one always hears about relate to those who try or use marijuana. And the fact that those figures are staggering only makes it seem all the more surprising that a dramatic number of people have *stopped* using the drug. Remission (as the Washington statisticians call it) is occurring in all age groups and all classes of people. According to a 1979 National Institute on Drug Abuse survey in which respondents were asked whether they had ever used marijuana and whether they had used it in the last year, over 38 percent of former users now in their early twenties have stopped, over 48 percent of people twenty-six to thirty-four years old, 63 percent of people over thirty-four. Those are the categorical pot teetotalers. Add to these figures the vast number of former heavy users who now smoke very occasionally—only a few times a year—and you start to get an idea of a remarkable trend.

And why? Nobody knows. The phenomenon appears to be unremarked so far in the scientific or popular press. The statisticians and researchers in the field to whom I spoke when I first set out to write about this subject weren't even aware of the "remission rate" figures, which have so far remained dispersed and buried in the masses of government data about current marijuana use.

So what's going on? There are two possible explanations: either different types of people are smoking marijuana, or else something has happened to the people who used to smoke it. Or both. The drastic rise of "remission" with age seems especially significant: although more Americans of all ages are smoking more marijuana than ever, most of the very people Ginsberg was speaking for in 1965, the people who were college students in the sixties and whose heroes were the Beats and the blacks, the illustrious kids who initiated the popularization of marijuana among the middle class, who turned on America, those are the people who aren't smoking any more.

They're scared, they say. They get paranoid, anxious, stupid, bored, or physically disabled, they say. Some would rather snort cocaine, others would rather drink. A surprising number of the largest and most famous group of thrill seekers Western culture has ever produced say that in fact they would rather not alter their consciousness at all.

Paranoia or The Dog Is Us

In order to narrow the field a bit, I focused my attention on people around my own age, those I personally started smoking marijuana with, went to school with—or could have—in the mid- to late sixties. Persons in this group, perhaps in part because they're so often examined by the media, tend to be both articulate and self-conscious: they provide an unusually loquacious sample for this sort of inquiry. Their motivations almost certainly differ from those of other age groups or socio-economic classes, but it seems to me that they represent a good place to start looking.

The people I went to school with were the "heavy users" when it all started; they used to smoke marijuana to come *down* from other drugs. After a fierce LSD trip or a psyche-twisting speed bout, they'd light up a joint to cool out. Many of them would smoke first thing in the morning, and last thing before making love to the person they were spending the night with. The Ginsberg sign comes to mind because, as one of my old school friends puts it: "Hallucinogens were unreal and real life was unreal; it was when we were high on marijuana that everything seemed most real." At least from a historical perspective, one can't help wondering at the answer to this question: why is it that so many of the self-appointed shock troops of what some social scientists have called "the hang-loose ethic" don't want to touch the stuff any more?

To get the facts straight, despite all the grandiose talk about consciousness raising, and notwithstanding the insufferably predictable political-demonstration anecdotes from people who went to school in the late sixties, much of our time then was spent simply lolling about in indigent stupor. If you're the wrong age to have been in college at that time, or if you were too straight to smoke, here's your chance to snicker disdain-fully. If you're around my age, as humiliating as it may be, try casting your mind back to a typical stoned dormitory scene, the kind we individually enacted hundreds of times. Sitting in a shabbily furnished room, or maybe lying under a tree on a campus, there's a bunch of people in a state of pleasant quasi-stupefaction. They're listening to music and staring at the spaces between one another's heads. Maybe someone said something a few minutes ago, but most of the people there have either forgotten the last remark that was uttered or else are considering one by one the infinite number of repartees that might have been made. In any event, at some point in the proceedings a dog walks in. Wow. Naturally, everybody there looks at the dog. They actually become mesmerized by the dog; they can't stop watching it. And then, invariably, they start laughing. It strikes them that the way the dog is walking about, the way he sniffs, his rheumy eyes, his matted fur (fur!), or, especially, the way he sometimes stops and hesitates with one paw in the air, is somehow extremely funny. In fact, for some reason the dog's appearance and everything he does and even that he's there at all seems INCREDIBLY RIDICULOUS.

Of course, there were variations: some people used to watch their cat on catnip, some people used to watch their mom and dad, some people used to watch Lyndon Johnson, or Charlie Company hacking their way through the jungle, on TV. Almost anything or anyone could be the dog. Some people just used to lie down, look out their window, and laugh because the whole universe was the dog, but the point is that this was my generation's idea of a good time: to take note of the absurd and to laugh at it.

But now it appears that many of us can't take it any more. That's why most of the people I've talked to say they've stopped smoking: it gives them attacks of ego-chewing paranoia. Now that we're in our mid-thirties, what often happens when we get high is that we see the dog again, but now the dog is us. And it's not funny.

Rather than outward, the anxiety-ridden pot smoker's attention is directed toward self-scrutiny, eventually generating a kind of paralyzing self-consciousness. When I asked people why they had stopped smoking marijuana, many responded with wails of misery. It's not that they no longer have a desire for a recreational drug, these people say, but that turning on has come to mean opening a file at the emotional hard-case bureau.

One of my friends, a guy who used to buy dope by the kilo, says, "All the things that I used to like about being high just make me anxious. Every time I try it again out of the old curiosity, as soon as I get high I ask myself, 'Why did I do this?' My lower lip gets so dry it feels like it's hanging off my face. My heart starts beating really hard and it reminds me that I'm going to die. And I never want to tell the people I'm with how I'm feeling, because no matter how close friends I may be with them, I suddenly decide they couldn't care less. So I make up an excuse to leave so I can go back to my apartment and be by myself to think how I'm going to die. And I get absolutely compulsive about leaving. The last time it happened, I was in a car. I demanded to be let out and had to walk on the highway all night to get home."

Another of my friends, one of the many people who would *never* turn down an offer to share a joint, told me that now she's become too paranoid to get high in a group. For a while she continued to smoke, but only when she was alone: every night she'd put on earphones and get high, to unwind. But even those days are over. She declares: "If I get high with other people, I become convinced they think and have always thought that I'm pathetic. So I start saying things to prove I'm not pathetic, and then I think about the things I've just said and I realize I'm much more pathetic than they even think I am. It's worse if I'm by myself. I think about my career and it seems a total sham to me. I start reviewing my relationships with men and decide they're shallow and based on lies. I can't bear to look in mirrors. And the worse thing is that I feel that the perceptions I'm having are the correct ones, and that even when I come down I'll still feel this way. Fortunately, it's not true. And coming down feels *great*. Safety, at last. I'm never going to take it again. Who needs this?"

Pot anxiety has a peculiar characteristic: in its mild form, you can sometimes will it away, or, rather, remove yourself from it by making a sort of mental object of it to be examined and manipulated or discarded as you choose. Ideally, of course, the *anxiety* should become the dog. But when it strikes in its most ferocious version, many of us aren't able to laugh at our fears and make a mental object of our dread. We're sometimes just too tired or too bored or too sad or too mad or too frightened.

Enough Edge Consciousness, Thanks

One of the things marijuana researchers seem to agree about is that set and setting, the user's environment and the mood he's in when he starts to smoke, affect his emotional state once he's high. Whether we acknowledge it or not, our present lives may be so filled with stress, repressed and otherwise, that we can't afford to let go. The people I know have a hard enough time as it is without cutting these wide swaths in their emotional-stability quotients. "I don't want to be sensitized!!!" a friend fairly yelled into the phone when I asked him why he'd stopped smoking. "I want to be DE-sensitized! I'm OVER-sensitized as it is. That's the last thing I need!"

Suppose the simple truth is that, as a group, we suffer from deplorable mental health to begin with and that we simply can't afford to make waves. When we were merely youthful neurotics, part of the very point of taking drugs (I refer, of course, to hallucinogens—marijuana was *nothing*) was to prove to ourselves that we could go to the edge and come back. In fact, we learned to live—we deliberately trained ourselves to do so—in a state of perpetual edge consciousness. But maybe we've had too much of a good thing. It's not easy to forget that many of our friends checked out, or burned out. Those of us who managed to get through the sixties and its aftermath without either dying or otherwise irrevocably deteriorating always secretly figured we'd be better when we grew up. But now that we are—at least on paper—grown up, we find that we're better only by the most careful management of our unpredictable emotional resources. So even under the once-benign influence of marijuana, we simply can't afford to tap into our preconscious (at least not without supervision).

Research has shown that even though marijuana often has a deleterious effect on short-term memory, long-term memory can improve while one is in a state of intoxication. Now that we're older and have, uh, lived a little, we're carrying much more baggage. Lying dormant behind the bars of reserve memory banks are some grim, long-forgotten events, places in the unconscious emotional landscape we never want to visit again.

And besides, let's face it, when all you can think of is that you're going to die, that all your acquaintances think you're pathetic, and that you are, in short, a dull and worthless speck in the universe, you tend to lose your sense of humor.

Intrepid Tripper Declines Spliff

In many cases, even those still hardy enough to want to continue to hover over the precipices of consciousness have abandoned marijuana. One man I know loves drugs so much that I thought he'd never stop smoking marijuana. He's an intrepid tripper, an unreconstructed sensation-seeker who'll sample any bizarre chemical he can get his hands on. But he recently said to me, "Pot was the first illegal substance I had access to, and what a relief it was to start taking drugs! But since I found myself weeping in a muddy gutter in a Pakistani town, I never smoke weed any more. All it does is make me feel sad and lonely, and it has no compensating factors for me. Thank God, though, it *does* lead to other drugs! [Sic.] It's just a waste of time. With LSD you rocket, with pot you putter. With horse you soar, with pot you become petty and get hung up on your own ego. I believe in raping my mind, I really do. But pot just makes me ask myself banal questions with uninteresting answers."

Fear of Socially Unacceptable Behavior

It's been suggested that the reason for the well-known fact that many people do not get high the first time they smoke is that they don't know how to be high. Eventually, their friends show them how by teaching them a set of expectations. "The taste for such experience is a socially acquired one, not different in kind from acquired tastes for oysters or dry martinis," wrote pioneer marijuana-researcher Howard S. Becker in his 1953 study, "Becoming a Marijuana User."

Perhaps, similarly, once a pothead's friends stop smoking, he may become tempted to do so as well, not because his peers are exerting any undue pressure, but, rather (or also), because his acquaintances' reports of unpleasant experiences on marijuana cause him to change his expectations about his own highs. Ironically, therefore, many of us may be stopping for some of the very same reasons we began: the kind of high we get is influenced by what our friends tell us.

Here are some of the negative testimonials I've gotten:

—Cosmic Anxiety: "Remember that time when I took some mescaline and I was wandering around campus in a state of terror because I felt time had stopped? Every time I smoke marijuana it reminds me of that." (A number of studies show that the notorious acid-flashback syndrome can be elicited by cannabis.)

—Fear of Freaking and other socially unacceptable behavior: "Frankly, I never liked pot. But in the sixties it was just out of the question to turn it down. I'd developed this whole technique of sucking it in and holding it in my mouth without inhaling. But the last time I had it was at a Grateful Dead party at the Chelsea Hotel, and the stuff was so powerful it got to me. I became so oppressed I had to go hide in the bathroom. I locked the door and lay down on the tiles. People kept knocking on the door and saying, 'Are you all right?' It was horrible. Finally I emerged and made a fast getaway. It's the most humiliating thing that ever happened to me." (Once it was all right, even desirable in certain circles, to act weird. Now acting like a lunatic is considered antiquated behavior.)

—It's become a low-status drug: "When you see Wall Street bankers smoking on their lunch break, you know pot has had it." (A hard knock for the old psychedelic pioneer spirit.)

—Pot is the tool of a sexist society: "I guess I only smoked because my boyfriend did. After we broke up, I tapered off and finally just stopped thinking about it." (Men have always smoked more than women. The profile of the average heaviest user of marijuana in the late sixties was male, from an upper socioeconomic background, single but—interestingly—statistically more likely to be involved in a relationship of long duration than an occasional smoker or nonuser. [One could hazard some interesting speculations here....] Whether or not some of these guys are still smoking, their former girlfriends have gotten off the bus.)

—The Dreaded Amotivational Effect: "When we were at school, life just seemed like one big softball game, and it didn't really matter whether you were on the team or in the stands. Now, when I go to a party with my colleagues, I don't want to take the chance of becoming either so paralyzed that I don't want to talk to anyone or else too aggressive so that I'll botch up situations which should be handled with more subtlety. I feel I have to be alert now in social situations." (The expression "uptight," one of the most pejorative words in sixties lingo, is so irrelevant to our present needs that it's fallen into desuetude.)

—It's a drag to get it: "In the old days, you could buy it from your friends. Now you have to deal with professional pushers. It's not worth it. And there are better drugs than marijuana now. If you want mild euphoria, there's alcohol. If you want tranquilization, there's Valium. If you want a social drug, there's cocaine, though personally I don't care much for cocaine anyway, or for using drugs socially at all, for that matter." (If you're using drugs for therapeutic rather than social purposes, alcohol and pharmaceuticals are far more

convenient. They're easier to acquire, you can carefully reg-
ulate the dose, and you don't have to spend time scoring,
sifting seeds, rolling joints, and creating stashes in your home.)

—Who wants to hang around when the party's over?: "I
stopped smoking cigarettes too. Whenever I had any grass
around, I'd smoke it all up. I decided I hated being addicted
to anything." "It distracted me from my depressions. I'm more
depressed now, but I think I deal with things better." "I used
to love to mess myself up, to see how high I could get; now
I can't imagine wasting my time that way." "It just isn't a
thrill any more. And I can't work when I smoke." (An un-
expected symptom of adulthood: the urge to exercise self-
control. This syndrome is generated, in my view, by the recent
change in psychocultural predilections from the Dionysian—
ecstatic, intuitive—to a preference or, not to put too fine a
point upon it, a *craving* for the Apollonian, rational. Excess
seems passé, almost quaint.)

—Losing the habit of dissociation: "I don't want to smoke
all the time any more. I still get high every once in a while,
but I'm careful about how I pick my situations. I wouldn't
want to drool in public." (Occasional smokers have to exercise
prudence. In a way, it's easier to smoke more. It's not certain
whether one develops a tolerance to marijuana, but at the
very least, its effects are less shocking if you're experiencing
them on a constant, long-term basis. The people I talked to
who still smoke all the time tend to be prosaic about it. They
say they use it to function, though their evidence is fraught
with contradictions: "It helps me sleep" and "It helps me stay
up" are two reports I've heard. One guy I talked to told me at
one point in our conversation that he used it to stay alert for
work and, at another, to relax so he could sleep. It's just
possible that he may be right on both points, but I've decided
to discount this interview, since he was high at the time and
our discussion kept stalling during the long pauses while he
tried to remember answers to questions such as "When did
you start smoking?" To boot, he abruptly terminated the interview by saying that all he could think about was his tuna-
fish sandwich, and he'd have to call me back. In any event,

the people I spoke to who now smoke only occasionally tend
to be cautious. They often told me they had "rules" they followed: "Never at work"; "Only on vacation"; "Only at parties";
"Never at parties"; "Only to go to the movies"; "I make an
agreement ahead of time with my wife that if the phone rings,
she has to answer it.")

Wrong Answers and
Pot Research Perplexities

Many people haven't bothered to wonder why they've stopped
or cut down. For them, the change has come as naturally as
cutting their hair, throwing out their pea coats, and putting
the Moby Grape records in the closet. However, when asked
to ponder the question, many came up with one of these two
answers, which they often prefaced by saying "It's simple...":

1. *It's become a hard-hat drug. We've stopped because marijuana is now used by the same people who hated us in the
sixties. It doesn't go with our life style.*

Wrong. Statistics for remission show that blue-collar smokers are quitting with greater frequency than the people from
upper socioeconomic backgrounds or the so-called upwardly
mobile. According to a recent National Household Survey,
people who haven't completed high school are stopping over
20 percent more frequently than college graduates.

2. *It's just part of growing up. You get older and you have
more responsibilities and you can't afford to put yourself out
of commission.*

This is a conjecture I heard not only from former users but
also from a number of psychiatrists and experts in the field,
who patiently explained to me that these people were merely
"getting involved in what we call the social roles of adulthood,
which are incompatible with getting high every day." Well,
of course. But this factor alone is an insufficient answer. After
all, what about all the adults who only started smoking marijuana in the eighties? They don't seem to find getting high
incompatible with *their* adult roles. "It's true that there's a
big drop-off at around age twenty-six," says George Farnham,

national director of NORML. "But the total number of people smoking in America increases each year by the rate of about three million, and that increase is not from adolescent smokers, it's from the category of over thirty." According to National Institute on Drug Abuse figures, five out of six consumers of marijuana in America are adults.

There aren't any "simple" answers, and now that government funds for research in the field have been drastically reduced, we're probably not about to get any of the more complicated answers either. It is true that there seems to be a "maturation" factor at around age twenty-six, but the psychosocial and/or biochemical reasons for this have not been established.

It's possible, for example, that after years of marijuana smoking, it may be metabolized differently, the nervous system may react differently, or, plausibly, the sophisticated user's perception of the biochemical effects of cannabis may be different from the neophyte's (for better or for worse). If this were true, it would undoubtedly affect the complex mind-body relationship of marijuana intoxication. That is, if our physical response to marijuana changes after a number of years of use, our mental state may be consequently altered. Do long-time users of marijuana suffer a greater incidence of tachycardia, tracking difficulties, defective psychomotor functions? Or, on the contrary, do they develop, with tolerance to marijuana, an ability to compensate for these disruptions of their biochemistry, and therefore become jaded to the effects of the marijuana high? None of the scientists I spoke to knew of any research findings in this area. A recent Institute of Medicine report, *Marijuana and Health,* poses more questions than it answers, and its authors lament the lack of objective research material on the physical effects of marijuana (let alone mind-body problems).

In addition to the margin of error that exists in all new areas of scientific inquiry, the questions related to marijuana use are further obscured by the pro- or anti-pot bias of most researchers. And, finally, there is the problem of the complicated plant itself. "The major difficulty in any discussion of the

'properties' of acute cannabis intoxication is that the effects
of this herb are extremely variable and unpredictable—from
one occasion to the next for each individual, and, more strik-
ingly, from one person to another," writes Harvard psychiatry
professor Lester Grinspoon in *Marihuana Reconsidered*.

The Two-Tier Pot System Blues

To compound the confusion, the current proliferation of types
of marijuana available on the market has turned pot smoking
into a veritable mind-body Russian roulette.

"I know that many of these people still have a certain nostalgia for their marijuana days," says Robert Dupont, president
of the American Council on Marijuana. "But, with all due
respect, the marijuana they were smoking ten years ago was
a different product. It averaged two-tenths of a percent THC.
Today marijuana averages 5% THC."

Marijuana grades differ so much that estimates of actual
THC content (THC is cannabis's most active ingredient) are
anybody's guess, but undoubtedly the stuff is much stronger
now. Also, in the sixties the average joint was probably smoked
by half a dozen people (each of whom therefore got a pro-
portionately small dose). There was a time when it would have
been unthinkably rude not to share. Now it is not uncommon
to attend a dinner party where one person simply extracts a
prerolled joint from his cigarette pack and smokes it by himself, after a perfunctory gesture to the group at large. Marijuana smokers have come to expect that their companions
either are not smokers or are unwilling to try somebody else's
stuff when they don't know how strong it may be and how
they will react to it.

"In the sixties, when people were smoking Mexican, it was
much simpler, both financially and in terms of the high you
got," says Andy Kowl, editor of *High Times*. "In the seventies
people started smoking Colombian, but then the Colombians
got really greedy and started trying to squeeze in more growing cycles for their crops, which caused a decline in quality.

So now there's a two-tier pot system. At the low end, the pot is weaker than what the people you're talking about used to smoke. The crummy Colombian street stuff that's selling for thirty to fifty dollars an ounce is usually garbage. At the high end, the $150-to-$250-an-ounce sensemilla and so forth gives you a very intense, heady high. It's much more potent than anything that used to be available ten years ago."

In fact, a surprising number of the people who are still smoking are simply growing their own. One of my old school friends still smokes several times a week, but he told me that he sticks to his own homegrown and his neighbors'. "It's part of the clean-living philosophy in these parts," said my friend, who lives in a Maryland suburb, in a community of people he describes as "pseudo–blue-collar." Certainly, many oil riggers, cowboys, and construction workers, pseudo and otherwise, are still smoking reefer out there around the country, and carefully tending their marijuana crops. But the rest of us have neither the space, the horticultural skills, nor the inclination to do so. And we also have no interest in putting in the effort toward frequenting dealers, sampling exorbitantly priced products, and generally becoming dope-consumption connoisseurs (which brings to mind—perhaps unfairly—the sort of aging hipster who refers to getting hungry as "the munchies"). However, if we don't grow or purchase our own, but merely accept the occasional joint or toke now and then, we quickly learn that this sort of casual impulse-smoking can lead to spending around four hours grappling with the monsters of the id. Many of the unpleasant effects of marijuana are directly dose-related. And according to Robert Dupont's estimate of THC levels, the marijuana we're smoking now can be *twenty-five times* stronger than the stuff we grew up on. Undoubtedly this is a factor in my sample's "remission" rate, compounded by the fact that the occasional smoker is affected much differently from the regular user.

Several of the researchers I spoke to agreed that this hypothesis might be valid. One psychiatrist, however, scoffed. "Is it possible to imagine that these people simply aren't as adventurous as they might once have been?" he asked. "And besides, these are sophisticated users. Why don't they just smoke less of the stuff?"

It's entirely possible that we are, indeed, not as adventurous as we may once have been. In fact, as has been well documented by the many newsweekly articles on this generation, we may simply be becoming old, conservative, and boring. But whatever one's opinion of this debatable point may be, it is clear that being adventurous needn't mean being masochistic. Turning down a joint can mean avoiding expanding our vistas, as they used to say, but it may also be a perfectly healthy avoidance of pulverizing brain pain. Or anything in between, and *there's no way to know in advance*.

"I never know what to expect any more," laments a disgruntled ex-smoker. "One little toke can hit me like a ton of bricks. I can't stand being out of control like that. There was a time when I'd never turn down an offer to smoke. Now I often refuse. Then I watch the other people in the room get high and become catatonic and I know I'm right."

The question arises again, however. Why aren't all the *new* people turning on suffering from the two-tier pot system blues? What's different about the people who started smoking in the sixties?

Subculture Flags, Class Identification, and Bolinas

If you smoked in the sixties, as likely as not, all your friends smoked. When you went to visit someone in his dormitory room, you wouldn't be surprised to find him with one of those ubiquitous shoe-box tops, sifting seeds or something. At the time, this didn't seem so ludicrous. This guy was more likely to be your friend than the average straight-arrow mossback. You were attracted to people who smoked: you had more in common with them. Marijuana was one of the indicators of a certain subculture, a kind of freak flag.

Now we no longer need the really obvious indicators of the sixties; in any event, marijuana itself no longer indicates any

subculture we want to belong to. "I smoked marijuana because it was part of the community I wanted to belong to,"
says a former activist. "It went with long hair, rock 'n' roll,
and challenging the rationalist ethos of a decaying imperialist
structure. I wanted to be part of a community of people who
felt as I did. Marijuana was a crucial identifying factor. Now
that community is dead. Once marijuana was a sociopolitical
and philosophical gesture. Now it just means spending hours
in my room by myself looking for objects I keep misplacing."

That the "community," such as it was, no longer exists is
debatable. Certainly, many people suffer from sixties nostalgia, but in my view this may be due more to regret for their
youth than for the "community." Of course, we're more isolated, and many of us suffer from psychosocial loneliness.
But, aside from the ideal fantasy now and then, who wants
to stay in college all his life? In any event, I believe that the
old bonding devices have left their traces, and that marijuana
was one of the crucial ones.

Some might remember how we used to divide people according to whether they were "straight" or not. This was in
the old days, when "straight" referred to drugs and sensibility
rather than to sexuality. In the forties and fifties the term was
used to refer to someone honest, and not a drug addict. But
in the sixties it began to be used to refer to not being high
(as in: "I'm staying straight to study for my exam tomorrow").
Finally, it came to refer to someone who didn't smoke marijuana or take any drugs, and denoted that this person was
uptight, square, unhip, uncool, a potential drag, bummer, or
bring-down (depending on the year in the decade). If you said
about someone that he or she was straight, it was almost
always a put-down, at least among the people I knew, who
preferred to view themselves as being outside the "straight
world."

Interestingly enough, all of these people (including the ones
who no longer smoke) say they can still make that distinction,
although it is no longer necessarily a put-down. Almost all
the people I spoke to say they still, almost automatically, divide
people they meet into straight and nonstraight.

In the eighties, now that all of the obvious components are missing, the criteria for this peer-identification process are mysterious. None of the people I interviewed were able to state exactly what enabled them to separate the straights from the nonstraights now, but all of them said the registration occurred within seconds. "It's like the wink of an eye," says one of my friends. Perhaps, like all class and subclass distinctions, this disparity can be characterized by almost imperceptible and apparently insignificant visual and auditory clues: pants worn one size smaller or larger are a signal; a choice of jewelry sends a message; an ostensibly casual remark connotes an interior universe to the knowing interlocutor.

However, we're far more tolerant now than when we were adolescents—though whether it's because we're nobler or because we have no choice is another matter—and we no longer necessarily choose our friends or even our lovers on the basis of whether they're straight or not; or, rather, we have a new definition of "straight" and it has nothing to do with drugs.

Personally, I think that's a good thing. If two of that subculture's goals were avoiding "conformism" and respecting the dignity of the individual, these would not have been achieved if we had stayed together as a group. Witness the fact that the remaining sixties enclaves are for the most part dull, sad communities. As hard as it may be for some of us to face, all of that search for beauty and naturalness may have ended only in uniformity and ugliness.

"But have you ever been to Bolinas?" an old friend asked me after we'd spent some time pleasantly reminiscing about the psychedelic past. "It's a beautiful town on the Pacific, about twenty-five miles north of San Francisco. My wife, Linda, and I had heard that it had dramatic scenery, rocky cliffs, charming houses, that there were a lot of poets and artists there who were still living the so-called Life. We were curious, so we went. It was hard to find: Bolinas people are so intent on isolation that the signs have been removed. When finally we got there, we took a walk on the beach, and we suddenly noticed a little girl playing on the sand. Now, I'm not kidding you, this little girl had a tail! We couldn't believe our eyes. So we got closer, and then we realized that this little child had real long hair growing out of a birthmark, and that it had been *braided!* Linda and I looked at each other and I said, 'Let's get *out* of here!' That calmed my sixties nostalgia down for a while...."

Sex and Dope

When being high on marijuana was a way of life, we made it an aspect of many, if not most, of our activities: you always turned on before going to the movies, for a drive, for a walk. This was an unquestioned practice: in a group of friends, there was always someone who—without even inquiring—would start rolling a joint for the group whenever an activity had been decided upon (which often meant that the said activity was promptly forgotten or deemed inconsequential by all members of the group as soon as they were stoned).

Very quickly, those of us who had started smoking recreationally in high school or in the first year of college found ourselves smoking before doing most anything. (Or was it that college life simply became one big recreational period, a kind of four-year recess?) But marijuana seemed especially propitious for certain activities. Listening to music, for example—or anything that might provide an interesting sensual experience.

And so, of course, there was a sexual element too. In 1965, if you were a woman at the college I attended, one of the ways you knew if a guy liked you was when he suggested turning you on. I'd hazard a guess that the people I went to school with had most of their formative sexual experiences under the influence of marijuana and other illegal substances. Yet when I recently asked them whether they missed the sex-and-marijuana combination, most of these people hadn't considered the possibility for so long that they drew blanks just trying to remember what it was like. This seems interesting in view of the fact that some researchers maintain that marijuana has aphrodisiac effects, or at least heightens the user's sexual perception.

"It's true that I used to be under the impression that sex was better with marijuana," said one of my friends after she'd thought over my question. "But that could have been because sex was pretty new to me too, so that everything about it seemed new and exciting."

Now the women I know would feel insulted if their lovers invariably smoked marijuana before coming to bed. And enthusiasm for marijuana as a sexual adjunct seems positively déclassé. But it's hard to say whether this has more to do with changing drug habits or with altered attitudes to sex, or both.

Changing Fashions in Psycho-Aesthetics: Is Marijuana Cool or Cold?

To many of us, the chimerical nature of the marijuana high no longer seems enticing. After some years, one can grow weary of contemplating contradictions and pondering the implications of implications.

Could it be that there are changing fashions in psycho-aesthetics, and that the kind of high one gets with marijuana has simply gone out of style? There are historical precedents: some nineteenth-century French Romantics went for hashish in a big way; in reaction, the straighter Naturalists discarded cannabis intoxication in favor of the more comforting lure of absinthe.

Those of us who felt comfortable smoking in the sixties may have been attracted at the time to a kind of paranoid aesthetic which no longer interests us. Fifteen years ago, we felt that paranoia was a palatable or even valuable state of mind, because it could be a correlative to an ultimately pleasurable and imperatively needed trip to unexplored consciousness. Though they have often forgotten it, many of these former smokers suffered from marijuana-induced anxiety in the sixties as well (though probably to a lesser extent, because of the lower THC content and other factors outlined above). Studies performed at the time invariably reveal that a significant number of users suffered from dysphoria. One 1971 study on the effects of marijuana use reports that over a third of their respondents *usually* or *occasionally* felt "brooding or morose" (42 percent), "sad or despondent" (39 percent), "can't tell if happy or sad" (33 percent), to say nothing of "numbness over body parts" (44 percent), which could make anybody feel brooding and morose, as far as I'm concerned. At any rate, when I cast my eye down the long column of dysphoric symptoms, I was struck by the fact that the big winner, at 57-percent total of "usual" or "occasional" occurrence, was "less self-confident." In other words, *most* people occasionally felt paranoid, even then. So why did they take it?

In an interesting sense, sixties thought—with marijuana as one of its crucial catalysts—may have been merely a point in the continuum of the psycho-aesthetic trends of the last hundred years, rather than the beginning of a new consciousness. Just as the Decadent Romantics reacted to industrialization with a search for what Baudelaire called "The Artificial Paradises," the sixties generation, overloaded with unprecedented input of technology and information, turned once again to the soothing distraction of marijuana intoxication, precisely because it enabled them to enjoy contemplating otherwise unbearable contradictions.

The propensity for "mind expansion," then, becomes clear. A line can be drawn from the lust for hallucination of the French Romantic movement to the similarly feverish passions of Surrealism, the apotheosis of paranoid ideation. Salvador Dali, for example, defined his entire work from the "paranoia-critical" viewpoint: "All my art consists in concretizing with the most implacable precision the irrational images I tear out of my paranoia," he declares in *The Unspeakable Confessions of Salvador Dali*.

This paranoid aesthetic inevitably coexists with alienation. True to historical pattern, sixties thought eventually echoed that of the French Existentialist fifties (which had influenced it in the first place via the Beats). "No one can begin to think, feel or act now except from the starting point of his or her own alienation," wrote R. D. Laing in *The Politics of Expe-*

rience (published in 1967). "My feelings precisely!" would have replied Sartre, Camus, et al.

In other words, the sixties and their inevitable backlash may have simply been a rehash of the old consciousness-explosion-to-alienation cycle: After all the mind-expanding drugs, all the rock 'n' roll, all the much-heralded free love, all the attempts to explode the presixties fortresses of alienation, we still dwell among the absurdists' emotional props.

So, a decade and a half later, what's the point of continuing to explore that avenue? Why persist in confronting what we most dread if we have neither the emotional nor the spiritual tools to come out ahead? If it's true that we've come full circle, then our real problem boils down to good old fifties-style disaffection. If we don't enact this principle as flamboyantly as our "New Wave" successors, it may be because we're just too old, too tired, too busy, or too cool.

But, as you've probably noticed, being "cool" is out too, for this generation. Perhaps we have grown to find it tedious to maintain perpetually a conscious posture of emotional nonchalance. "To be natural is such a very difficult pose to keep up," wrote Oscar Wilde. We seem finally to have wearied of keeping up the pretense of emotional invincibility; the deliberately casual (read: inachievable) looseness; the insistence on sustaining the perennial observer's power over the more vulnerable participant.

Some of us may still exhibit the symptoms of a flattened affect, but that is perhaps more a matter of style than of psychological veracity. It's harder for us to change our behavior than our beliefs: few concepts were so carefully inculcated in us as the imperative necessity at least to *act* cool (whether or not you felt cool), out of regard for your friends' aesthetic sensibilities if for no other reason.

Marijuana is anathema to this new "uncool" mentality. Despite its historical characterization as a social lubricant, as a "mellow" agent, the former smokers I spoke to invariably declared it to be a "cold" drug. They say it makes them antisocial when they smoke it and, when used on a long-term basis, negligent of important emotional details in their relationships.

They say it separates them from other people. One man I spoke to had only recently ended a five-year period of smoking several times a day. "Marijuana kept everything at arm's length, like television. I feel better being straight, because I've come to like being more emotionally uninhibited. Pot does the contrary: it makes you intellectually uninhibited and verbally uninhibited, but emotionally it bottles you up. I'm more depressed now that I've stopped, that's for sure. But that only makes me think that I was keeping a lot of feelings under the lid of marijuana."

The really compulsive tough, hard-core outsider is no longer socially acceptable, let alone a role model. It's ironic, in a way, because we fought so hard back then to stay outside. But these days, alienation has become something about which we may consult a psychiatrist—if we can't get rid of it, at least we may learn how to ignore it (or, in modern parlance, to "cope" with it).

Certainly, the last thing we want to do is to flaunt it. For some, the image may still have its nostalgic value, but who wants to have dinner with someone who is still laying down a third-rate simulation of Marlon Brando in *The Wild Ones*? ("What are you rebelling against?" "Whaddya got?")

A Personal Note from the Writer
Relating to Public Matters

I'm one of those who decided in the recent past not to take a chance with marijuana any more. Lately, as it happens, I've opted for no illicit psychotropic alterations whatsoever. I'm the kind of person who gets upset if someone reminds me too early in the day that the universe is finite yet boundless. For better or for worse, like many of my contemporaries, I've come to prefer alcohol for purposes of dissociation. While I was working on this article, however, I thought it should be part of my research to smoke a bit. So I acquired a joint—good stuff, medium potency, I was told—and waited for a propitious moment to smoke it. It lay in a drawer of my night table, and every time I saw it I'd think about lighting it up and then I'd tell myself, "No, I don't think I'll rock the psychic boat tonight." Finally I gave up. Who knows, I told myself, if I smoke it I might decide not to do the article. I might decide I don't want to do any article, ever. I might start to wonder why I do *anything* ever.

But I could easily be wrong. Maybe I'd have a good time. What I'm getting at—and this is a personal note related to a public matter—is that, whatever my circumstances may be, these are my problems, and I would like the right to change my mind, say, next week, if I feel like it. I don't wish to add fuel to the witch-burning fires of the New Puritans. Certainly, no moral judgment is being made here about people who do smoke, and, at any rate, the criminalization of marijuana possession is an outrage to smokers and nonsmokers alike. Last year, close to half a million people were arrested on marijuana charges, and this despite the increasing number of reports published that it neither is addictive nor necessarily leads to other drugs.

When I talked about all this to Dana Beal, the Yippie leader who has been described as "the Lenin of the marijuana movement," he promptly told me: "Well, I still smoke, and all my friends do. But what's interesting about what you're saying is that it proves that we've been right all along: you *can* stop." Beal opined that the trend away from marijuana may be due in large part to the recent government crackdown on smokers. "They're now spending most of their budget on pot," he told me, "thereby diverting funds from the really serious drug problems. There's been a changing pattern in drug use. In the seventies, along came cocaine, and there was an incredible mass-merchandising trip to make cocaine chic to upwardly mobile white people. And then white powders became acceptable. So the real story since 1978 is the tremendous upsurge in heroin use. And 1978 is the year the government decided to really prosecute marijuana decisions again. I'll tell you something: the end product of the system is junkies." Indeed, it was recently reported that the number of heroin users has risen exponentially. In New York City, for example, one out of every forty residents is estimated to be a heroin addict. And this while the Supreme Court has ruled in its Roger Davis decision that it was not cruel and unusual punishment for the Virginia courts to have sentenced a black man to jail for forty years for possession of nine ounces of marijuana.

There are many people who started smoking marijuana in the sixties and continued to do so without harmful effect, and they would take exception to the points I have made here. There are others who stopped for some years, but then resumed smoking, at least on occasion. One person I talked to described himself as being in "postremission." For all I know, there may be in the future a trend away from restraint. Why shouldn't this be a matter of personal choice?

And besides, if marijuana was legalized, its production and distribution regulated, many of the deleterious effects I've described here might become obsolete. One could purchase a desired dose of a specific brand: cerebral highs, body highs, cosmic or comic highs would be made available to those who wished to indulge. What's wrong with that idea, especially when it's compared with the sometimes calamitous current system?

No Regrets

Aside from the fact that many former smokers tend to be civil libertarians, they are tolerant of other people's marijuana use because they usually have no regrets about their own days of indulgence. "That was then and this is now" is the prevalent position.

This is perhaps partly because whatever the lessons of marijuana use may have been, they are still part of our view of the world, whether or not we continue to smoke. In fact, this was the original plan. "Unquestionably, this drug is useful to the artist," wrote William Burroughs in 1964. "I have now discontinued the use of cannabis for some years and find that I am able to achieve the same results by nonchemical means

... especially by training myself to think in association blocks instead of words, that is, cannabis, like all the hallucinogens, can be discontinued once the artist has familiarized himself with the areas opened up by the drug."

Carl Sagan suggests in *The Dragons of Eden,* his book of speculations on the evolution of human intelligence, that the effects of marijuana may have a relationship to the cerebral cortex's division into the left hemisphere, which processes information sequentially, and the right hemisphere, which does so simultaneously. He writes, "I wonder if, rather than enhancing anything, the cannabinols... simply suppress the left hemisphere and permit the stars to come out." Perhaps, if you've smoked enough marijuana over a sufficient period of time, you can learn to tap this source even when you're not intoxicated.

To put it another way: once you've seen the dog, you don't forget the construct, and you remain conscious of its applications.

Lately, I've been thinking of another long-forgotten sixties expression: "goofing." A product of marijuana-induced double consciousness, to "goof" meant to *act* straight in your confrontations with the straight world, all the while you were in a state of (you hoped) imperceptible stoned mind expansion. Goofing was performed partly because people were afraid of being busted, but also because it was a funny mind game. Kids used to goof all the time in restaurants and bars. They'd goof on their teachers in class and on their parents in the family living room. Lots of temeritous guys went and goofed on their draft boards.

Some of us have never completely relinquished the practice of goofing, even now that we are—ostensibly, at least—enacting the "social roles of adulthood." On the negative side, this may well be one of the things that now make so many of us anxious when we get high: after a certain age, it's no longer goofing, it's simply faking, and it means we can never take ourselves completely seriously. Sometimes in the middle of the night we find ourselves inexorably drawn to ask, "What

Am I *Doing* with My life? I must be kidding with this job and this marriage! My whole existence is INCREDIBLY RIDICULOUS." This can be a pretty devastating notion to the individual who has made a conscious commitment to the idea that his or her job or marriage (or whatever) is a better channel to well-being than continuing to wallow in the wrecked crash pads of the mind.

But if we suffer from this sort of disastrous double vision every once in a while, that's the breaks. And on the upside, I think that the people in this generation, in part because of their profound and sometimes implacable irony, are infinitely more interesting than their perhaps calmer, potentially non-alternative selves would have been.

Much of the sixties marijuana legacy seems banal and stale to us now, especially since it has been so completely co-opted by the former straights. But all the time we spent tantalizing our psyches wasn't wasted. The people I interviewed for this article had often chosen paths and adopted modes of behavior that wildly diverged from their sixties expectations. But they still had in common a strange, enticing quality that I can only describe as the ability to disturb. This can be manifested in subtle ways; in the midst of a conversation, in the course of the casual encounter, there is the sudden bold remark, the audacious twist. So you look into these people's eyes and you think: "This person's capable of *anything!*" There's nothing more seductive than this ones tentatious capacity for daring, whether or not the intention is consummated. One can choose to lie low. Perhaps precisely because they've chosen not to continue their engagement in the world exclusively through the ultimately limited visions of marijuana smoke, many of these people still personify that old insistence on maintaining a special attitude toward their environment. I don't know what name to give that attitude: in the last decade and a half we seem collectively to have lost the desire for defining and naming such phenomena. In the sixties, one might have referred to it as a special awareness. I think this is a valuable insistence. It reminds me of a device Huxley used in his utopian novel *Island*. On the island there were signs that simply read "Attention."

Are You Scared of the Dark?

So we keep our irony from a bygone era, even as we come of age in another. As for the rest...

"In college, I did my senior thesis on Hesse's characters' search for self-revelation, a hot item at the time," a friend told me recently. "And when I met with my adviser to discuss it, she asked me, 'What would have been the result of these characters' quests if they had achieved it?' I thought about it, and I finally had to answer, 'They'd be dead.' 'That's right,' she said. 'Why wasn't that in your paper?' I didn't have any answer. I guess I couldn't face it at the time, but now I know you eventually have to detach yourself from most everything you wanted so badly then, because achieving it meant to die."

"There are truths which are not for all men, nor for all times," declared Voltaire. If we have allowed the sixties *Zeitgeist* to become diffuse, it's probably, to some degree, a matter of self-preservation.

Maybe we're not incredibly ridiculous after all. We're just doing the best we can.

TERMINAL COOL

A JAZZ fan dies and goes to heaven. When he gets there, he's greeted by Saint Peter, who shows him around, and it looks exactly like a jazz club, with crummy lighting and café tables and waitresses in tights and everything. When the jazz fan sees who's in the club, he says, "Oh my God, this really is heaven." At one table, Lady Day is sitting with Lester Young. At another is Thelonious Monk having a drink with Charlie Parker. "Man, this is too much," says the jazz fan to Saint Peter. Then he sees a figure sitting alone at the bar, dressed in black and wearing neck jewelry, with his back to the audience. "Who's that?" asks the fan. "Oh," says Saint Peter, "that's God. He thinks he's Miles Davis."

Strictly Nostalgia: When Cool Was Cool

CONUNDRUM: *You aren't always what you pretend to be, but sometimes you can become it.*

For sixties adolescents, there were many types of cool to choose from: biker cool, streetcorner cool, Zen cool, Jewish-comic cool, antiwar-movement cool, John Kennedy–button-down cool, coffee-house-intellectual cool—not to be confused with folk-song cool, which was largely enacted in coffee houses but also had contingents in city parks, in people's living rooms, and in subway stations while they waited for trains. By the mid-sixties, the variants of cool were already too numerous to name, and I'm just thinking about the East Coast. In the West, they had surfer cool, prankster cool, and God knows what else.

Miles Davis comes to mind because back-to-the-audience cool was precisely what the people who were my friends in high school and college aspired to (although they would never have worn neck jewelry). Unlike some other brands, this type of cool wasn't occupational or situational; it was a state of mind and emotion, one that closely resembled the dysfunction psychiatrists refer to as the flattened affect: distance, neutrality, impassivity, and all the other symptoms of anhedonia or the inability to feel pleasure (though what was really sought was the inability to feel pain).

What was coolest of all was to maintain one's flattened affect in the most extravagant, exciting situations: when you thought the motorcycle was going to crash, when your mind was in hyperdrive on some weird drug you'd never taken before, when you were about to make love with someone for whom you hankered, for the moment anyway, with psyche-grinding teen-age passion. When their lives were punctuated by the most violent sensations they could find, the *modus vivendi* the people I knew then adopted was to create for themselves a kind of neutral zone, a padded bubble into which they could retreat at will from the tumult. That's why it always seems wrong to me when people talk about the sixties as an explosion. "Explosion" is a correct description, perhaps, of the events, but certainly not the mood. The mood I remember was that of the eye of the hurricane, the mood of ashes. Distilled quiet, almost melancholy. Like a long bout of postcoital *tristesse*.

In the mid-sixties, many thousands of intellectually befuddled, morally perplexed, acne-ridden adolescents became incredibly cool, by sheer will. It may have seemed important at the time to be naturally cool, but in fact it wasn't. Almost no one is naturally cool anyway: the genetic odds are against that odd combination of intelligence, wit, alienation, and low metabolism. But if you were too agitated, insecure, romantic, or goony to come by cool naturally, you could still look cool and act cool, if you wanted to badly enough. Eventually, with practice, you could actually organize your psyche according to cool principles to a surprising degree. In a way, just wanting to be cool (even if you didn't think of it that way but instead, more vaguely, as having a certain relationship to your environment) took you halfway there, because the very nurturing of the desire meant that you had already gotten rid of untold amounts of uncool baggage.

Besides, even those with supposedly natural (biological or circumstantial) cool were posing, in a way. This became clear when, some years later, they opted for other modes. The first thing John Lennon did when he decided he'd had it with being cool was to get undressed and scream primally. To put it somewhat reductively, most of modern psychology seems to indicate that the most truly natural human act, once out of the womb, is to cower in a corner, whining. It follows that one has to do quite a number on oneself to ride enigmatically into the sunset, or stay behind in Casablanca.

Terminal cool purported to be a rejection of traditional values, but like honor, which it resembled in many ways, it was a learned abstraction: artificial and therefore highly civilized.

CONUNDRUM: *Cool was a pose, but it was the most honest attitude we could come up with.*

It would require a ridiculously convoluted history of the morals and moods of postwar America to untangle the web of cultural threads that led to the mass juvenile depression of the late fifties and early sixties, but clearly, by the mid-sixties, this collective depression was molded into a style of deportment that conferred status upon those who could elaborate it with elegance.

As soon as we went away to college and no longer had to put up with irritating adults exhorting us to be cheerful and mocking us for our predilections for bohemian values, we could be as despondent as we pleased. It was kind of fun

doing it as a group. Of course, no one then admitted that it
was fun. ("Happiness" was a word never even mentioned, like
"marriage" or "business.") Fun was too mundane, like your
parents' cocktail parties. Thrills were all right, though, and
the more extreme the better. Thrill seeking, after all, was a
classic tactic of the disenfranchised, and a stylistically correct
balm for clinical ennui.

"A lot of it had to do with the fear of being square," says a
friend who was around when that fear seemed like an ethical
imperative. "It's what was left once you'd eliminated all the
bullshit." It seemed like a historical necessity, a form of sabotage against the empty and incomprehensible effusions of
the adult world. And if it was highly egocentric, it was also a
type of sensitivity, and philosophically generous. It was a
transparent coping mechanism, but also the indicator of an
elaborate aesthetic that implied intelligence, irony, insolence,
whimsy, nonaggression, grace, and, most of all, integrity. It
may not seem like that now, but actually it was humanistic,
compared with the savage conformism of the times. Someone
I still know from those days recalls, "It wasn't much of anything by itself, but it subtly enhanced whatever personality
lay behind it. Sort of like monosodium glutamate." Cool was
a terrifically convenient aesthetic for the besieged adolescent
psyches of the sixties, because it was both a code of ethics
and a form of sex appeal.

CONUNDRUM: *So many of the trappings of sixties-style cool
have been co-opted by mass culture that even the people who
were instrumental in its propagation have forgotten its original purpose and function.*

Sixties college kids didn't invent cool. In many ways, the
form of cool they engaged in was a refinement of all the cool
attitudes that had preceded it. In fact, by then you could even
read about cool. Norman Mailer had already defined the White
Negro and pitted Beats against hipsters, though this distinction had become fuzzy by the mid-sixties. Several years earlier, Paul Goodman's *Growing Up Absurd* had been published,

differentiating the Early Resigned (young beatniks) and the
Early Fatalistic (juvenile delinquents): these were the Adam
and Eve of a family tree of cool whose branches were now
conclusively entangled in an incestuous confusion. All of the
various fashions for the alienated mind were merged in the
turn-your-back-to-the-audience cool, which the kids I knew
fancied so much. In a way, this was the last flourish of the
disaffected style. For many reasons, you might call it terminal
cool. Shortly after it had its apogee in, say, 1965, the deluge
of hippiedom began to pour into the public consciousness,
largely because of the herculean efforts of the media. And no
wonder—hippies made better copy because they were the
most overt (read: uncool), and they were by far the most
photogenic.

By the mid-seventies, all the gazing at flower children in
Time magazine had done its work, and the hippie sensibility
wound up hogging all of the territory in the Sixties of Memory.
Now all the versions of sixties cool are blurred together in an
irremediably murky hodgepodge, like the muddy brown you
get when you mix all the colors together. So annoying. And
it's not just our parents who populate the sixties with dazed
and scruffy street children. It's particularly irritating to discover this disremembrance among people who should know
better. Not long ago, to my amazement, I heard a guy I went
to school with refer to himself as a former hippie. I didn't say
anything—what's the point of reminding him that fifteen years
ago a hippie was someone with whom he would have had the
most peripheral relationship, and to whom he would have
referred, with amused condescension, as a "freak." He never
had any contact with hippies, except maybe to buy dope from,
or to sit next to at a rock concert. He was reading Antonin
Artaud while they camped on the streets of Haight-Ashbury.
He was dressed in dark and neutral colors, and nothing could
have induced him to wear a fringed leather jacket, let alone
a flower in his hair. He ate hamburgers and Mars bars—God,
no grain, no yogurt, please. Like them, he listened to the
Beatles, Dylan, and the Byrds, but also to Stravinsky, and
certainly not to Grand Funk Railroad. They lived in tribal

units; he had no acknowledged group loyalty. They had communal sex, while, once or twice, he may have gotten into bed with two girls at the same time, and it had been *their* idea. If he had sexual contact with "hippie chicks" (sorry), he probably would have treated them the way townies were treated by the Ivy League boys: if it was great, he might spend a week shacked up in an abandoned bus in a Cape Cod town on his summer vacation with some lovely airhead, but he'd never bring one back to school with him.

Like his parents at the time, my friend no longer knows how to distinguish among all those kids who all had long hair. But maybe he doesn't want to remember the old distinctions. After all, at some point in the late sixties or early seventies, a lot of his old friends washed out or canceled out. And at around the same time, any leisure-suited joker could light up a joint and go to a wife-swapping party when he was through mowing the lawn and declare himself liberated from establishment values. Suburban ladies made appointments with one another to attend happenings after lunch. "Counterculture" became a slick media buzzword. By now, cool has become a sloppy trivia concept. A paperback book has just been published called *The Catalog of Cool*. Paper dresses, the "Andy Griffith Show," "Hullabaloo"? They must be kidding. Cool is something my friend now associates—condescendingly—with other generations. He's amused by his elders' version of the cool principle: the tough but vulnerable image of the Frank Sinatra hipster (now degenerated into the intolerably silly detachment of the Adolpho Man.) His New Wave successors, on the other hand, adhere to a meta-cool, automaton aesthetic, which entertains but does not absorb him. New Wave cool is completely uncool by his old standards: too overt, too visual, too much eye contact, too much eye shadow. It's look-at-me cool. He was once used to subtler nuances and more profound convictions. Well, but that was then.

Now that the idea of cool is almost never brought up by people in their thirties without derision, it seems like an emblem of many of the goals we once had. Most we didn't reach.

And those that were fulfilled evolved into something we either couldn't handle, didn't want, or simply ceased to care about.

These days, the old nuances of the terminal-cool aesthetic as a code of moral behavior seem about as relevant as *The Tibetan Book of the Dead* and Ravi Shankar records. Even its moral aspects have come to seem hopelessly passé. I haven't heard anyone use the phrase "selling out" in years. If it's something people still think about, it's certainly not a matter of discussion at the dinner parties where the women in angel-shag haircuts and the men in their Armani or Armani-inspired sports jackets exchange professional gossip.

Yet one woman I know recently confided, "I miss it. There's a thing I used to tell myself that ran, 'Every day, in every way, I'm getting cooler and cooler.' And that kind of comforted me. I don't have any religion or any organized ideas or anything. So I used thinking about cool to keep me from getting sub-human."

Only a woman could have made that remark. After all, guys were always much too cool ever to talk about it....

Was Sex Cool or Uncool?

CONUNDRUM: *Girls were often more courageous than boys, according to terminal-cool criteria, but boys were always cooler.*

Cool had a lot to do with sex, sex appeal, and sex roles. Girls have never received enough credit for the fantastic leap of the mind they took in the sixties when they turned *their* backs to the audience. In these post–women's-power days, we've come to take a lot for granted. But when the seventeen-year-old girl from the comfortable home started adopting some of the attitudes of the black jazz musician, the lessons of centuries of class and gender indoctrination were dumped in the trash along with the pink plastic curlers. And gladly, too.

Yet boys were always cooler. Cool boys were much more feminine than their sloshed and rowdy frat-house counter-parts, but basically all the characteristics of the cool personality were male traits. All of the cool prototypes were males: cowboys, hoods, male homosexual poets, basketball players, bass guitarists, Bogarts and Brandos.

"Cool girls were extremely independent" is what most people recall. "Nobody told them what to do. They went where they pleased and did what they felt like doing. They still had feminine sexual allure, but they also presented themselves as equals. For a girl to be cool, she had to have both." Perhaps females were more talented at being androgynous than males, or more willing because they felt they had less to lose.

It wasn't something we thought about, but, looking back to college days, I'd have to admit that my girlfriends and I imitated boys a lot. We dressed like them and talked as they did. We tried to imitate their attitudes—at first when we were in their company, later with one another, and finally even to ourselves. And why shouldn't we have? What else was there to imitate? Aside from F. Scott Fitzgerald's heroines and maybe Margaret Mead, the feminine role-model pickings were really slim. Postwar America certainly hadn't yielded anything satisfactory once you rejected all the establishment females. The so-called offbeat prototypes from old films, the Katharine Hepburns and the Gloria Grahames, were basically only putting up a good front in reaction to men. Some antiestablishment types appealed: the Supremes, say, or Anna Magnani, or Susan Sontag. But while one could admire these women, it was difficult to identify with them. Other counterculture types already seemed like hopelessly corny cartoon figures, such as the Vivian Darkbloom pointy-glasses dragon ladies (too silly) or the female Beats in dirty hair and sweatshirts who were the inevitable appendages of chess players and the like (too pathetic).

No, the boys we went to school with were on to much more sophisticated material, and we had more in common with them than with any women of the past or present. Besides, they were clearly having fun—in a grim, alienated way, of course—so we weren't about to be left behind. At my old school, the girls became champion thrill-seekers and aces in the I-can-take-it department; they were thought of as pals by their male friends and as wild (or worse) by everyone else (especially their mothers).

It's a mistake to ignore the obvious: the first thing they did was to imitate male sexual behavior. And it turned out that as soon as the label "fast" became obsolete—at least in the view of this subgroup—all of feminine behavior could be altered, because most of the circumscriptions had existed only to achieve the *demure* model. Once the sexual demureness barrier had been shattered, the other constraints became irrelevant as well, and ever so much easier to dismiss. So girls stepped out of their skirts and put jeans on, talked less, went hitchhiking around the country, took the most mind-bending drugs available, loved and left, had adventures, courted danger, and occasionally went to sleep drunk with their boots on ... just like boys.

I distinctly remember a guy at school who made my heart leap in a fierce way saying to me, "Lesbians are so cool." The funny thing is, I think that was his way of making an advance. It worked too: I knew he was right and it made me feel really jealous.

Yet, if you were still attracted to boys, you wound up retaining a good deal of your feminine emotional equipment, and in fact all the time you were evolving in the male-oriented context you were also growing as a woman. My God, were we confused, continually adding one more illogically acquired trait to an already hopelessly ambiguous personality. We were like guests with an eclectic appetite at a buffet dinner, piling an incongruous assortment of foods onto our plates. I'll have some of this, some of that, and, boy, am I hungry. No wonder personalities were indecipherable. One of my college friends recalls, "To be cool was either total affectation or total lack of affectation. With the coolest girls, you could never tell which they were. They'd behave in a fascinating way, but you could never know when, if ever, their behavior was a sincere reflection of their real personality."

If boys couldn't understand us, it was because we really weren't like them, notwithstanding all our efforts. And it wasn't only biochemical either. There were too many concepts in the terminal-cool mentality that we could grasp but not absorb. For example, girls may have been enticed by black music and style, but few could match their male friends' crucial and rich ambivalence—infatuation poisoned by envy—toward black culture. After all, most girls only had the crash course. And in matters of style, even though they had traveled a much longer road, they could never really be as cool as boys: the voice was still too inflected; the eyes too expressive; the hand gestures, the tilt of the head never successfully contained— the style of the powerless, of the participant observed by the infinitely cooler outsider. So in the end, in timeless fashion, the best way females could conquer power was to seduce it.

CONUNDRUM: *Cool purported to be the defiant rejection of an uptight mentality, but it was perhaps above all a variation on it. It was the aesthetic of inhibition.*

Like the courtship patterns of all inhibited cultures, the terminal-cool seduction was, of course, tremendously titillating. In addition to normal human nostalgia for Sex of the Past, I'd bet almost every woman who's experienced them still harbors wistful affection for these seductions. They were so well suited to feminine erotic-emotional predilections: drawn out, restrained, indirect, subtle, with exquisite attention paid to detail. Never mind if this was due as much to adolescent fear as to flair for sensual drama. The combination somehow made for wonderfully complex and preoccupying social activity.

For one thing, these attractions were so meandering. *Does he want to? Do I want to?* At my old campus, kids used to go down to the riverbank and lie down together for hours on the pine needles, drive each other crazy, not doing or saying anything, just watching the sun glimmer on the waterfall. Then they'd walk back to their classes and maybe not speak to each other again for weeks.

The languid pace of these seductions was compounded by the fact that, as of 1965 or so, the girls I knew still did not overtly initiate sexual encounters—though whether this was due to old leftover sexual mores or the new girl-cool code is

beyond the scope of my memory. The trouble was that by
1965 boys didn't want to overtly initiate sexual encounters
either. Pushy, you know. Aggressive. Risky. Uncool.

The coolest boys, the real heartbreakers, seemed inaccessible to the point of cruelty. Unless a girl happened to be good
friends with him, the most attention one of these guys would
show her would be maybe to say, "What are you up to?" when
he put his tray down at the table where she was sitting in
dining commons. And that was if he really liked her. So, after
lunch, she'd go back to her room and brood and try to talk
herself out of caring about it. ("Well, then, fuck *him*.")

Even if this guy was her friend, he was so enigmatic that
she'd develop a helpless compulsion to climb into his brain.
She somehow knew he liked her, but she couldn't be sure of
whether he felt *that way* for months (or at least weeks, which
seemed like an eternity at the time). But, finally, one night,
when a bunch of people had gone down to the local bar together, she'd catch him watching her dance with someone
else. And if she smiled at him, then, later when they all left
he would stay next to her on the walk back to campus and
he'd wait for the group to assume a propitious formation so
that he could speak to her in a conversational tone but not
be overheard and say, probably, "Do you want to get high?"
in the most casual way.

When the group reached main campus and disbanded, none
of the others would say anything as she walked away with him
toward his dorm, and the two of them wouldn't say anything to
each other either. Once upstairs in his room, they'd both sit on
his bed, leaning against the wall, but he wouldn't touch her,
except to pass a joint. He'd put on a record, and perhaps he'd
tell her something funny about one of his teachers, or show her
some object in his possession, a book of Francis Bacon paintings maybe. Hours would go by like that in the little dimly lit
room, and she didn't know any more what to expect. He stopped
putting records on and now they became silent; they could just
hear faint music coming from other people's rooms. And then,
if she stayed very still, he slid away from her so he could put her
foot on his lap, and he slipped off her boot.

When he finally leaned over to kiss her (maybe not until afterward), his eyes were closed and his mouth very open and his teeth somewhat in the way. But her eyes were open and she saw that he had an expression that was a bit like pain on his face, which made her feel a queer mixture of joy and malaise. Why malaise? It wasn't until years later, if she remembered it, that she'd realize that the expression was simply tenderness, and that she had known it even then but hadn't believed it.

These boys always seemed to have a secret. It should have been easy to see that the secret was only loneliness, but it was so effectively encapsulated by irony and nonchalance that we were fooled every time. They were so mysterious that we could idealize them to an absurd degree. And so we did, not understanding that to do so was also a form of cruelty. A really cool guy seemed like an irresistible challenge, but ultimately the challenge was to get him to be uncool, or tender. It's only now, all these years later, that it's become clear that a lot of what seemed so cool was probably simply shyness and fear. Only a few years earlier they'd engaged in the normal centuries-old teen-age fumblings, awkward gropings with standard clammy hands and excess saliva. Suddenly they found themselves in this absolutely amazing sexual funhouse, with all the girls they liked apparently available, and these poor boys were stuck with having to act cool when they were, well, scared. *Is she really willing?* is what they were thinking while we were racking our brains to figure out why they tormented us. And we were as thickheaded as they were to deny the evidence that they were as willing to give us tenderness as we were to be seduced.

But, then, there's all the more reason to ask: why malaise? Well, perhaps it wasn't only thickheadedness; perhaps we didn't want to process the evidence, because it would have meant wrecking our fantasies.

CONUNDRUM: *By its very nature, cool was a type of sex appeal that could only be destroyed by sex.*

Time passed. And with experience, these sad but sweet scenes degenerated, as inhibited tenderness hardened into cynicism—a far more dangerous form of fear. Eventually, it began to seem that the coolest sexuality was vicarious, remembered, imagined, removed. "After sex you could be cool," a friend says. "During wasn't cool at all, of course. And before, it could be pretty cool, but it was really too tense. But afterward, you could feel terrifically cool."

As an affront to the uptight standards of society, sex was cool, but how could you be cool while you were having sex? According to the cool subgroup standard, then, the coolest form of sexuality became sexual tension: the sex you didn't consummate, the night you spent with someone on LSD when you never took your clothes off; the look you once exchanged, by accident, with your best friend's lover. The coolest relationships were ambiguous friendships, often with someone you'd slept with once but it seemed so long ago that it only mattered in the sense that it was something already taken care of.

Of course, there was an unprecedented amount of sexual activity. But if you were actually going to engage in sex, at least it could be kind of somber (thereby preserving distance). Although so-called sexual liberation is always situated in the sixties, it wasn't until the next decade that the whole "joyful" sex syndrome materialized—except, of course, for the indiscreet (vulgar) hippies. *The Joy of Sex* wasn't published until 1972; the manuals of the mid-sixties conveyed the solemn and controlled sensuality of Eastern cultures, *The Perfumed Garden* and *The Kama Sutra*.

And precisely because there were so many casual affairs, the approach was rather... minimal. Eventually, not even making love was exempt from those outward signs of cool behavior which were also the symptoms of depression. For example, it was quite silent. It was silently requested, with a single gesture, only a touch perhaps, and silently acquiesced to, with a glance. Except for the record player in the room, the act itself was silent too. Between cuts, there wasn't a sound. In the mid- to late sixties, kids must have reached millions of orgasms without a word or a moan, and afterward lain next to one another silently. At the time, even "Did you come?" would have been considered an irremediably uncool invasion of privacy.

So many lonely children. So cool. And the lonelier they got, the cooler they became, and the lonelier they got.

When Cool Became Uncool

CONUNDRUM: *While cool meant staying free, it also meant staying out, which eventually revealed itself to be a form of imprisonment.*

I think that's what wrecked the cool aesthetic: it was simply too lonely. People started wanting to have long-term relationships, and after they'd failed at them a number of times because they were so damn cool, they decided to bail out of cool. As horrendously difficult and humiliating as it may have been to turn toward the audience again and say, *Please love me,* it wasn't as hard and as painful as that terrifying solitude you felt in a stranger's bed if you'd succeeded in becoming detached enough to make all your lovers into strangers, or the uneasy solitude you felt with even your closest friends if you'd become cynical enough to make all your friends mere cohabitants of a sad planet, or the devastating spiritual solitude you felt if you had messed yourself up enough so that even the original joke—that everything was a joke—became a joke, and *that* was really too sad to laugh at any more.

Curiously, the final death blow to the terminal-cool mentality came not from the outside but from its own entropy. Because of the nature of their interactions with one another—or lack of them—within just a few years many of these kids had become almost intolerably isolated. And that isolation was compounded by the psychological effects of the drugs they took. Tolerance varied: some people bombarded their systems with every drug they could get their hands on for years. But there always came the night when you had to crash from one

Black Beauty too many. That was a bad night. A very uncool night.

For others, a few really harsh LSD trips were enough. Psychedelics offered possibilities for the most extreme applications of cool, but were ultimately the instrument of its demise just because the ego, at least as it's constituted at present, is simply not designed to withstand such battering on a sustained basis and still remain intact. Most of the people I knew then became unwilling to pay the price of psychedelic solitude for the psychedelic thrill, and anyway, by that time, for many, it was no longer a thrill at all. "It got to be so the best part was re-entry," one of my friends recalls. "I'd realize I was coming down and I'd think, *Thank God, back to the world.*" That's what happened: suddenly the soiled, messy, ridiculous, completely uncool real world started to seem more alluring than the endless mazes of the pure but cold territory of the perpetual outsider. So one by one, and eventually by the thousands, they defected from the terminal-cool ethos. There's been a good deal of smug commentary about the return of this group to straight America. But I think it's unfair to mock these people for acquiring the three-piece suits and the mortgages and the lawn furniture, and for starting to use words like "business" and "marriage." Essentially, they just came in from the cold.

All these years later, the cool concept seems laden with contradictions. But the ultimate conundrum, it seems to me, is that many of the people who were adherents of that code in the sixties and then willfully abandoned it in the next decade, when they opted to be part of the world, really haven't succeeded in completely ridding themselves of its constructs, even now that it's become so uncool to be cool.

Actually, it's only lately that I've noticed this, so maybe it has something to do with the times, or with the stage my particular age group is in. "I'm going right from an adolescent identity crisis to a mid-life crisis without so much as a two-week vacation," a friend of mine mused recently. I laughed after he said that, and so did he. If we ever needed to use the cosmic-bulldozer sense of humor we developed in the mid-sixties, it's now that we have to deal with the, shall we say, final issues. You know, the futility and/or necessity of love, procreation, planning the architecture of one's life, and—we'll take all the help we can get on this one—mortality.

But cool's gone underground, in a way, just where it was before the sixties. Of course, old sensibility types haven't remained intact, but you can still locate them if you're in an archaeological frame of mind. The signifiers are subtle now that the really dramatic differences have been settled and people go to the same hairdressers and see the same movies and have the same politics or lack of them and have similar marriages, or lack of them.

Naturally, I'm not talking about the pathetic sixties casualties who still brandish the flag for a long-defeated cause: they were always uncool anyway. Too overt. The people I'm talking about look and act almost like everybody else. But soon after you meet them you hear them make a slightly incongruous remark—ah, you remark to yourself, *dissociation*. Upon examination, the logistics of their lives don't seem quite to hang together—*nonchalance*. They may be successful in their careers, but even if they exhibit the kind of maniacal ambition that's become a *pro forma* requisite for just hanging in there these days, they don't appear to support the system they've become a part of—*disaffection*. And then you catch them with a carefully neutral expression on their faces at a strange moment, and that's the conclusive tip-off—*inappropriate irony*.

Spotting these people is like looking for markers on a road where no one travels any more. Often, they're well hidden, but that only makes them seem...uh...*cooler*, no? So even though the old terminal-cool code turned out to be a failure as a way to organize your mind, maybe there are other, better forms of cool to be found in the future fashions for the mind.

As for Miles Davis...in a recent biography entitled *Round About Midnight,* there is the following passage in which Davis is talking about the time he spent in Paris with Jean-Paul

Sartre: "I knew that Sartre was a lot like me. I knew that the Nobel prize was just a lot of bullshit to him, just like all the awards I've won are to me. I told everybody that he would turn it down—I knew that he would." As it turns out, though, Miles Davis himself has received and accepted many awards, and his biographer recounts that the wall behind his piano is laden with plaques, so he asked Davis to explain. "I like nice wood," said Miles Davis.

CAN YOU SAY MORE?
WHAT PEOPLE WON'T TELL
THEIR THERAPISTS
═══ OR ═══
I'D LIKE TO APOLOGIZE
FOR THIS ARTICLE

I WON'T talk to my therapist about shit. As far as she's concerned, I haven't gone to the bathroom in the three years she's known me, and I hope she has therefore deduced that I have in fact never gone to the bathroom, and that excrement has nothing at all to do with my life on any level whatsoever.

I don't feel in the least guilty about this: very few of my friends, as I've discovered recently, talk to their therapists about shit. "Who'd want to discuss such a thing?" one of them offered. You may agree. In a way, I agree. But...

Let me digress for a moment. Frankly, I hate this subject. Oh, I'm in trouble. I'm already digressing. I'm already self-conscious. I'm already feeling guilty. Which reminds me:

Before I continue, I'd like to say I do feel rather guilty (I have no trouble talking to my therapist or anyone else about feeling guilty, since I consider this a safe subject, only mildly embarrassing—that is, it's unlikely anyone would seriously dislike me for it, unless I talk about it compulsively and become a bore, in which case I change the subject) about writing this article, because I figure people who aren't in therapy will read it and this will confirm their suspicion that therapy is silly and a waste of time. As it happens, many people in therapy waffle through phases during which they also think therapy is silly and a waste of time, though most of them carefully avoid talking about this with their therapists.

"I go through periods," says one woman I know, "when I think it's a total loss and why am I saying all these things to this person who only listens to me because he gets paid for it."

"And do you talk about it?" I ask.

"Of course not," she says. "Only afterward, when I'm out of that phase and back in a good mood. I can't tell him while it's going on, because I don't want him to think he's not doing a good job."

People will go to extraordinary lengths not to tell their therapists that they sometimes think their therapy is a silly failure and that they're angry at their therapists about it. "Patients protect their therapists from their aggression," a psychiatrist explained to me. One man I know has on a number of occasions complained to me that he feels his therapy isn't doing him much good, yet when I interviewed him for this article he mentioned that he shaves and dresses carefully for each session "so that he'll think I'm in good shape and his treatment is successful."

Mental note to myself: Must remember to talk about body language.

Back to the point. What was the point? Oh, yes, lately I've been systematically asking people I know what they don't tell their therapists, and here's a partial list of other topics many people are reluctant to discuss with their mental-health professionals: sex, money, love, work, art, politics, drugs, violence, loneliness, death, and mental health.

In fact, people will lie about or omit just about anything. And then use other lies and omissions to cover up the initial ones. "The hardest thing to say," says a friend, "is 'I lied,' even when you regret the lie." Just like real life, but worse.

People gave many reasons for lying or omitting, and often these seem odder than the falsifications or omissions themselves, until it becomes apparent that they are invariably a function of the very problems people went into therapy for. Some were aggressive: "I keep him on a need-to-know basis." Some were defensive: "I want the benefits of therapy without ever having to lose complete control. Nobody wants to feel bad in public, and I consider therapy to be public." Some were self-denying: "I don't want to hurt his feelings." Many were painfully insecure: "I want to avoid anything pat or banal"; "I don't want to be a boring patient." Many reflected resentment of authority: "I don't want to be hassled"; "I don't want to be programmed." A few were philosophical, reflecting the difficulty of conveying how thinking and memory and the mind's imagery work: "There are things I don't say because it's impossible." One was frank: "I don't want to resolve my ambivalences." One was fashionably semiotic: "What you don't say is a moot point; language is only an inexact mediator between your unconscious and the world anyway."

"There are things that are unthinkable and things that are unsayable," a psychotherapist told me. Often, the connection is mysterious.

"There are a lot of things I don't tell him," says one woman. "It's as though, I don't know how to explain it, it's as though I don't want him to know my dirty little secret."

"What's the nature of your dirty little secret?" I asked.

She paused. "I don't know!" she said. "I just know that I have one."

Of course, there's the plain fact that some people simply find it hard to talk to other people, but the funny thing about doing these interviews was how willing people were to tell me about the things they don't tell their doctors. "What a relief," said one person, "to confess." Though I'll tell you right now, so you won't be disappointed later, that the raciest thing I heard is that one of my friends has sexual fantasies about paraplegics. He did get around to telling his therapist about it, he assured me, but it took him several sessions. And the most often told lie, as you might expect, is "It was the traffic." In fact, it's a mystery to me how tens of thousands of psychotherapists across the country keep a straight face at the beginning of the hundreds of thousands of sessions that start with the words "I'm sorry I'm late. It was the traffic." But you can't win with these people—they will tell you that even that lie is significant: "Of course it's a desire to avoid punishment," a doctor explained to me, "but it's also the expression of a wish. In fact, the patient may really believe it was the traffic that delayed him, rather than having to tell himself, 'I didn't want to come today.'"

Reasonable, or not? I don't know. They have explanations for everything. If you're in therapy, you're stuck accepting the basic concept that there's an explanation for *everything*, yet you constantly find yourself wondering, "What if he's wrong?" What's more, there's no doubt that therapists are, after all, sometimes wrong.

"I won't talk about politics," says one of my friends. "I started analysis during the Vietnam war and I would talk about it during my sessions and so everything was related and therefore reduced to psychological factors, because therapy is about the individual, not the society. So now I won't talk about it, even though politics is a big part of my life. I don't want my passion and my anger defused."

I think he's right. I think some subjects should be left out of therapy altogether, yet the distinction between the personal and the societal is often tricky. For example, two psychiatrists mentioned to me that, in order to avoid talking about their own relationships, women patients will digress into indictments of sexism. "They'll talk about *Playboy* magazine or something, instead of what's really going on in their life." I only happened to have noticed it because both psychiatrists mentioned *Playboy*. The controversy over the magazine itself is neither here nor there, but, however women may choose to articulate it, is it impossible that the issue of gender politics has a daily, constant effect on their personal lives? Maybe I should point out that both of these psychiatrists were men. I think some of these guys may be kidding themselves too.

But, that aside, I have to say that, with one or two exceptions, most of what my friends won't tell their therapists is simply outrageous. Why? I did a good deal of speculation about this while I was talking to my friends.

"Maybe all these people were enraged during their child-hood and adolescence at having their privacy invaded," I pondered in the course of a conversation with a psychotherapist.

"That could be one factor," he said. "But everybody needs to have secrets."

"Do you go along with your patients' needs to have secrets?" I asked.

"To some extent, at least in the early stages," he said. "But also, with some people you'd not only go along with it, but you'd be glad of their capacity to conceal things. One of the differentials between somebody who is potentially psychotic and somebody who isn't is that, often, somebody who is in real trouble is incapable of keeping secrets. With somebody who is very disturbed you value their being able to maintain their own boundaries."

"Because people protect themselves with secrecy?"

"Yeah, or anyhow they have a sense that they have a self that they can keep things in. If you don't possess that sense of self, you're in real trouble."

I mentioned all this to a friend of mine.

"Good news," I said. "It means you're healthy if you can keep secrets."

"I must be really healthy," he said, with some bitterness.

"Can I interview you for this article?" I asked.

"I'd make a lousy interview," he assured me. "I try not to *think* of anything I can't tell my therapist."

Of course, my friends may have lied to me too. A psychoanalyst I spoke to immediately said, "Money and sex—that's what people omit most often. Men especially won't talk about sex. They'll talk about their erections, but they won't talk about their feelings." Apparently, it's quite common for men to talk about the status of their erections, or the lack thereof, but this subject was curiously absent from the sexual material my male friends told me they did cover during their sessions. (The reason, I know, is that, as it happens, most of these men talk about sex so little that it was easier to list what they did talk about than what they didn't.) Anyway, after I spoke with the analyst, I called several of these guys back to check on this, but only got a chorus of "no"s and distasteful comments. As in:

"Only when it comes up."

I said nothing. By then I'd heard a lot of these James Bond jokes.

"Ha, ha," said my friend.

I guess this is a digression, but I think it's interesting that people made the worst jokes about sex and shit.

(Maybe I should get the subject of shit over with now? No, I'll get to it later.)

To tell you the truth, I have a problem with this article, because I figure my therapist will read it. For example, even though I started the piece talking about shit, which makes me *appear* to be audacious (an old, old therapy trick), and (somewhat disgustingly, in my opinion) frank, in my heart I know very well that's not the hardest thing to write about. Or talk about.

Of course, there are some things that are just plain hard to talk about to anybody. But, as it turns out, there are fashions in taboo subjects.

"There's always one subject in particular that is taboo in psychoanalysis," a psychiatrist told me. "In Freud's time, around the turn of the century, it was sex. Then came shitting and pissing and toilet training. And it's still the case that people are much more willing to talk about sex in a sort of genital way than oral, or than they are to talk about shitting and stuff. I mean, that still hasn't reached a point where it is as accessible a subject as sex is. Then something changed again and recently, in the last twenty years or so, it turned out that the big subject of anxiety was food."

"Food!" I said. (What a disappointment.)

"And all of a sudden," he said, "people became conscious of their weight and their shape, and anorexia became a popular phenomenon and diagnosis."

Come to think of it, I hadn't even talked to any of my friends about fat, which I suddenly realized must be a significant omission, especially with my women friends, since as a rule it is against the laws of nature for two women who know each other well to have a conversation about anything at all and not wind up talking about thighs and such.

"But lately," he continued, "the big taboo has been money. People can't talk about money. And what's more, analysts can't talk about money either. They're as conflicted about it as their patients. And that's what gets omitted all over the place. It's a bigger source of embarrassment than sex or anything else."

Money. What a dull revelation. Duller, if possible, than food. I'd like to apologize for this article. There's nothing I can do about it: all of this pans out with what I heard from my friends. Everyone I know said they either lied about money, or at least were embarrassed to talk about it.

Actually, Freud himself was on to this: "The analyst does not dispute that money is to be regarded first and foremost as the means by which life is supported and power is obtained, but he maintains that, besides this, powerful sexual factors are involved in the value set upon it; he may expect, therefore, that money questions will be treated by cultured people in the same manner as sexual matters, with the same inconsistency, prudishness and hypocrisy."

Does this Freud quote belong in this section? I only have two Freud quotes I'm sure I'm going to use. Do I have the best possible Freud quotes for this article? Probably not. Should I feel completely fraudulent? Frankly, I had terrible problems researching this article. The interviews were easy: all I had to do was have twenty-five or so most interesting interviews with friends and acquaintances and talk to a half dozen mental-health professionals, all of whom seemed quite interested in this topic. "There's nothing written about it," one said. "Everybody concentrates on unconscious repression, not conscious suppression." Yet it was clear that there was an important relationship between the two and that I ought to do a hefty amount of reading on resistance, and on what Freud called "the impulse to banish an unwelcome guest." But I got medical-school syndrome while reading the psychoanalytic literature. I did read a bunch of books, and riffled through some more, but I quit after perusing David Shapiro's *Neurotic Types* and finding myself identifying with every single dysfunctional type and variants. I have to admit I had a personal preference for passive-impulsive, but I may be flattering myself.

A couple of days after I spoke to this psychotherapist, a friend told me he'd lately lost all interest in gourmet food and expensive restaurants. "It's weird," he said. "After years of consuming interest in elaborate cuisine, now all I want is a nice roast chicken."

So then I told him what the psychotherapist had told me about trends in neuroticism and how all this had to do with childrearing and what our mothers happened to have been conflicted about when we were infants, and that when we were born there was a lot of contradictory advice to mothers about what and how to feed their babies. "But now that's waning," I said. "Now it's money."

"Money!" he said. "It's true. I'm so neurotic about money. It drives me crazy."

"It's not your fault," I said consolingly. "It's a trend."

"But why do I have to be so fashionable?" he said. "I hate the money thing. I hate it. I liked the food thing much better."

"Me too," I said. "In Freud's time it was sex. I wish it were sex again. I'd like sex much better."

"Money is horrible," he said. "I'm so sick of thinking about money."

"Maybe it'll end soon," I suggested.

"How long did the food thing last?" he asked.

"I think about twenty years," I said.

"Oy gevalt," he said.

Wait. I'm wandering.

Money: why are people so reluctant to talk about money to their therapists?

"Of course," says an analyst, "there's a realistic meaning, which is that they're afraid it will be taken away from them."

Some of this would seem entirely rational, considering the fees being charged these days. "No, I never talk to him about money," says one woman, "but it's true it often occurs to me that instead of seeing him once a week I could be out buying clothes that would make me feel good."

One man I know told me one of the biggest omissions in his therapy is that he's uncomfortable about the fact that he thinks his therapist doesn't charge enough, but can't get himself to bring it up.

People who are profligate seem to have as much trouble talking about money as people who are greedy. Almost no one tells his therapist how much he makes. (Of course, several of my friends don't even know how much they make.) Almost all the people I talked to admitted they tended either to inflate or to reduce whatever vague notion of their income they conveyed when the subject came up. Even people with serious problems regarding money try to avoid the topic: one person I know attends DA meetings (Debtors Anonymous, believe it or not) because she occasionally goes on such maniacal spending sprees that she often owes a year's salary to various department stores, but she doesn't discuss the subject with her therapist.

Even people who can talk about sex lie about money: my friend who had the fantasy about the paraplegics has not told his psychiatrist about his last two raises at work. One woman I have been going to lunch with for years (which has enabled me to observe her writing numerous checks without ever filling in the stubs) told me that she has discussed with her analyst her incestuous fantasies about her son, yet she will never discuss money. "It's my one area of intense chaos, and I have the feeling it's the same for him," she says. Another friend told me that he has not told his analyst about his sizable trust fund. I thought this was particularly funny because this was one person who actually said "Of course!" when I asked whether he ever talked about shit. (This is where people in analysis really get separated from people in therapy, as it turns out.) "In fact, several times I've had to leave the session to go to the bathroom," he said. "Usually when we've been discussing anal intercourse."

By the way, in traditional psychoanalytic terms, money *is* shit. "That's the classic meaning," the analyst explained to me. "But, depending on what money means to an individual, it can cover the whole gamut of psychological factors. It can be shit, it can be love, it can be self-worth. It may have to do with fantasies of being robbed, or being raped sexually—for both men and women—of being penetrated and having something taken out."

But I think there's a level on which the reality that can't be faced is that therapy is paid-for intimacy. One of my friends...

No. Can't use that.

Note to myself: must be careful to protect my friends' identities. You know, I really have very serious problems with this article. My therapist will read it. My *friends* will read it. My MOTHER will read it.

Where was I?

Money. I don't think I'll continue this topic. Too vulgar. No concern to me.

Actually, regarding the protection of my friends' identities, I was amused to note that the only time people asked me to be sure they were camouflaged was when they talked about their therapists' shoes. But I'll get to that later.

In any event, most were amazingly cooperative. Though it's true that one person said he had certain things he wanted to tell me about sex and power and control but couldn't go into it at the moment because his wife was at home and he couldn't talk. He said he'd call me back, but I haven't heard from him in the three weeks since that conversation, which is kind of odd since we usually speak every few days. In fact, come to think of it, this is the first time in the seven years I've known this person that he hasn't returned my calls.

Anyway, only one of my friends overtly balked, at first.

"Have you had a dream you haven't told your therapist?" I asked.

"And you expect me to tell *you!*" he asked.

"Yeah!" I riposted.

But then, he did.

"Well," said my friend. "Well, I dreamed that I was standing outside at night on the sidewalk. It was probably in New York. There were four-story buildings. And I had to take a leak. So I went over to the side of a building." He paused.

"Yes?" I said.

"Well, it came out blood."

"Blood?"

"Instead of urine, I mean."

"Oh," I said. "Why didn't you tell your therapist?"

"I analyzed it myself."

"How did you analyze it?"

"Well, what is blood?" queried my friend in a didactic tone.

"I don't know. What?" I said. (I wasn't even going to take a shot at it—I hate rhetorical questions.) "What?"

"Life," he said, impatiently. "I'm pissing my life away."

"Oh," I said. "Why couldn't you tell him that?"

"So you buy that analysis," he said.

"What analysis?" I asked.

"About pissing my life away. Because I have a friend who's a shrink and I told him the dream and he said my analysis was faulty."

"Do you mean," I asked, "that you told another shrink, but you wouldn't tell your own?"

"Right," he said. "It's funny, because I even had a session the morning the dream occurred."

"Hmm," I said.

"It was too disturbing," he said.

"Maybe it's because it was about sex and death," I opined.

"Yeah, it was connected," he said.

"Do you talk to him about death?"

"Yes."

"Do you talk to him about sex?"

"Very little. It's not a problem," he said.

"Oh," I said.

"Though it's true," he said, "that I have better sex with women who are less challenging, when I'm fully in control."

"Well, and do you talk about that?"

"Not in any depth," he said.

Where am I going with this dialogue? Do sex and control have anything to do with blood and urine? Probably, but I think I don't want to know.

I liked listening to my friends' dreams. Though, of course,

I may have heard particularly weird ones, since they were only the ones people recalled not telling in their sessions. Several people told me they'd had sexual dreams about their therapists they hadn't told. (I've never had one of those, thank God.)

One woman didn't tell her doctor she dreamed he was fondling her. (Male therapist.) One man never told he'd dreamed he'd had his session in bed. (Male therapist.)

I think I'll change the subject. Don't want to talk about sex yet. Anyway, I got sidetracked. I was talking about people's being surprisingly cooperative. As to why they would be willing to tell me all these things, my theory is that the bigger the omissions, the more approval they got from me (at least for the purpose of the interview). And a lot of this has to do with approval problems.

"Isn't it ridiculous, all the stuff you don't tell your shrink?" someone said to me. "You know why? It's because they really are your mother. Or whatever. All that transference stuff actually works. You want them to love you."

So, even though you're in therapy because you know you're in trouble, you find yourself helplessly trying to make yourself look good:

"I want him to think I'm a moral person," says a friend. "I won't tell him if I've gone to a party and acted flirtatious and tried to get attention from a lot of men, because that seems frivolous to me, and I want him to think I'm a serious person."

"I only tell him about the good stuff that happens at work. That is, I'll bring up the humiliating things, but I'll try to gloss over them so that I don't appear like a failure."

(If you're not in therapy yourself you may be wondering by now how I can have so many friends who are such maniacal approval-cravers. Contrary to what you may think, I have not selected these people as my friends because misery loves company. [Well, actually, that may not be entirely true, but this has little to do with approval craving.] In normal life, many of these people do not appear any more insecure than anyone else. But the notorious regression syndrome that occurs in the course of a psychotherapeutic treatment of any depth causes them to have a childlike need for approval from their therapist–parent figure. I don't think I'll go into any more explanation about this; you'll have to take my word for it that it winds up being an important part of the treatment. If you think that's ludicrous, just imagine how *we* feel.)

In an interesting twist, some people, in an effort to win their therapists' approval, will only emphasize their worst traits and their most unfortunate behavior. "If anything really great happens to me, I often don't mention it, or else I'll let a few sessions go by. And even when I do, I talk about it very casually. I know why too. One of the things I hated the most about my father was that he was such a braggart, and we've talked about it. I don't want my therapist to think I'm that way too. And besides, I feel I have to be casual about the stuff I'm actually proud of, because I don't want to appear like a pathetic little lemon telling Daddy how well I did today."

But in general, most of the people I talked to seem to want to work hardest at fulfilling what they imagine their therapists' expectations of them are.

"I never told my therapist that when I was in college, I went to bed with about three hundred guys," says a woman friend.

"Literally three hundred?" I asked. I think I was impressed.

"Yeah," she said. "I know I should probably tell her about it, but I only talk about my childhood or the present. My adolescence and my twenties were just too horrible to talk about. I'd probably tell her if she asked, but luckily it's never come up."

"For a long time I played down my homosexuality," says another friend. "He knew I had sex with both women and men, but I talked as if they were equal to me, which they weren't. Then I broke down and really talked to him about it, and felt great about it. But I still am not myself with him. It's as though I spent such a long time convincing him that I was another person that I don't want him to know how much I deceived him. He has too much of a stake in me."

"I always tried to go in with the good news," says another one of my friends. She had a long-standing affair with a married man, which she would not discuss with her therapist. "And when he tried to bring it up, I became an ace at changing the subject, at starting a topic and then veering off. I'd even talk about money rather than talk about that. Of course, I didn't have much of a choice past a certain point, since the checks I gave him kept bouncing. But, anyway, there's almost nothing I wouldn't have talked about rather than this affair. It was too embarrassing to me. I think that when you first go into therapy, you're a complete wreck; so you tell this man what a terrible person you are, you know, how you're completely fucked up, you really need help, this is rock bottom. But after a while, after you've made some progress, he becomes a new authority figure, a parent you want to do well for. So, on the question of my affair, I never broke down, I never got beyond wanting to make him believe that I was not a shmuck in the relationship, that I was an intelligent, strong, modern woman in a modern relationship, and aren't I terrific for that. I was always trying to go in there with a good report. 'I got really angry yesterday and I showed my anger,' I'd say. And he'd say, 'That's terrific. That's really progress for you.' And I wouldn't tell him that an hour before I came to the session I'd let someone walk all over me and not said a word. I'd tell him the good things, as though he'd become a kind of teacher. Good girl, you've done your homework, you've pulled through, now you get an A today."

"Did you realize you were doing that?" I asked.

"Yeah," she said. "I even talked to him about it. I'd say, 'Don't let me do it, don't let me use my tricks on you.' We would talk about it and we would both feel good. He'd feel good he had been able to break through the façade, and I would feel good that I had been able to come clean. And then I would leave for the day, and then the next time I came in it would start all over again."

"And do you think you were replicating a pattern you have in your other relationships?" I asked.

"Oh, of course," she said.

"And what did you do when the cycle became obvious?" I asked.

"Well, you remember," she said. "That's when I decided it was an opportune time to go to Europe for a few months...."

"As trust develops, one barrier after another will come down," a psychiatrist told me. "The biggest problem in therapy is people fleeing."

But you can flee *within* the process.

"No, of course, I don't tell him when I sleep with anybody else," says a married woman. "For one thing, I have these affairs to simplify my life, not to complicate it. I don't want to have to go in there and wreck it by *talking* about it. And, besides, I know he'd disapprove."

"How do you know he'd disapprove?" I asked. (This wasn't such a stupid question—I'd already been told by a doctor that patients project their own moral standards onto the therapist, and that what they imagine would be the therapist's disapproval is really only a reflection of their own attitude of disapproval of themselves.)

"Because I'm sure he thinks I should be working at my relationship with my husband. And I'm sure he'd think that, instead of spending a perfectly pleasurable afternoon in bed with someone else, I should be home having some earnest talk with Tom about mutual needs or something."

I laughed. She laughed. Though we both know it's not so funny. Well, maybe it is funny. I mean, all of this is either really funny, or not funny at all. I hope my friends don't think I'm making fun of them in this article. No, I think they think all this stuff is funny too. Well, I don't know. Maybe it's just me: I prefer to think it's funny, but I know this is one of my problems.

Another thing that bothers me is that I read in a book called *The Heart of Psychotherapy* by George Weinberg that one of the few categorical rules of therapy is that you're not supposed to talk about your therapy with other people. "There are people who make a travesty out of every intimate relationship by discussing it with others to get their opinions. Also, their discussing the sessions cuts down the intimacy of their relationship with the therapist..." points out Weinberg. He adds, "The patient who discusses his therapy with loved ones or acquaintances creates other problems. Knowing he'll repeat to them what he says in sessions, he disposes himself to censor what he says in the sessions themselves."

I think that rule's ridiculous. (For one thing, I don't know that I think anyone who uses the locution "loved ones" has much credibility to begin with.) It's well known that most patients go through a phase in therapy where that's *all* they can talk about. You go to their houses and *before* they've even asked if you want a drink, if you ask them how they are they'll lean their head on their hand and say, "Very sad. You know, everyone has always left me, my whole life, starting with my parents."

Or you ask, "What have you been up to lately?" and an otherwise perfectly reasonable person with a full life, an absorbing job, many interests will reply with ferocious intensity, "You know what I found out this week? My relationship with my sister is an *exact* duplication of the relationship my parents had with each other. *Exact!* It's really amazing."

You learn to put up with this sort of thing, since it usually doesn't last long. Or, rather, a new phase will start, and those who were obsessed with the sorrow of loss last week will this week have become tremendously upset because they've discovered they don't make enough demands ("All right, I'll pick the restaurants from now on"). Usually these people are easy to console. "You won't *always* have trouble expressing warmth," you must reply to the nocturnal plea. "No, no, it's fine to call me at 3 A.M., and I'm really glad to know that you love me." If you've had enough psychotherapy yourself, you get pretty good at this soothing business. When your friend calls to say he can't work because he's finally understood that he once *literally, literally* wanted to fuck his mom and kill and eat his dad, you learn not to find it silly to reply, "Well, yes, it's not unreasonable to think that you're having trouble working because you don't want to compete with your father, though there may be other factors too." If your friend refuses to drop the subject and continues to exclaim, "Kill and *eat* him—literally!" this may be a good time to suggest going to a movie.

The worst phase of all is when people get hung up on their mothers. This can last for months, or even years, what with relapses. One of my musician friends has been in this phase for quite a while now and, as he recently pointed out to me, "While I'm working on a song, I often stop and think, 'Would my mother like this chord?'"

People who are in therapy will often have really silly conversations with one another in which they will complain that their therapists are goading them into irritating areas. "Working on your relationship" is a good one. Can you believe that phrase: *working* on your *relationship*? But there's a seemingly endless number of indignities.

"Do you know what she said to me yesterday?" I tell a friend. (I always try to say "she" or "my therapist." In fact, one of the things many people won't say in a session is their therapist's name. I haven't asked any professional about this, but I bet it's something ridiculous like that they're the "other" in relationship to the self. Or something.)

"Do you know what she said to me yesterday?" I tell a friend, in a tone of indignation.

"What?" he asks.

"That I have a Problem with intimacy. Well, she didn't say that exactly, but we were talking about something else and she said she thought it had to do with a Problem with intimacy."

My friend prudently says nothing.

"Do you think I have a Problem with intimacy?" I demand to know.

"It's not the first thing that would come to mind," he says cautiously. He's had a lot of psychotherapy.

"Exactly," I say. "Though of course now I'm spending a lot of time trying to figure out if I have a Problem with intimacy. It's really humiliating. Talk about therapy clichés: to have to be told you have a Problem with intimacy."

"I know," he says. "I have to sit there and endure being told I have a Problem with anger. But the really humiliating thing is that they're right."

Of course, these conversations only occur when there are

no nontherapy spies around to jeer. (In fact, this article is one of the greatest acts of disloyalty I've ever committed, I think.)

For some reason, the subject of loyalty reminds me of my mother.

Mothers. How did I get back onto the topic of mothers? In fact, I'm completely off my subject, as usual.

It's as though there's something I don't want to say in this article? What could it be? I don't know.

Okay. I'll try again.

One man I know, a painter, when I ran down my checklist with him, gave me "no" answers to almost everything. Love: "I don't want to spoil its mystery." Sex: "It's none of his business." Work problems: "Therapy is too reductionistic to apply to art." Drugs: "He wouldn't understand." Money: "Not an issue." Early childhood: "I don't remember."

I couldn't imagine what they talked about.

"It's true," said my friend, "we do have long silences."

"Dreams?" I asked. "How about dreams?"

"Usually I can't recall them," he said. "Though of course sometimes I do, but I don't like telling them when the meaning seems obvious."

"Gee," I said.

"I don't tell my therapist anything," my friend cheerfully declared. "It serves him right."

He was only slightly kidding. I mean, it's not that much of a joke. You might say this guy must have had some Problems with his father. Well, but who didn't? Another of my friends blithely declared that she had lied through her teeth about almost everything in the several months she spent in therapy. "I'd go in there and spout out these complete inventions. But the funny thing is that it still made me feel better. In fact, I consider my therapy entirely successful: I went for writer's block, and making up all those lies twice a week got me out of my rut."

If these are extreme examples, they only dramatize the rule. In my talks with my friends it became clear that there was a pattern of excising large chunks of one's interior life, sometimes even unwittingly.

"I'm pretty open," says one of my friends. "That's what I'm there for, after all."

"Can you think of any big areas you don't tell him about?" I asked.

"The trouble is," he said, "that there are some areas that I feel are not the purview of therapy, but it always turns out I'm wrong."

"Like what?" I asked.

"Work, for example. For years I thought work was something I dealt with very well. Even though I knew that it was filled with tense relationships and that my particular pathology forces me to act in certain ways, and causes me a lot of trouble, and I agonize over it. But for some reason, for years, with all the various therapists I had, I thought it was something I could and should handle on my own. But suddenly, last year, after all these years of denial, I also suddenly realized that work takes sixty to seventy percent of my waking time. It was most of my life I was leaving out, the canvas on which most of my problems with authority were being acted out, in both subtle and obvious ways: how to deal with it, how to exercise it, how to admit to myself that I was subject to other people's authority. In other words, all the screwball problems I have with everything else too."

I wonder whether these interviews are representative. Are my friends abnormal? "Are so-called creative types crazier?" I asked a psychotherapist. "Well, that's a real hard question," he said. "But without really getting into it, I would say that people who are creative are probably more aware of what they're thinking and feeling than people who aren't, so more of their withholding is going to be conscious or preconscious than for people to whom it never occurs to reflect about what kind of sensations they're having, or who don't have names for them."

Many of my friends won't talk about their creative work either. "When I'm in a phase where I'm working on something that really absorbs me, I won't talk about anything much at all in my session, because the catharsis you get in the therapist's office overlaps with some of the catharsis you get from creation, so I don't want to use up that tension in the therapist's office," says an artist. "Anyway," he continued, "part of what I do and why I do it and how I do it is mysterious to me, and I don't want to wreck that mystery with all that reductionistic therapy talk; I don't want everything reduced to pat personal, emotional terms."

"Does this person have problems working?" asked a psychiatrist to whom I cited my friend's statement as an example and asked for an analytic explanation.

"Yes," I said.

"What this has the ring of," he said, "is a re-enactment of an intrapsychic conflict. Let's say that this person's work has a particular kind of significance to him—that the work represents something forbidden, so that he is in conflict over it. So what happens in that operation is that his own negative self-evaluation about his work is projected onto the therapist. There's a very common notion among people that analysis will steal a person's creativity. It's true of many creative syntheses, not just art but other types of work, or love. Someone may not want to let the therapist into the interior of the phenomenon for fear that the creative synthesis, which to the patient is a kind of magic, will disappear. Yet it's not true, though patients fear it all the time. I've never heard it happen that an artist comes to treatment and loses his artistic talent. It's the opposite that happens. The forces that go into being an artist are so great that a little thing like therapy can't possibly knock them out."

The next time I saw my friend, just to see what would happen, I repeated these remarks to him, and patiently explained to him that his refusal to talk to his therapist about art was a re-enactment of an intrapsychic conflict. "Oh," he said, "sure."

Not everyone is so snide. One of my friends answered my initial question with "Of course I tell my therapist everything. You know I tell *everybody* everything. Why should I make an exception for my shrink? I want to get it all out, tell her every little thing." But, he called back to tell me, he had suddenly realized that he'd never been able to tell her how much he appreciated her, and that he felt grateful to her. "Somehow I can never get myself to say it," he admitted. Also, now that I mentioned it, he'd never talked to her about the fact that he had a thought or two about her wearing a sari.

"She wears a sari?" I asked.

"Yes," he said, firmly. His tone seemed to indicate this was not a joking matter.

"Oh," I said.

"She's from Sri Lanka," he was willing to explain.

"Oh," I said.

"And, no," he said, "I don't have any sexual fantasies about her."

"You don't?" I said.

"No," he said, "though she says I do. Every time I have a dream or something and there's a large brown object in it, she says it's her."

"And you don't talk to her about her wearing a sari?" I asked.

"No," he said. "I've gotten used to it."

I didn't find that so surprising: by this time one of my other friends had already told me that she had not once brought up the issue of race with her black psychotherapist. "It's too weird for me," she said.

Based on my own (admittedly highly unscientific) sample, the worst taboo in psychotherapy is not sex or defecation, or even money, but the therapist's appearance. Yet the impression I have is that many a patient's supposed stream of consciousness is constantly interrupted by unspoken disapproval of the therapist's appearance. Among the people I know, there was fierce general opprobrium regarding dress style, especially vis-à-vis male therapists. Clashing plaids were a major complaint, as were polyester, silly ties, absurd blazers, belt buckles with logos or initials, distasteful cuff links, and banal mustaches. "He dresses exactly like a substitute biology teacher," one friend complained. "He wears briefcase-carrying nerd clothes" was another's description. In fact, I haven't heard the word "nerd" used so much in years. "It's the revenge of the nerd style," one of my friends suggested. The "nerd" look seemed to fall into three categories:

1. The hipster: "He's kind of in the folkie style," explained one of my friends. "Although I know there are worse things. But his sideburns are ridiculous!"

2. The parody of the traditional Freudian: "He's a terrible dresser. Though I guess maybe he would have looked hip in Vienna at the turn of the century," said another man. "No, come to think of it, he could never have looked hip."

3. The wimp: "He's the kind of guy who in high school would wear his pants much too high and have white tape on his glasses and pens in his shirt pocket."

But the most virulent invective was directed at psychotherapists' shoes. Hush Puppies were the worst offenders. (Attention Hush Puppie Corporation: I think you should advertise in the *Journal of Narcissism and Borderline Disturbances,* or whatever—this is your market!) Close on the heels of Hush Puppies were Wallabies and white buck shoes, and anything in patent leather. Revulsion for red sneakers was also expressed. Ditto loafers with tassels. Slippers were mentioned, with considerable dismay. And one of my friends says her therapist wears sandals. "With thick soles," she added, "and he has hair on the top of his feet."

Actually, women therapists are not totally exempted from this sort of invective. I did not speak with this person myself, but one of my friends told me that one of her friends quit her therapy not too long ago, the crowning blow being that her therapist came to a session wearing peds with sandals.

"Why *do* they wear such ugly shoes?" I asked a psychiatrist.

"It's true," he said. "Most analysts dress with extraordinary dreariness. A fetish is made of neutrality. And they don't deal with visual reality, so there is a disavowal of its importance and of the pleasure in looking and in being seen, especially of the analyst."

In any event, the passion generated by the subject of shoes does lead one to wonder why people stare so much at their therapists' feet. "When they're on the couch," the psychiatrist told me, "that's all they see if they turn their heads." But what about people who sit up? "You want to avoid eye contact," explains a friend, "but you don't want to look at his crotch, so you stare at his feet."

She has a point, but beyond that, shoes and clothing are totems, artifacts of subcultures. So even while one part of your mind tells you it's perfectly ridiculous, you find yourself wondering: Can someone who dresses like that really understand my problem, grasp the texture of my consciousness, be able to help me define and fulfill goals that may not conform to establishment standards? Does this person perceive the world as I do? Obviously not, and yet he or she has a tremendous effect on my life and the choices I make concerning it.

The problem is, ultimately, that shoes and clothes are among the most obvious signifiers of class. You could also throw in anything that is a symbol of personal style, posture, physical quirks, office furnishing, speech patterns and accent, what you can infer about his or her politics, even the choice of magazines in the waiting room—the question is: Can this person understand my reality?

"He has this ugly new carpet. I hate that carpet," said one of my friends. "And he's so proud of it too."

"Did he tell you he was proud of it?" I asked.

"No," he said. "But I can tell. I can tell he wants me to say how nice his carpet is, which I refuse to do. It's disgusting. He's such a Long Island Jew."

"But..." I started saying.

"I know, I'm a Long Island Jew too. I've spent my whole life running away from that aesthetic; that's why I understand it so well."

"The people I interviewed said they were unable to discuss socioeconomic differences between themselves and their therapists, even though they often wondered whether this was not an obstacle to their treatment," I mentioned to a psychotherapist.

"It's realistic," he said. "Of course there's a class problem. Many people in therapy are from upper socioeconomic backgrounds, while therapists are generally Jewish academics from the middle and lower-middle classes. But it works the other way around too. If you're an Italian from a tough neighborhood and you walk into an office and see three Ph.D.'s on the wall and a guy wearing tweeds and metal-rimmed glasses, and in your family there's always been contempt or anxiety regarding these people, and you've been told all they care about is money, you're going to have some problems for a while relating to the guy."

This is probably why most people one talks to say they are unable to say anything to their therapists about personal style. Besides, they know that *in theory* this makes no difference.

Or am I kidding myself? This was the subject on which many of my friends became most voluble, most derisive. Maybe this was one area where they could allow themselves to express the hostility they feel toward their therapists but which they will not allow themselves to experience with regard to "substantive" issues.

Or maybe it has nothing to do with either cultural artifacts, socioeconomics, or hostility. Maybe it has to do with... what?

Shit?

No. Too far-fetched.

Sex. That's it. How about sex? Everything always comes down to sex. And clothes are worn, after all, uh, on the body.

"I absolutely refuse to say anything about his appearance," said one of my women friends, the one who dreamed about her therapist fondling her. "I don't think I would tell him if he had his fly down."

"You wouldn't?"

"No. I don't want to believe that he's a person."

"Or that he has a penis," I suggest.

"Oh God!" she gasped. "Forget it."

But she's only been in therapy a short time. Women in deeper therapeutic waters have no trouble speculating about their therapists' penises (though they don't mention the subject to the therapists), and didn't mind at all recounting their speculations in the course of our interviews (though they certainly don't plan to mention that they did so at their next session); in fact, they often fantasize about sex with their therapists when they masturbate (a subject they do not discuss in therapy).

"Do you think of him when you're making love with your husband?" I asked one of my friends.

"A lot," she said. Then she laughed. "Oh, all the time."

"Have you told him?" I asked. (I meant the analyst, not the husband: I may be indiscreet, but I'm not stupid.)

"Oh, no," she said. "I never discuss my sexual fantasies about him."

A number of people vigorously assured me that they do not have sexual fantasies about their therapists. Of course, scientifically speaking, this is about as reasonable as the assumption that the universe was created in seven days by a tall man with a white beard: wishful thinking.

After all, two people (the gender permutations are probably immaterial) must sit together in a quiet room. For hundreds or thousands of hours, they discuss the most intimate matters the human psyche can yield. Fantasies. Dreams. Wishes. Yearnings. Fears. Secrets. They sit fairly close together. They can almost smell each other. They can almost touch each other. They look in each other's eyes, and sometimes at each other's mouth, breasts, groin. There's no doubt about it: it's sexy. How those two people can sit there and pretend that as far as sex is concerned they're dog meat is either a tribute to or a tragic indictment of what we call civilization.

Well, but all this makes sense, actually. The therapy session itself may be the quintessential testament to the notion that you do have control over your behavior and that you are not compelled to enact your fantasies. That is, it's the ultimate denial of the suspicion that all any human being really wants to do with his spare time is fuck and kill, since one or the other, or both, is probably what every patient wants to do to his therapist, and, I assume, vice versa.

Anyway, almost none of this is ever mentioned, let alone acted on, at least by the sort of people I have dinner with, and doctor and patient manage to maintain this astounding discretion, month after month, year after year (except maybe in California, as I've been told, but that's another article).

Psychiatrists are well aware of the problem, and they at least have the relief of intellectualizing this stuff by writing and reading about it in scholarly articles on countertransference and so forth. Patients are left with the unpleasant alternatives of (1) repressing it (and, if they stay in therapy long enough, having to undergo the humiliation of being told that they're repressing it); (2) suppressing it (that is, being aware of it consciously but not talking about it and having to undergo the guilt of knowing they're not really coming through with their feelings in therapy); or (3) talking about it, which, for most people, is simply unthinkable.

On the other hand, some people tell me that what they're thinking and not saying is not that they're attracted to their therapists, but that they think their therapists are attracted to them.

"I know he's jealous," said one person who'd told me he'd recently become sexually bored with his lover, but hadn't brought that up in therapy. "He wants me to concentrate on our relationship, not the relationships I have with other people. I think he would like me to be celibate, because he thinks sex is a distraction from my therapy."

In fact, though some of my friends said they were pretty open about sex in general, and though I'm sure that the people I know are not especially prudish, there seemed to be a nearly unanimous discomfort about discussing the act of sex itself in any detail. According to one psychiatrist I spoke to, heterosexual men are the worst at this, and will only talk about sex in the most abstract terms. Generally speaking, he said, homosexual men are somewhat more frank. Oddly enough, or not, women are the most frank.

A few of my female friends exclaimed "Never!" But others said they did talk about sex, though they picked their language carefully and often resorted to technical terms.

"For the first time in my life," says one of my friends, "I found myself using the word 'cunnilingus.' *Cunnilingus!* I wouldn't even know how to spell it...."

(I have to admit I had to check the spelling myself. I can't believe how many dirty words I've used so far in this article.

Maybe my mother's friends will read it. Is this material suitable for my mother's friends? No, but, let's face it, I've already burned my bridges, though it still bothers me somewhat. Is the secret of life that you don't want to upset your mother? This is a very sad thought.)

(*Maman: je t'expliquerai tout cela un de ces jours....*)

Back to sex. (It's true, this is much easier than shit.) (Actually, there really is nothing very shocking in this article. I'm kidding myself. I mean, even my mother's friends must have heard of cunnilingus.)

(Does anybody go down on my mother's friends? Oh my God.)

Back to sex:

"No, unless you press them, patients won't talk to you about the details of their sexual experiences," says a psychoanalyst. "Men, but women too to some extent, have a hard time talking to you about specific fantasies used to achieve orgasm, or union and merger experiences at the height of climax, the dissolution of boundaries. They will tell you that they had good or bad sex, but the details of what they experience sexually beyond the narcissistic measure of their performance are very hard to get to."

"Isn't the therapeutic relationship itself inhibiting?" I asked.

"Well, to some extent it has to do with their fear of getting excited, and the specific erotic transfer, and there is always an element of shame or embarrassment, where the therapist is cast as some kind of judgmental figure. But it also has to do with the threat to the self posed by sexual experience, and the elusiveness of some of the phenomena. There's a blurring of body boundaries, self-boundaries, of perceiving with parts of the body and imaginings of the other, which don't have to do with our normal modes of perceiving and representing the world as visual and ideational. These phenomena are very hard to articulate and they threaten everyday consciousness."

So this is the good news: we are reluctant to speak explicitly about sex not because we are prudish petits bourgeois, but because the experience itself threatens our consciousness, and dissolves our sense of self. Which may in fact be the whole point to sex, now that I think about it.

The bad news is that it is often this very material, relating to primary process, as they call it, that, when an attempt is made to articulate it, will give us the most vivid clues to our true selves.

"Do you remember when I was completely obsessed with Michael?" one of my women friends asked me.

"Yeah," I said. How could I forget? She'd talked of nothing else for months.

"That's all I could think of," she said. "That's all I'd talk about in therapy, about that he was being cold to me and that it was driving me crazy. And my therapist would ask me what I wanted from him and I'd say, 'I want him to love me, I want him to be tender with me.' If she asked me what my fantasies were about him, I'd say I wanted him to hold me and caress me and protect me and that kind of stuff, you know?"

"Yeah," I said.

"But, meanwhile, I'd always fantasize about him during sex with other people, or if I masturbated. And my fantasies were always something like seeing him fucking someone else. Which hurt. Or I would imagine him looking at me making love with the man I was actually with, and then turning away, because he wasn't interested. And that would make me *come*. Afterward I'd wonder, you know, about myself having these fantasies. And then they started getting worse and worse. I mean, he was more and more cruel. Until finally, one night, I had an orgasm imagining myself lying on the floor and he was kicking me."

My friend sighed. Neither of us said anything for a while. I guess neither of us thought it was funny. For once, even I was stumped for a joke.

"I can see," I said after a bit, "why it would have been difficult to talk about it."

"It was impossible," she said. "It was impossible because I would have had to accept that that's what that whole thing was about, and that what I really wanted from Michael was only pain, that he was giving me exactly what I wanted, and that it turned me on to suffer. How could I accept that about myself? It made me feel totally doomed. So I didn't talk about it, and I still haven't. It's stupid, really. Maybe it would help. I don't know. But, you know, the odd thing is that, by that point, I understood what those fantasies meant anyway. I mean, I'd had enough therapy to be able to figure it out. At the time, I just couldn't go that last step to make it real, by saying all this out loud. And then, later... I don't know... it never came up."

Actually, I think that conversation was not about sex but about love, which means this article is going to get even less funny.

For many people, it takes years of therapy to be able to talk about love or, as it's often referred to these days, primary relationships. Many people protect their lovers, omit or gloss over bad traits, bad habits. Even people who seem to be talking of nothing else will not really tell the truth about problems in a relationship.

"I wanted it to be something I knew very well it wasn't, and probably couldn't be," says a friend about a relationship that lasted a number of years. "I would have had to face that if I talked about it. It's not that I lied, exactly. I'd talk about it, but I wasn't truly honest. Lying, in that sense, is detail work, fretwork. I'd be talking about it and seeming to tell the truth, but if a depressing thought occurred to me, I'd push it away. I mean *really* depressing, not just 'We had a fight the other night and she threw something at me and I was pissed off.' That's nothing. That's not hard. But that lightning-fast depressing thought you have that tells you this is a dead end, that's what I couldn't let go of my feelings about."

"What did you do," I asked, "when you had those thoughts?"

"I changed the subject. I became conscious of the noise outside. Anything."

Women especially, or so it seemed to me, protected their husbands and lovers, not exactly lying about but underplaying character traits that were harmful to the relationship.

Some women won't talk at all.

"When I first started therapy," says one of my friends, "I mentioned Philip's name, really as part of my bio, that this was the man I lived with. For the next full year and a half, I never mentioned his name at all. It was as if he didn't exist."

"You didn't even mention him in passing?" I asked.

"No," she said. "I didn't even notice it for a long time, but then I started realizing that I was leaving out a hell of a lot about everyday life, about my personal life. I didn't talk about home. I talked about my erratic behavior, about how my irresponsibilities were affecting work. I talked about my anxieties, I talked about fears, I talked about how I thought talking about it helped me change all these bad habits. I talked about the past a lot, about my mother and my father, about growing up as a Catholic and a good girl. But I never talked about Philip."

"Did you talk about love in the abstract," I asked, "or sex?"

"Sex! Are you kidding? With my Jewish therapist! Not a prayer. I didn't even talk about holding hands. Then, about a year and a half or two later, he said, 'Don't you think it's time we talk about Philip?' I said, 'Philip. Yes. I think that would be very good. I think it's time we moved on to Philip.' And then we sat there for fifteen minutes staring at each other without saying a word."

"Did you really sit in silence?" I asked.

"We sat in silence."

"And he said nothing?"

"He said nothing, and I said nothing, except occasionally I would interrupt it by saying, 'This is ridiculous, I know that I have a lot of things to say about Philip.'"

"Do you remember what you thought about?"

"My mind became a total blank. All I could remember was his name, nothing else. So at the end of that session, my therapist said, 'I think it's probably a good idea for us to talk about Philip.' And I said, 'Yes.'"

"So, then, did you, afterward?"

"Yes, but it was always very hard for me. I'd start talking about something that had made me furious, usually something at work, and my therapist would say, 'Do you think there's anything else you may be angry about?' And I'd think and I'd say, 'Well, I'm probably angry with Philip too.' Almost because I knew that was what he was driving at. It was the right answer for the teacher. So then I could give him a good song and dance about why Philip drove me crazy about certain things, like his being a slob around the house and expecting me to take care of the quotidian of our lives all by myself and thinking the dirty laundry magically disappears and magically returns in the form of clean shirts, stuff like that. But it took me years to get beyond that."

My bet is that an enormous amount of therapy time is spent by women talking about laundry, dishes, and clothes not put away and other drearily traditional women's complaints. After all, this is the one area women have always had permission to be angry about. Besides, the household chore is not a bad metaphor.

"Do you think you try to make your husband look better than he is?" I asked one of my women friends.

"Not too long ago," she said, "we got into the whole issue of financial responsibility, who's going to take financial responsibility for the family. He agreed that this was my husband's role as opposed to mine, and that this would solve a lot of anxiety on my part about role playing, that I could be more of a... if he were more of a..." My friend was obviously having trouble just getting the words out. Then she spoke quickly: "... woman if he were more of a man."

"Yes," I said.

"Well, and that one way he could be more of a man in my eyes would be to assume the man's responsibility for the family. Not even to make more money, but to just take care of paying the bills, which I usually do. But the notion of trying to teach him how to write a check and pay the bills was so insurmountable in my mind, so difficult.... It was ridiculous. So we talked about it and we agreed that I would try to get him to do it."

"And what happened?" I asked.

"Well, as soon as I got home I realized that there was no way in hell that my husband would ever understand this and there was no way I could teach him without really going right immediately into divorce court." My friend laughed. "So I totally backed off and then completely lied to my therapist. I mean, I said, 'Yes, fine, he's doing all the bill paying now.'" My friend laughed again. "So I guess that answers your question about making your husband look better. I couldn't admit to him that I was married to a man who literally does not know how to write a check, or make a deposit."

Does this sound absurd to you? Are you thinking: "How can anyone in the world pay seventy-five dollars an hour for this?" I hope not. This is why these people are in therapy in the first place. All these offhand remarks and jokes and laughter are often the deflected expression of terrible pain.

"I had an abortion about six months after I started seeing my therapist, and I didn't tell him," one of my friends said. "I felt guilty about it, but I felt it would have been too creepy to talk about it. I didn't want him asking me voyeuristic questions about how I felt."

"He must have been able to tell that you were depressed," I said.

"Yeah, I'm sure he was. But I would come up with other things that seemed like valid explanations, the loss of something else, the loss of a friend, something nostalgic. I would pick an equivalent event that could bring up the same feeling, almost like actors do when they need to display a certain emotion. But I couldn't tell him that what I'd lost was my baby. It was... very private, a very private kind of grief that I was going through."

I don't think I'll continue with this love material. I'm getting depressed. I HATE this article. I don't even feel like making any jokes any more.

Why is this so hard to write? It brings to mind an Otis Spann line:

The work wasn't hard
But my boss was so doggone mean.

Maybe I should have a paragraph or two about how in blues lyrics the boss is a metaphor for the superego. No, that's just the sort of trick I'd pull.

Let's see. What could I digress to?

"Helen Gurley Brown," said one of my friends. She'd spent half her session last week talking about Helen Gurley Brown.

"Hmm," I said.

"I really learned a lot," she said.

"Do you ever talk about your marriage?" I asked.

"Oh, no," she said. "There's nothing to discuss."

Much of therapy time seems to be spent digressing. Some people veer off into anecdote, but this is the least subtle method of avoidance. Some talk about ideas instead of feelings. Others, on the contrary, will unconsciously make only the pretense of approaching a sensitive subject but will then attempt to drown their therapist in an infinite flood of words, endless vignettes, and torrential unnecessary description.

"Just as in normal conversation people hold forth differently, and people protect themselves differently," a psychiatrist told me, "you try to categorize the defense. Some become silent, some cover things up with endless detail. Some digress to another topic, a topic that may even be important but is in fact a defense against a more important subject."

There are some days, though, when the truth about anything at all private seems so painful that the most determined patient will find himself compulsively digressing.

"Something really humiliating happened last night," he'll start. Cough. Stare at a cuff link.

"Mm-hmm?" says the mental-health professional.

"Oh!" exclaims the patient with sudden vigor. "I'll get to this in a minute, but I just remembered something very important I thought of right after our last session."

"Mm-hmm?" says the mental-health professional, who (1) according to his diagnosis does not feel the time has come yet to coax his patient into resolving his ambivalences, or (2) is a human being capable of compassion and/or is sensitive to his patient's need to hold on to his defense structures, or (3) is busy anyway having a vivid sexual fantasy about the psychiatric nurse he met poolside in San Diego last week at the Paranoid-Schizophrenic Disorder Conference.

Some people won't even bother to kid themselves into thinking there's not a minute to lose in revealing some important "insight" they've had on another subject. Some people will settle themselves comfortably in the chair or on the couch and begin a frame-by-frame description of the movie they saw last night. Some people will discuss important insights they've had about their friends' therapies. My friends have told me they often talk about movies, books, clothes (not the therapist's), gossip about people they don't know, or simply babble aimlessly about the meaning of it all and if anything has any meaning at all.

Actually, I am not one to cast a stone in the direction of metaphysical speculation as a diversionary tactic. My own specialty, when I began therapy, was astrophysics, a subject about which I know almost nothing but my own apprehension. But in the course of my early sessions, I carefully explained to—okay, let's call her Monica—my theory about the boundlessness of the universe being a metaphor for The Void. Fear of The Void was one of my favorite subjects, though you can only talk about it in the abstract for so long. I seem to remember, however, a lengthy diatribe on the important difference between the English word "void" and the French word *néant*, which then led me to certain valuable cerebrations regarding psychosexual and intellectual disparities between Anglo-Saxons and Latins.

I still think about The Void, but nowadays I tend to do it on my own time, so I'll spare you the rest of the details. I'm not sure why I stopped talking about it to Monica. I may have noticed her crossing and recrossing her legs once or twice. But if so, I wouldn't have told her.

Instead, I turned to expressing my views on the small- and big-bang theories, black and white holes, my problem wrapping my mind around the idea that any other galaxies exist at all, and, worst of all, that the sun will one day turn into a red giant, then a white dwarf, then will collapse, turn nova, and explode. (Or something like that; I never did do my research for these sessions.) The end of the sun was (in fact still is, now that I think of it) one of the saddest things in my life, but a certain something in the air, a *je-ne-sais-quoi* of disapproval, seemed to hover in the room when I expressed my feelings about these matters to Monica instead of talking about, oh, say, my mother (a subject I consider entirely too predictable), certain of my other personal relationships (honestly, Monica, I just can't think of anything of any interest to say), or my father's death (I didn't want to depress her). So now, for the most part, I've piped down about astrophysics, though I might drop a remark here or there about my anxiety regarding the Doppler effect, just for old times' sakes.

"They use it to figure out the speed at which stars are moving away," I explain to Monica.

"Mm-hmm," she says.

"I don't know why, something makes me anxious about the idea of stars moving away," I admit.

She recrosses her legs.

"Can you say more?" she asks. (I'm really fond of Monica.)

So these days I generally force myself to concentrate on the mundane. But I'm afraid Monica may still not be pleased. ("Why should it matter whether I'm pleased or not?" I bet she'd ask me if I could ever get myself to tell her any of this.)

But about digressions, "Sometimes," she once said to me, "when you talk to me I'm reminded of a ritual tribal dance. There's plenty of action and drama in the dance, and it seems endlessly interesting to look at. But behind the dancers there's a tent. And in the tent there's someone who is ill and in pain."

I love this tent image. I spend a lot of time trying to imagine what's in the tent. But I can only come up with B-movie images: Eyes narrowed by fatigue and pain, someone lies in the tent, drenched with fever, driven mad by the sound of the tomtoms. On the ground, next to the straw mattress, is a pith helmet and a bottle of quinine.

Maybe I'll add a native approaching the tent. A knife is clenched between his teeth. He advances silently, stealthily, glistening under a relentless moon.

Can moonlight be relentless?

I'm completely off the point now, aren't I?

Well, I'm getting close to the end of my word limit, and I've left out a number of important items. Religion, menstruation, death (out of the question to write about this—can't afford it), inorgasmicism (is that a word?). Termination of treatment. And, of course, I've left out one of the biggest—and often unuttered—questions: "Is this person competent?"

"I know he expects me to complain sometimes, so I give him harmless kinds of criticism. I'll humor him with remarks about his lateness or something. He loves it when I say something like that, because then we're talking about us. But if he was unsatisfactory in dealing with an issue of mine, I won't tell him. If I think he's doing a bad job as a shrink, I never mention it."

"But you must have a conflicted desire," I suggested (I was getting pretty sly by this time), "to give him what he really wants by expressing dissatisfaction."

"No," my friend said. "Because my sense is that even though he's asking for it, he doesn't really want it. But, you know, a lot of this has to do with my mother, who is an extremely fragile woman. She's a shrink herself, by the way. And so many of these fragility things could be total projections. I don't know how true they are, though I know what they come from. Yet I keep acting on them. Anyway, despite all the mistakes he makes, he still helps me."

"Do you ever feel grateful to him?" I asked.

"Yeah," he said, "sometimes."

"Do you ever tell him?"

"No," he said, "I don't want to give him the ammunition."

I also haven't mentioned my friend who won't talk to his therapist about his preoccupying fantasies about little girls. About my friend who won't tell her therapist when she's going through a period during which she thinks a lot about suicide, because she's afraid he'll commit her. Or my friend who won't tell her therapist that the man she lives with has a pretty nasty cocaine dependency. About my friend who takes a lot of drugs himself and, in fact, spends every weekend, all weekend, stoned on something or other: "I don't even tell him I smoke." Or my friend who couldn't tell his first, second, or third therapist that he had masturbation fantasies about men beating other men, but finally told his fourth. Or my friend who's heard from someone else that his doctor has had major heart surgery, and doesn't tell him how much he worries that he's going to die. I haven't talked about the man I know who for years had two complete quasi-monogamous relationships with two women. Not only did the women not know of each other, but neither did the therapist. That is, for about a year he discussed one of these relationships with his therapist as though it was the only one. Of course, he was so exhausted he probably couldn't think straight anyway.

And there's more. It's astonishing, really, how much I heard in the few weeks I spent asking these questions. I no longer think therapists have boring lives now that I have an idea of what it's like to be on the receiving end. Though I realize, of course, that I heard these revelations under very different circumstances, in a very different mood from that of the therapy session: on the phone (safe), my questions couched in jaunty locutions (safe), in a spirit of camaraderie (not only safe but ego-reinforcing).

"Therapy is a vulgar necessity of modern times," says one of my friends. "You have to do it, but it's important to keep your dignity."

The sarcasm didn't surprise me. I mean, it's par for the course. And it's not just unconscious resistance either. I think there's something else at work here.

Most of the people I know went into therapy reluctantly, as a measure of last resort, with a strong suspicion that it wouldn't work, but feeling that they had to do something, anything, about this depression/anxiety/confusion—whatever. Not that depression, anxiety, confusion, and all the rest were anything new, of course, but all of a sudden formerly reliable escapes didn't work, or only made things worse. At some point in the seventies a lot of the old remedies came to seem useless: drugs were a failure, for sure; sex with strangers was either too complicated or too boring; fun suddenly seemed scarce—adventure of any kind was difficult to arrange, and sometimes even to conceive of. Clearly, the party was over, and if you didn't face that you'd wind up sitting there forever in front of an empty glass. So then there was a big scramble among people my age to drop the kid stuff and go after Goals That Meant Something, which was widely interpreted as love, work, or money, or some combination thereof.

So for a while you got yourself wrapped tight, and kept your mind off the street while you were busy pursuing various tangible items. But after a bit, when you got some of that stuff you'd been so busy pursuing, you had to face the fact that you *still* didn't feel tip-top. In fact, you often felt terrible. TERRIBLE. And even when you didn't feel completely terrible, you never felt quite right. And now you had all these concrete problems to deal with too: routine (*Routine! This can't be me! This can't be my life!*), obligations, pressures, responsibilities. Routine, obligations, pressures, responsibilities. Routine, obligations, pressures, responsibilities. Routine, obligations, pressures, responsibilities. Some of these people began to hear a scream, an unscreamed scream, reverberating endlessly against the walls of the corridors of their minds. Others were too repressed to hear the scream. I don't know what they heard. Maybe a whine, or a whimper.

And, to boot, now that you were in your thirties, there seemed to be an awful lot of accumulated psychic gunk, which seemed increasingly to interfere with functioning. Certain patterns had become irritatingly apparent. You couldn't get into a meaningful monogamous relationship with anyone, or you couldn't stay in one, or you couldn't get out of one that was clearly a bust. Ditto work. It really seemed too unfair: here you'd been trying to toe the line and you were STILL depressed and/or anxious.

Of course, when you were seventeen you felt just as bad, if not worse, but somehow it hadn't seemed quite so serious, painful, frightening. Besides, when you were seventeen depression was attractive, in a way. Peppiness was okay for parents or other degraded types—religion majors, cheerleaders—not for you and your friends. And craziness was seductive, for political reasons because it was the ultimate expression of antiestablishmentarianism, and for personal-style reasons since it was thought to be conducive to creativity as well as interesting friendships. There was a time when a spacy girl in a miniskirt was very sexy. It was entertaining never to get a straight answer from her. A pathologically uncommunicative boy (if he was smart and good-looking enough) was an irresistible attraction. But now none of that garbage worked. Lately, mental illness had lost its charm. Neurosis lay on the psyche of the woman in her thirties about as attractively as the micro-mini would sit on her hips: just didn't quite make it. Sadness lost its romance—it now seemed, after all, tedious, monotonous. Suddenly, you couldn't take it. It didn't seem funny any more not to function, or not to function well. And the thing is that once you got into your thirties you suddenly were backed into the grim perception that you might be in for depression and/or anxiety FOR THE DURATION.

So even the people who'd resisted all of the various "help" fads, those who'd scorned self-help literature, who'd sneered at Yoga, who'd laughed at est, who'd groaned at analysis— even they were finally forced to commit themselves to one of the hokiest trends in the culture, and when the time came to pick your poison, psychotherapy seemed the least humiliating. And then, whether they believed in it or not, they found it interesting, really interesting, even if only as an intellectual exercise. And it actually helped to talk to someone. It was painful and embarrassing but, as it turned out, it was a relief too. And it was, at least, a fascinating investigation of their exhibitionistic potential. And, what do you know, this or that seemingly insurmountable problem could actually be resolved by applying some of the concepts they had absorbed in their therapy. In other words, willy-nilly, they were helped. So they continue treatment. But only under the utmost duress. Anyway, they can salvage some of their pride by having a bad attitude. Just as they always had.

You might say this is a generation that specialized in problems with authority.

"I think of the things while I'm there, but I don't tell him anything really important. I don't tell him any extremes of degradation or heroism that I feel. On the other hand, I have told him *that*. Then he says, 'Let's talk about it.' But then I don't talk about it; I have a way of seeming like I'm going to talk about it but then I don't. For one thing, I don't want to give him the satisfaction. By the way, have I ever told you that spite was the central driving motivation in my family? But, aside from that, if something's bothering me that's really important, I don't tell him at the time, because I have to sort it out first."

One of my friends tells me he has never forgiven his therapist for telling him that he's "not in touch with his feelings." What my friend objects to is the banality of the cliché, but beyond that I think there's a problem of style. This is someone who subscribed in the sixties to the terminal-cool ethos and made it through the seventies with all of his psycho-aesthetic equipment intact: impassivity, imperturbability, the laconic, taciturn manner, the perfectly controlled, modulated voice, the impeccably neutral facial expression. The whole *point* was not to be in touch with his feelings; how else could he have carried it off? Now in therapy ("I had no choice"), he's being bombarded with powerful pressure to relinquish what has been his exterior and, he had once hoped, interior personal style for decades.

"I can't really relinquish myself to therapy," he says, "because I'm afraid of what I'll turn into when I find out who I really am."

"Who do you think you really are?" I asked.

"I know that deep inside I'm just another Jewish showoff," says this master of the flattened-affect demeanor. "Jerry Lewis! That's it! If I have enough therapy, I know I'll turn into Jerry Lewis."

People are afraid to lose control. Me too. Why? What will happen?

Phew, I'm almost done. What's the big deal? Don't know why I'm having so much trouble with all this. What's shocking? I don't know. Nothing's shocking any more. That's why all this censoring is so stupid. We all know it's stupid.

Well, this is not productive.

This is not a normal article.

I'm not normal.

But what's normal? There's no normal any more either.

Anyway, who wants to write a normal article?

What's a normal article? I once knew. I once wrote normal articles. I think. Maybe not. Maybe I've never written a normal article. Only pretended.

What's normal? The more I think about it, the less sense the word makes.

Oh, no, now I'm getting onto the subject of eccentricity, which inevitably reminds me of my father.

Mental note to myself: must absolutely keep any reference to my father's death out of this article. No one wants to hear about this; it's not funny.

Why is it so hard to tell the truth? I guess I can't answer that question in this article. For one thing, all the emotional business of psychotherapy is only a part of it. To talk about this intelligently, you'd have to draw on other disciplines: linguistics, sociology, anthropology, philosophy, metaphysics. In fact, for hundreds of years people have been writing about the nature of what can't be said; cf. Parmenides, Plato, Socrates, Hume, Kant, Wittgenstein. Would a strict Freudian tell us that maybe all those guys were just trying to avoid saying they wanted to kill and eat their dads too? I don't know.

This is not an article.

No, that's ridiculous. This *is* an article. It exists, therefore it's an article.

Of course, it's not a perfect article. Let's face it, it's not a good enough article.

Why am I blaming myself again? Don't I have better things to do?

Why am I blaming myself and obsessing out on my inadequacy when I should be running around making demands or something?

I don't know. I think it's because this article demands I admit something else. But I don't know what! What haven't I admitted? Okay, I'm a terrible writer. No, a terrible person. How about that? And also bad, ugly, angry, jealous, lazy, dirty, smelly.

Actually, I didn't make that last bit up: I read it in a book

by the Swiss psychoanalyst Alice Miller. *Prisoners of Childhood,* it was called in the hardcover edition, though in paperback it was changed to *The Drama of the Gifted Child.* (A
big mistake to change the title, in my opinion.) In the book
Miller explains that there's a false self designed to hide the
true self, which the child early learned to dissimulate in order
to win a parent's love. "It is one of the turning points in
analysis," she writes, "when the narcissistically disturbed patient comes to the emotional insight that all the love he has
captured with so much effort and self-denial was not meant
for him as he really was, that the admiration of his beauty
and achievements was aimed at this beauty and these achievements, and not at the child himself. In analysis, the small and
lonely child that is hidden behind his achievements wakes
up and asks: 'What would have happened if I had appeared
before you, bad, ugly, angry, jealous, lazy, dirty, smelly? Where
would your love have been then? And I was all these things
as well. Does this mean that it was not really me whom you
loved, but only what I pretended to be?'"

So that's how I know this is the thing I and everyone else
don't want to admit.

I like that sentence, "Where would your love have been
then?" I think it's true. It feels as if it stays true all of your
life: Where would your love be if you saw me as I am? Will
you hate me if I tell the truth? Let me tell you only part of
the truth, so that you'll help me but still love me.

The hitch is, it doesn't work.

Here is my other Freud quote: "It is a most remarkable
thing that the whole undertaking [analysis] becomes lost la-
bour if a single concession is made to secrecy. If at any one
spot in a town the right of sanctuary existed, one can well
imagine that it would not be long before all the riff-raff of the
town would gather there."

One psychiatrist I talked to was surprised and saddened by
the list of things I told him I'd heard were omitted from therapy. "The whole point," he said, "is for the doctor and the
patient to be in an honest interaction, an alliance against the

patient's subconscious resistance."

"I just don't want to get into a big thing about it" is a remark I heard over and again.

But in fact most of my friends told me that when they did finally come clean on whatever they'd been putting so much energy into hiding, they invariably felt much better. No wonder: as you might expect, every psychiatrist and therapist I spoke to told me that whatever was being avoided was inevitably the gateway to the patient's fundamental problems. "The structure of a therapy is its content, and therefore also what's missing from that content," one doctor told me. Despite their frequent rationalizations, my friends know that too. Yet they continue to equivocate about some matters, to lie, to omit, to joke, to downplay, to engage in obfuscating sophistry, to digress. "I don't know why," said one man. "Some of the stuff I hide is so stupid anyway."

But often the lie or the omission, seemingly innocuous in itself, is precisely, as one doctor told me, "the gatekeeper to a string of thoughts the individual wants to keep out of therapy."

Lying and omission are defense maneuvers and adaptive maneuvers, these doctors explained to me, and can mean many things psychiatrically. Lying may have been a lifelong adaptation in situations where there was really no other good way out. It can be an identification with somebody who once lied to the patient as a child; it can be an adherence to long-forgotten family rules, an appeal for approval, for sympathy; it can represent a wish, a fantasy. "It can be many things," an analyst told me, "and there's a great deal to be learned about this person if you study the lie together. The problem in therapy is not if a patient lies; the problem is if the patient doesn't bring the lie in for examination."

"Do you let some omissions or lies go by even when they're obvious?" I asked a psychiatrist.

"Initially you don't want to frighten somebody and stir their fears of disapproval. But eventually you want to be able to allow them to take in your own ability to be tolerant and to scan all of their internal life. So you can't go along with this kind of vulnerability, this felt vulnerability. You analyze it. Why do they need the approval? What is it that they're afraid of? There are a lot of things people won't talk about because of shame or embarrassment, but also, if you analyze the associations, you might find that the reason for the withholding has to do with guilt over destructive urges that hadn't been manifest. Or the real fear might be of getting too close to the therapist, too intimate, which might have a sexual implication, or just be a threat to somebody who needs a great deal of composure and compartmentalization."

"Are there some people who are better off not being honest with themselves?" I asked.

"Yes," he said. "Certain extremely vulnerable, disturbed patients who, if they would confront—say—their incestuous wishes or murderous impulses would be so terrified that they would regress, decompensate, and become like infants."

"Is that rare?" I asked.

"No," he said. "It's not so rare. You have to make a good diagnostic judgment about somebody. And if you see decompensating, or a transference psychosis, then you shift the treatment and don't do too much probing."

"What does 'decompensating' mean?" I asked. (I had a nasty feeling about this.)

"It's a psychiatric term. It means that their adaptation to reality begins to crumble, and the underlying psychosis..."

Some jargon followed here. But, finally, I had my answer. I really think that's what the answer is. It's not just that the truth hurts, it's that it can make you *crazy!*

"Is that what everyone is afraid of?" I asked.

"Everybody is afraid of being crazy. But it means different things to different people. It could mean genuinely hearing voices, but for some people it means to be overly sexually excited, or for certain obsessions to be out of control, or to have diarrhea, or to be overwhelmed, or to attack. So you have to make a determination about how radical a treatment somebody can tolerate. But I'll tell you one thing: most people have great adaptive abilities—even the most disturbed ones—and they will send out the cues, and circumscribe their vulnerabilities."

Well, I don't know about you, but I feel much better now that I know that my disquisitions for Monica's benefit on the subject of astrophysics were not a cheap cop-out but a circumscription of my vulnerabilities.

Maybe I should stop making all these stupid jokes. I really feel guilty about this article, especially since I made the mistake of showing what I'd written thus far to a friend who is a psychiatrist.

"What kind of therapy is this?" he said. He was upset.

"It's the kind of therapy everybody has," I said. "At least, all the people I know. What's more, most of them feel that their therapy is a tremendous help."

"All this mockery!" he exclaimed with some consternation. He was looking down.

"I know," I said. "It does sound a bit like the kids trashing Mom and Dad behind their backs."

"I think you've trivialized the whole process," he said. "That's not what it's really like. It's a much more powerful and moving process than what you've described," he said.

"I know," I said. "We know. But maybe it's precisely because the psychotherapeutic session can be such a powerful experience, can make you feel so vulnerable and yet safe at the same time, that afterward, when you go back to your terrible real life, you need to protect yourself with something. And humor is as good as anything."

"I'm sorry," he said, "but I don't agree. I really can't understand why you even wrote this."

I said nothing. I was too busy feeling guilty, so I didn't say what I was thinking: But it's the truth! Yet I felt bad.

"Did I make you feel bad?" he asked. "You know I usually really like your writing."

"No, no, it's okay," I hastened to reply.

"And the other thing is," he said, still looking down, "I have very wide feet. These are the *only* shoes I can wear."

So then I looked down too, at his loafers with tassels. Oh my God, I thought.

Is he right? No. Yes. No. Well, I can't make up my mind, to tell you the truth, whether all this is funny or sad. On one level, it's funny for sure, to lie to your therapist. Or sadly ironic, anyway. But what's really sad, ultimately, is never to allow yourself the chance to give another human being tremendous power over you, and find out they won't hurt you.

I think that's it. Is there anything I haven't admitted yet?

Okay. Monica, it's true, I don't really trust you either. I mean, I can't, completely. I wish I could. It's not your fault: you've given me every reason to do so, for years now. But I think it's not really my fault either. I think there's something awful in the culture these days that makes it still harder than it ever was for people to trust other people, to trust anyone, even someone who is only there to help.

But I think this is not what you want to hear, because, as my friend says, "Psychotherapy is not about society, but about the individual."

Maybe I shouldn't have said that, about not trusting you. What will you think? How will you feel? Will you be upset? Disappointed? Exasperated? Angry? Or pleased that I've gotten to the point where I can reveal such a terrible secret?

And now what, anyway? Nothing. You reveal a terrible secret, and it maybe isn't such a big deal after all. It only hides another secret. There's always more because it's a process. And because there isn't any truth, really. Whatever you truly feel one moment, whether you reveal it or not, will be gone the next, and there's only forty-five minutes anyway, and there's the interruption of the sound of the door in the outer office when the next patient comes in, and the difficulty of selecting what's important, and the intrusion of sexual tension or gender problems or missed class-communication codes, and the hardship of grappling with the inaccessible, the ineffable, and the just plain random. Just like real life, but worse.

"Yeah, I have a dream I haven't told my doctor," said one

of my friends. He's the one who's been in analysis for many years and can talk about shit and everything, so when he said that, I had high hopes for a really jackpot dream.

"Great," I said.

"I dreamed about a spunky, black-haired, short, vivacious, beautiful woman named Vadge Mandell."

"Vadge?" I said.

"Vadge," he said. "Mandell. I was in San Francisco and I was hanging around with some people and we ended up at Lew Alcindor's house."

"Who's Lew Alcindor?" I asked.

"A basketball star, Kareem Abdul-Jabbar. And then outside this house was this girl I used to know in college. She came out and said 'hi.' And then I got arrested by this very silly, old, frightened cop. He was afraid of me, and trembling, and he had his gun out. So he arrested me and brought me inside this luxury condo so that Lew Alcindor could identify me, and there was a young couple, sort of like a *New Yorker* liquor ad. They were eating but then they went upstairs. Alcindor came home, and he was furious because he didn't know I was there. And he was angry that I wasn't in uniform. Then we went outside, after he relaxed, and I found a whole bunch of watches on the lawn, and they were part of the plants. Then I saw a whole bunch of TV commercials in which sports stars appear as great artists. Alcindor was Michelangelo. I thought he needed some sort of over-the-counter tranquilizer because I was afraid he'd get so angry that he'd break the top of the Sistine Chapel. There was also Wayne Gretzky, he's a hockey player, appearing as Dante. Wandering around with him was this other guy I knew in college, but then I got some very pretty girl into a sportscar and started making out with her."

He paused.

"Hmm," I said.

"That's it," he said. "It's a great dream, isn't it?"

"Why did you never tell him?" I asked.

"I don't know," he said. "It just never came up."

PART TWO

TILT!

Why I Hate to Go Below Fourteenth Street

As far as I'm concerned, Fourteenth Street represents the limit of the civilized world. Now don't get me wrong: it's not above but *below* this thoroughfare that the hinterlands begin, among the charming streets that fit within no grid, where it always seems colder than any other part of town. Yes, it's about time that someone said out loud what New Yorkers who live north of Luchow's* tell each other privately: I wouldn't mind hearing that I never had to go below Fourteenth Street again.

Let's not even speak of SoHo, a preposterous address, which for some years has been fit only for those who maniacally insist on behaving as though they were characters in a Paul Mazursky movie, to say nothing of Tribeca, Nobeca, et al., all those doleful havens for stockbrokers with the most desperate symptoms of misplaced *nostalgie de la boue,* and other lost souls. Luckily, these dismal locations whose inhabitants live not in apartments but in "spaces" can be avoided altogether. It took me a while to realize this. Of course, I never went down there of my own free will, but I used reluctantly to accept occasional invitations to those parts. After half a dozen miserable expeditions I decided once and for all that nothing

---

* Since this article was published, even Luchow's has defected to midtown.

would ever make me return to Spring Street. After all, one might as well go to, say, Cincinnati: it's easier to get there, the food is better and cheaper, and the art shows infinitely superior.

Of course, one has to learn to say no. If you live uptown and are troubled, as I once was, by discommoding requests to throw away a day of your life (it always takes up an entire day, what with traveling time and brooding before and after), here is the strategy to follow: If you discover that a new acquaintance actually lives in that region, or if a previously trusted old friend betrays all standards of deportment by moving there, do not hide your dismay. Simply announce, sadly but firmly, that you will not ever, *ever* visit, although you are perfectly willing to continue the relationship as long as the Nobeca resident agrees to travel uptown. Be generous: offer to meet at a midtown restaurant, by way of compromise. If your acquaintance timidly insists, or shamelessly begs, that you make just one exception, all you need to do is to joke about it. Any joke will do, even a recycled one. "*Me*, go down to Nobeca! Why I'd just as soon go to Cincinnati!" These people are socially insecure, and they will laugh with you while they're secretly wondering whether it wasn't a mistake after all to move down there.

But the Village is another matter. Notwithstanding how carefully one plans, the Village, East and West, cannot be avoided in perpetuity. First of all, among the eight million (plus or minus) stories in this naked city, at least several hundred thousand take place in the Village (that area has a particularly high concentration of stories, since the apartments tend to be small and overcrowded), and, despite all precautions, some of them are bound to be those of close friends. No matter how careful you are, you'll wind up being obliged to go there several times a year.

Don't even attempt any Nobeca-type strategy; that's worthless in this instance. If you try to palm off an invitation with an old Cincinnati joke, you'll only lose a good friend. No, these people are too polished for that sort of thing. There's no point in laughing, since Village inhabitants are not only secure about their address, but, indeed, they themselves exhibit subtle but unmistakable compassion for those poor uptown squares who live in exile from what Villagers consider the city's sociocultural heart.

So, every once in a while, against all of your better instincts, you board a taxi headed downtown. You try to ignore the driver's glee when you give him the address on Perry Street and he chuckles because he's adding another digit to his bank account after doing a quick calculation of the number of miles he will cover getting down to Sheridan Square and then endlessly circling the area looking for Perry Street. Naturally, there is a "No Smoking—Driver Allergic" sign in Son-of-Sam lettering neatly taped to the seat, and you spend the half-hour ride observing the effect of the collapse of your smoke-starved lungs while you ponder the cruelty of life in the naked city, enduring the driver's cheerful chitchat about how "these goddamn one-way streets are always going the wrong way, but we gotta be getting close to Perry now," while your sight is becoming impaired as a result of your hypnotic stare at the ever-growing figure on the meter.

And when you finally arrive, it's not as though anyone will be grateful. No! For those who live there, the Village is a destination, and you're made to feel that you should be grateful to have been admitted. No one will emit the slightest expression of appreciation for the fact that you've torn yourself away from the real world and braved the perils of the elements and of financial destitution to go and drink jug wine or its equivalent in an eight-by-ten living room with an exposed brick wall or its equivalent.

What is it about that area that makes people who seem perfectly rational in every other way want to live up to a tradition of living down? Why are the seats never comfortable in their apartments? Why are the chairs too hard and the couches too low? Why are the dining rooms too small and always overheated? Why is the plumbing invariably inadequate and noisy? Why are there never locks in the bathroom? Why would anyone prefer to live in a neighborhood with no Central Park, no museum, no comfortable movie theater, no

normal coffee shops, and no available taxis—as you discover
when you walk back down the five flights of stairs from your
friend's apartment and stand on a drafty corner for forty-five
minutes while the only vehicles driving past you have New
Jersey license plates and are filled with hordes of beer-swilling
youngsters who yell obscenities at you as they cruise by.

I'll tell you why: these people are nostalgic for bohemia,
whether they admit it or not. Secretly if they consider themselves sophisticated, or openly if they don't, they're perversely
proud of the tradition of their neighborhood. The fact that the
tradition was dead before most of these people were born
seems to bother them not one bit.

Personally, they remind me of Hollywood folks; they're just
somewhat less vulgar. In L.A., people will say, "This was
Charlie Chaplin's house, you know," or "Preston Sturges lived
here." What's the difference between that sort of namedrop-
ping and the unspoken evocation of Eugene O'Neill, Edna
St. Vincent Millay, e. e. cummings, Carson McCullers, and
the *East Village Other*? Only the urban leaning toward the
literary.

After all, many of us associate the Village with our youth.
Those old enough to remember the Depression look back
fondly at the speakeasies on Eighth Street and the bowls of
spaghetti they used to get for a nickel at Mori's. Now Mori's
is the Bleecker Street Cinema. Aging housewives can still
recall how they arrived in New York in the late forties, suitcase
in hand, and headed straight down to the Village, in the style
of *My Sister Eileen*. Now the drugstores where young career
girls used to sip their cherry-lime rickeys at the soda fountain
are sixty-nine-cent stores, Orange Juliuses, and chain shoe
stores featuring Day-Glo cowboy boots. Once there were parties where guys wearing sweatshirts really did read poetry.
Now young singles invite dates to dinner in their studio apartments. And why shouldn't they? So once there were green
fields and now there are sleazy, junkie-filled all-night delis.
So what?

Allow me to say that I am not impervious to the sort of
sentimentality many New Yorkers harbor about the Village.

I even lived there myself in the seventies. And, what's more, I have a bundle of wistful memories from the sixties of traipsing down to MacDougal Street with my friends, absurd nymphets dressed all in black wearing Fred Braun shoes and carrying Greek bags (those of us who thought of ourselves as nonconformists wore all black and Fred Braun shoes but carried leather bags) to meet guys with beards at the Café Figaro who were always just about to make it as folksingers, poets, or chess champions. But that was in the early sixties, when the Fifth Avenue traffic still ran both ways, when Kennedy Airport was still Idlewild, and Charles Mingus was playing at the Village Vanguard.

But even that was ridiculous. I mean, let's face it, the Greenwich Village bohemia moved to Connecticut and Brooklyn in the thirties. If you want to see James Baldwin, take a trip to the south of France. We may all have bittersweet yearnings for the aesthetic of our youth, but living in a thousand-dollar-a-month one-bedroom apartment in one of America's best-known tourist attractions seems a bit like overkill.

Of course, there are those who'll say that a nice thousand-dollar-a-month apartment is a good find anywhere in the city, whether or not it is visited by the illustrious ghosts of the Beats. True enough. But, then, let's please curtail this "sociocultural heart of the city" business. After all, if you get down to specifics, the pickings are pretty slim. A theater or two, a little music, the New School, a Japanese film festival now and then. What else is there: Balducci's?

No, as far as I'm concerned, there are only two valid reasons to venture downtown. One of them is the second-hand bookstores, undeniably the best in the city. The other is the obligatory trek, under duress, to go see a good friend who will be offended if you never, *never* visit. You can only put it off for so long.

When I heard last year that one of my closest friends was moving from her apartment on Bank Street, I had a moment's delight. "Ah," I thought, "she'll finally live uptown in a grown-up neighborhood." Alas, I was sadly mistaken. She only moved a few blocks east. "It's not all that bad," she said to console me when she noticed my ill-disguised consternation. "At least I'm closer to the subway now. Think of the savings in cab fare. You should take the subway more often anyway, instead of wasting your money on taxis. You'll have more to spend at the Strand, which is also close by. I think it's a great location. And I'll be within easy walking distance of Balducci's."

Balducci's again. They're always bringing up Balducci's. Why, I remember when Balducci's was just another Italian produce stand where fruits and vegetables were left to ripen in outdoor stalls in the summer. Well, it doesn't matter. The years go by and it's winter now, and much too cold ever to want to travel down to below Fourteenth Street again. And so what if I remember the days when there were no curfews in the city parks and boys and girls would stroll among the trees on warm nights and lie down on the grass together to neck for hours under the violet summer skies.

A
RENDEZVOUS
WITH SLOTH

FIND myself growing increasingly irritated with the recent faddist clamor for "Quality Time." Droves of drearily earnest therapists and obnoxious self-help-magazine feature writers are relentlessly trying to prod Americans into spending Quality Time with their lovers, husbands, children, and friends. When this sort of well-intentioned nagging appears in the New York press it betrays, in my opinion, a profound ignorance of urban culture and its exigencies on the part of these sanctimonious cheerleaders. The truth is that New Yorkers who have any time at all left over after work, going out, personal grooming, and a certain minimum amount of TV watching are not in the least helped or improved by frittering away their precious few leisure minutes on so-called Quality Time with those close to them (for all the good *that* does...). No, the real self-help is going on in a clandestine manner in single people's apartments around the city. This salubrious activity could be labeled Spending Quality Time with Yourself. And it consists of an occasional, surreptitious, highly satisfying rendezvous with sloth.

I refer to single people because this is one of those things you can't do properly if you're living with someone. "At best you'll be observed, at worst reprimanded," says an acquaintance who's in the know. If you live with someone, you have to wait until he or she, mercifully, goes away for the weekend. Because I'm not talking about a stray half hour here and there spent doing nothing except staring into the middle distance, but of a good two or three days spent in your bedroom by yourself, the door locked, the phone turned off, the rest of the universe blissfully shut out. "It's the great escape," says a friend of mine who frequently indulges, "a pleasant and innocuous form of temporary death."

This mini-fugue can take any number of forms, but among the several people I queried recently on this subject, four elements seem to be interchangeably pre-eminent: eating, watching television, reading, and sleeping. These pretty much cover the range and indicate the quality of activity, although some variations include listening to music, staring out of the window on sunny days (walks outside are out of the question), and, oddly enough, pacing. I was surprised to discover that one of my friends actually paces, since, as far as I'm concerned, the most attractive feature of these escapes is an extended stay in bed, interrupted only by frequent trips to the kitchen. (I envy future generations who will have mute androids to bring meals on trays to the bedroom, or, alternately, sufficiently advanced technology to construct conveyor belts from the refrigerator to the bed.)

My own personal preference is that delightful combination of literature and (strictly junk) food. To my way of thinking, there is no higher form of self-indulgence than lying in bed reading a nineteenth-century novel while eating a sandwich— preferably bologna on toasted Wonder bread with mustard and tomato. But, then, I'm a purist, and far be it from me to proselytize to those who choose to prepare for themselves lavish *petits plats* and either peruse back issues of *Car and Driver* or stare hypnotically at the likes of "As the World Turns," Geritol commercials and all.

The mood of the bona-fide Indolent Interlude is an exquisite combination of self-pity and comfort. The appropriate attire is the (cumulatively soiled) nightgown. The artifact is the abominably cluttered night table (and in extreme cases, a two-foot area around the bed). In fact, since the whole point of this state of grace is to avoid all responsibilities, I would bet that most of us do absolutely no cleaning until Sunday eve-

ning. I say Sunday evening because most of us indulge mainly
on weekends. The problem, you see, is that one is very well
aware of the habit-forming potential of this sort of binge,
especially if one doesn't have highly structured work conditions.

Free-lance writers, for example, are treading treacherous
waters during these episodes. We have to be very, very careful,
for the knowledge lurks that these little idylls could stretch
into weeks and—one secretly dreads—into months, bills piling
up on the hall table, your name forgotten among editors who
once tolerated your presence in their office, your former friends
ignoring your existence once they grow tired of badgering
your answering service for a straight answer as to whether
you're out of town.

I suspect that participants tend to be of the female gender.
When I inquired of a few randomly chosen male friends
whether they indulged, most didn't even know what I was
talking about. "Do you mean needing to be alone every once
in a while?" "Yeah, right," was all I said, cutting the conversation short. After all, my time is at a premium. Only one of
my men friends immediately understood. "I do it at least once
a month," he said. "If I'm in fairly good shape, I order from
the market and cook myself meals. From there it descends
via Chinese to deli food to, worst of all, when I really want to
wallow in misery, ordering pizza and eating it out of the box."
This fellow also has a novel variation on principal activities:
he takes horizontal showers lasting anywhere from two to
three hours. "I lie down in the bathtub and let my mind drift
away. I can't hear anything because of the sound of the water,
so the world is even more effectively shut out."

In these ideologically touchy times, I won't venture to spec-
ulate why women apparently do this sort of thing more than
men, but I would like to point out that, aside from the ones
embroiled in motherhood or some other inescapably full-time
fate, the few women of my generation I know who never
retreat in this way are basically people who can't stand to be
alone with themselves. I suspect they're afraid of what would
happen if they let go.

Of course there are some (I refer, naturally, to the sancti-monious cheerleaders) who would call these episodes a form of depression. But I think the rendezvous with sloth is a form of convalescence. When we're tired of functioning, when we're suffering from overload, when our brain is screaming TILT, why shouldn't we devolve into slugs and enjoy a little Quality Time with ourselves? When tedium finally sets in, we can rise refreshed (and, in the case of persons with high metabolic rates, raring to go), ready to confront our other life. Which is more real? Sometimes I have doubts, I admit. And in the midst of my activities, I can't help sometimes feeling a twinge of nostalgia for those wonderful slow afternoons when it's just me, *Anna Karenina,* and the bologna sandwich.

TECHNOFEAR,
TECHNOLUST,
TECHNOAMBIVALENCE

MANY of us are secretly proud of our faults. For example, I've often been called a nineteenth-century person and, frankly, I don't mind. Of course, some of my acquaintances use the epithet fondly, while others barely conceal their derision. The latter, I usually tell myself, just don't know what they're missing. In fact, I don't have to be pressed hard to admit that I prefer most nineteenth-century values to those of our own era. Romanticism was an acceptable mode of consciousness. Art still had meaning then, as did falling in love. The clothes were better and, by all accounts, so were the dinner parties. Good deportment was so highly valued that it was admirably codified down to the smallest detail. Yes, this is my idea of a good time.

My preference for the last century dictates most of my predilections. If I feel like having a satisfying read, for example, given a choice between Balzac and John Barth, I do not hesitate. Ditto Beethoven and country music, Turner and Robert Motherwell, Nietzsche and Wernher Erhard, good table manners and the New Life Style. The direction to be taken is invariably clear, as far as I'm concerned.

There is, however, a discrepancy in my essentially nostalgic sensibility that I have a hard time reconciling with any of my dearly held principles: I have an irresistible weakness for modern technology. I can't help it, I love kitchen appliances, I'd do anything to own a computer, and I firmly believe that sophisticated pharmaceuticals are the best thing to have happened to the human race since the invention of movable type.

Shortly before his death, I had the pleasure of interviewing Marshall McLuhan. I was calling from New York; I reached him at his home in Canada. He seemed pleased to talk to me but he sounded pretty unhappy about the role of the telephone and other electronic media in our culture. "Over the telephone, we do not have physical bodies," deplored McLuhan. "We are discarnate beings. We become angelic or disembodied intelligences. When you lose your physical body—which you do at electronic speed—you become an image only; you have no real identity and no relation to natural law."

McLuhan was no less depressed on the subject of television. "It puts people in a trance," he said. "It's a powerful tranquilizer. Kids who watch television a lot go on an inner trip; they are in a drugged state. They lose the ability to pay attention to anything in other forms. Television watching is a very diseased form of experience."

I was having a hard time believing my ears were still subject to natural law. Was I really talking to the author of *Understanding Media: The Extensions of Man*? But according to McLuhan a decade and a half after the publication of his famous study, our electronic technology is causing the fabric of our society to disintegrate. "At the speed of light, which is now the speed of information, things fall apart. Communities and families lose cohesion; the individual loses identity. Our society can be called decadent in that our structures are literally falling apart. There are no goals in our society now. At the speed of light you cannot have a goal. You're already there. There are literally no goals, no values, and no morals. And no one has diagnosed the problem. No one is prepared to do so or to take any steps to solve it. People prefer somnambulism. They sleep too much."

I asked Dr. McLuhan whether he had any potential solutions.

"Pull out the plug!" he answered.

"The television plug?" I asked, surprised.

"No, you can't restrict it to any one medium. Pull out the

plug on all electricity. No human adaptation is possible to the electric speed. To adapt means having to become superhuman on every front, throwing out all of the old human hardware. You'll just have to decide to get along without electricity in our world, because as long as you have any form of electric circuit, your own nervous system is being projected into the environment, and at that speed you have no identity."

I pondered, for a moment, the idea of cutting out all electricity. "It does seem to me that this is a very distant possibility," I finally said. "Can you think of any less drastic options?"

Marshall McLuhan thought this over for a while. Then he said, "Well, any kind of rationing of electric services would help."

I must have sighed audibly. "I wish I could see some light down the tunnel," he said. "But it would be an electric light if there were one."

Luckily (perhaps McLuhan would disagree), I recorded this interview with one of my favorite possessions, my Sony Cassette-Corder TC-150A. If I hadn't recorded it, my slow scribbling and poor memory would have prevented me from being able to recall most of our discussion. Also, my IBM Selectric II enabled me quickly to transcribe the talk that we two disembodied angels had via the long-distance wires. (Is there really a wire between here and Canada? I'm a little foggy about how phones work.)

In the past couple of years, I've often thought about this conversation. It seems that the professor, after having made his reputation as a supreme manipulator of modern technology, as a man who saw the machine as an extension of the human soul and psyche, had turned out in the twilight of his life to be a nineteenth-century man at heart. His words are those of the lifelong atheist who on his death bed calls for the priest, hedging his bets.

I wish I had thought to ask him why he was willing to speak for posterity via the heinous electronic circuitry. It didn't occur to me. Now communications expert Marshall McLuhan is dead and has no more to tell us about the theory of communications.

I used to think that I had fundamentally negative feelings about using technology to preserve corpses on the chance that they could one day be resuscitated, their fatal diseases cured. But wouldn't it be great to have a "library" of the experts of all time? If McLuhan had lived long enough to take advantage of cryonic resuscitation, perhaps he could explain why people who communicate at the speed of light can't evolve new goals, other values, different from those of the past but no less uplifting. I'd also like to ask Descartes a few questions. I'd love to hear a new Mozart sonata.

Is this sort of reflection pure whimsy or a plausible projection of the future? If I indulge myself with these fantasies, should I also reflect on their consequences?

As I said earlier, I'm not too clear on how the telephone works. I don't really fit in with a society of individuals who have an easy familiarity with the design and function of sophisticated technology. According to Webster's, the word is from the Greek *technologia:* systematic treatment. The rhetoric of my old-fashioned mind is unsystematic and quirky, better suited to the evocations of poetry than to the intractable rigor of, say, physics. I'm therefore as unqualified as they come to discuss the specifications of our technologies. And it's precisely people like me, hazy on the structure of recombinant DNA, confused about the process of nuclear reaction, who must daily cope with the implications of these technologies in our personal lives.

After all, as much as I may care for the novels of Balzac, I still wear clothes with nylon zippers. And (perhaps because I am a nineteenth-century person endowed—or cursed—with an irresistible urge to generalize) I feel convinced that once I have allowed the nylon zipper et al. to enter my life, I am compelled to examine the moral aspect of all modern technology.

Perhaps you laugh (or snicker disdainfully) when I mention the nylon zipper. But think of all the fine buttonhole makers, dressmakers, lacemakers, milliners, tailors put out of work by zippers and sewing machines. Then think of printers who go on strike against cold type, musicians' unions protesting against the use of synthesizers, Freudian analysts railing against the use of mood-altering drugs.

This is not a new problem. In fact, what is astonishing about most of the technology polemics is that they seem relatively unchanged since the nineteenth century. In 1891, Oscar Wilde had this to say in *The Soul of Man Under Socialism:*

> I cannot help saying that a great deal of nonsense is being written and talked nowadays about the dignity of manual labour. There is nothing necessarily dignified about manual labour at all, and most of it is absolutely degrading. It is mentally and morally injurious to a man to do anything in which he does not find pleasure, and many forms of labour are quite pleasureless activities, and should be regarded as such. To sweep a slushy crossing for eight hours on a day when the east wind is blowing is a disgusting occupation. To sweep it with mental, moral or physical dignity seems to me to be impossible. To sweep it with joy would be appalling. Man is made for something better than disturbing dirt. All work of that kind should be done by a machine.

Wilde's position was that the only way there could be a successful classless society was if the machines did the work. And these machines, thought Wilde, should be owned by the people (the state), so that no individual could control the means of production. Then machines would not compete with, but serve man.

> There is no doubt that this is the future of machinery; and just as trees grow while the country gentleman is asleep, so while Humanity will be amusing itself, or enjoying cultivated leisure—which, and not labour, is the aim of man— or making beautiful things, or reading beautiful things, or simply contemplating the world with admiration and delight, machinery will be doing all the necessary and unpleasant work. . . . Is this Utopian? A map of the world that does not include Utopia is not worth even glancing at, for it leaves out the one country at which Humanity is always

landing. And when Humanity lands there, it looks out, and, seeing a better country, sets sail. Progress is the realization of Utopias.

In other words, Less Work for Mother! What's wrong with that? Personally, I'm willing to experiment. That is, if I accept nylon zippers (thereby going on record as rejecting a slavish advocacy of the work ethic), I'm also willing to try Elavil when I'm depressed or to write a novel on a word processor.

Besides, there is about the *image* of modern technology an agreeable flavor as one tosses it about one's mind. It is an evocation of pleasing, shiny metal, voluptuous plastics, knobs, dials, panels, the smooth movement of mechanized parts.

I first felt this way as a child of the fifties when, dragged away from my books, I was occasionally taken for a meal at the Automat. The old Automat cafeterias seemed sophisticated and reminded me of TV and spaceships. The food, behind its little window, seemed more real, had more impact, more personality as it sat in its isolated metal niche. It didn't matter that one knew very well that some guy on the other side was slinging the pies and Danishes in by hand. You put a nickel in, lifted the little door, removed your pie, and then, once the door had flapped shut, another pie *revolved* into view!

Now the old Automats seem as quaint, as obsolete as an eighteenth-century salon. But in our very homes, we can have computers, photocopying machines, televisions that are turned on and off with the human voice: objects that are, in my opinion, delightful not only for their function, but also for their conceptual aesthetic. These machines are so appealing that, just as people once used the objects of nature (trees, flowers, et al.) as metaphors, we now favor the characteristics of gadgets for the same purpose.

"I'm a member of the Duracell generation and I'm proud of it," says my friend Blair, who is passionately attached to her Sony Walkman. "Plug me in, fast-forward me, and put me in replay." Blair tells me there's a great deal of life she would prefer to experience in fast-forward. "I get so annoyed," she says, "by people who complain that with all this technology nobody has close relationships any more. I like that. You can do away with most emotional responsibilities."

It never fails: the most whimsical discussion of technology will bring up the question of emotional responsibilities. The ultimate decision, then, may be to clarify which emotional responsibilities can or should be gotten rid of.

I first started thinking seriously about all this in the course of working on an article about psychopharmacology. I found a tremendous resistance among health professionals and the public to the idea that seriously psychiatrically disturbed persons should be treated chemically. Risks were mentioned, of course, and disputes about the relative success of drug therapy, but the fundamental argument against psychopharmacology was, I believe, a feeling that people (including mental patients) should solve their problems in the old-fashioned way by coping, by working, by demonstrating will. But I had interviewed dozens of these patients and, clearly, at their nadir they were incapable of performing the simplest functions, let alone coping or working through psychotic episodes, hallucinations, clinical depression. What is morally wrong about the administration of lithium to manic depressives if it may in fact enable them eventually to reassert their will and resume their emotional responsibilities? None of the anti–drug-technology advocates really answered this question satisfactorily, but there was a lot of talk about "human dignity." How much human dignity does an unmedicated schizophrenic possess? A suicide?

The point is that once I'd made up my mind conclusively that psychopharmacology was in principle (if not always in application) a good thing, the door was open to all sorts of other questions. I felt curiously liberated. All right, so I wasn't a consistently nineteenth-century person; I'd succeeded in abandoning the need to preserve that image. Still, I didn't realize the extent to which I'd been indoctrinated into upholding the moral value of emotional responsibility.

The exact moment in which I was forced to re-evaluate not only my opinions, but also my fundamental attitude, was in the course of an idle conversation I had with a man I know.

We were discussing a news item relating to the newly discovered process by which a woman can become pregnant following the insertion into her womb of an embryo that has been fertilized in a glass dish by sperm from her husband.

"Soon they'll be able to carry out entire pregnancies in the laboratories," I said.

"Much better," said my friend.

"Well, yes, for those women who can't carry a pregnancy to term successfully," I said.

"I think everybody should do it," he said.

"I wouldn't!" I exclaimed.

"Why not," he asked, "if it were medically safe? In fact, it would probably be safer for the child. And you could smoke and drink if you wanted to. And you could remain mobile and not lose months of your life."

"But..." I started to say. Then I paused. I didn't have a good answer. All of the arguments that came to mind could be refuted with the query "Why?" In every instance, the justification for preferring *in utero* pregnancy resided in the insistence on continuing to lug around nineteenth-century baggage.

Anyhow, that's how I came to realize that one has constantly to be wary, not just of the future, but also of the past. It's a little disorienting not to have a consistent frame of reference any more, but it's infinitely more interesting. Technolust, technodread vie in my consciousness, positioning, repositioning their messages of pleasure and anxiety: video records, Thalidomide, mylar, Frankenstein, supersonic planes, artificial skin, Tang, Johnny Carson, microchips, Percodan, rock 'n' roll, holograms, World War III, motorized sexual aids, Excedrin, solar energy, computer dating, and the timeless desire to learn the landscapes of inner and outer space.

I read an article recently in *Science Digest* that speculated on the role of the stars in our consciousness. "Would we be fully human without the stars?" the author queried. "Do we owe our curiosity, our imagination, even our upright posture to the fact that our ancestors pondered, mapped and reached for the heavens?"

Perhaps. And, similarly, it seems to me that the invasion of technology into our personal lives, while it may impoverish us in some regards, ultimately enriches our sensibilities, makes us more interesting, intellectually richer—not simpler—people.

"Are you a 'nostalgist'? In what time would you prefer to live?" Vladimir Nabokov was asked in the course of a *Paris Review* interview. Nabokov answered: "In the coming days of silent planes and graceful aircyles, and cloudless silvery skies, and a universal system of padded underground roads to which trucks shall be relegated like Morlocks. As to the past, I would not mind retrieving from various corners of spacetime certain lost comforts, such as baggy trousers and long, deep bathtubs."

The future needn't be unpoetic, nor does it have to exclude the amenities of the past. As for me, I'm perfectly satisfied with the best of both worlds: I'll take a Concorde to London's National Gallery to view the Turners; I'll listen to Beethoven with the latest electrostatic speakers; and if someday I find myself reading a Dickens novel on a computer terminal with the capacity to store and display every great work of the nineteenth century, that's okay too.

THEY CAN'T TAKE THAT AWAY FROM ME

FRED ASTAIRE is my hero, and I don't care who knows it. "Gimme a break!" sneer the technocrats, the pseudo-dandies with the punk haircuts, all those who favor business lunches and open relationships. Yes, they will mock, but I don't care. Indeed, my sentiments regarding Fred Astaire are almost of a missionary nature. After all, everyone's got his prescription for improving the world: these days, social critics beg for less narcissism, environmentalists for conservation, and Republicans for lower taxes. I say Fred is our ticket. I say: Bring back moonlight!

Naturally, I speak of Fred Astaire as metaphor. Consider how certain concepts evoke, beyond themselves, the pinnacles of Western culture. The Acropolis. The sonata-allegro form. The British Museum. The Theory of Relativity. Fred Astaire. But whereas in the history of our civilization there are many landmarks of power, money, and, more seldom, beauty and wisdom, only Astaire consummately exemplifies casual elegance. I speak not merely of the now venerable dancer, but of the concept of the icon of finesse, the embodiment of grace, the paragon of romance. Fred Astaire is the *summum bonum* of debonair charm, a quality that, alas, is disappearing from our cultural shores.

I happen to believe that the public TV stations in this country should run Fred Astaire movies all night, every night. It would indeed be a public service. We could all go to sleep with the sets on and, just as we are subliminally influenced by commercials we thought we hadn't noticed, we might unconsciously absorb some of the glorious Astaire allure that we who are stranded in the eighties so desperately need. Think of all we'd learn: how to walk, how to dress, how to banter, how to dance "The Piccolino."

But no, we enthusiasts are left to peruse local listings for the sporadic appearance of our idol. He's always worth the wait for the "Late, Late, Late Show." The more I see of these films, however, the more a bizarre and compelling urge overtakes me. I want to find Fred Astaire. Not in *Top Hat,* not in *Carefree,* not in *Swing Time,* but, you know, in Real Life. Not the literal Astaire, of course. What I'm looking for is the Fred Astaire attitude, the mood, the subtle certain something that made life seem, how shall I say, worthwhile, in 1935....

Needless to say, my search so far has been perfectly futile. Otherwise I wouldn't be writing this. I'd be dancing on some parquet floor wearing a dress made of ostrich feathers. (And I'd be blond, but that's beside the point.)

Why can't I find Fred Astaire? Is his persona a total fiction? It's odd, but the Astaire character as I imagine it seems so plausible, so likely, that I simply can't understand why he's only to be found on celluloid. Why, there must be hundreds, maybe even thousands of Fred Astaires out there. You know, guys who can strike a jaunty pose next to a candelabra without getting their hair singed; guys who assure you that not only are they in heaven but they can hardly speak when they're dancing with you cheek to cheek. Most guys I know won't even dance cheek to cheek except as a joke, and it's usually with one another. But so far I'm not discouraged. I'm keeping my hopes up and staying on the lookout. One thing I'm convinced of: I'll know the real thing when I see it.

I'm sure Fred Astaire doesn't read paperbacks. (Whether he reads at all is another matter, but never mind, you know what I mean.) And he wouldn't own a digital clock. He'd never wake up angry in the morning. You couldn't pay him to be rude to a waiter. And he would never, *never* have a recording machine answer his telephone.

Speaking as a woman, I pine for Fred on numerous occasions. I pine, for example, when the man who walks into the restaurant ahead of me allows the door to slam neatly in my face. I pine when my lover comes to breakfast in his jockey shorts. I pine when my editor rudely insults me without subsequently tearing off my glasses and falling in love with me. (Actually, I believe it's Humphrey Bogart who tears off girls' glasses and falls in love with them, but you get the general idea. In fact, as it happens, I don't wear glasses.) I even pine for Fred Astaire seasonally. In the spring and summer, I pine for the tender hand-in-hand walks in appropriately bucolic surroundings. And in the fall and winter, I pine on schedule once a week, in splendid solitude, for the entire duration of "Monday Night Football."

I think the trouble with young men today is that they don't have any romantic ideals. And it's no wonder: all of their role models are hicks, schlepps, stiffs, or studs. After all, who is there? Richard Gere? Robert de Niro? Bill Murray? Please. I mean, in your heart, you *know* these people have terrible table manners. And as for their wardrobes, it's strickly heartbreak city.

I'm not saying they should bring back white tie and tails—though that would be lovely at crucial points in a relationship, the first time a man spends the night in one's apartment, for example. But let's be realistic; what with the frequency of one-night stands these days, the dry-cleaning bills would be astronomical. Certainly, the very least men could do, in memory of the great silhouette, would be to try and develop some Attitude about what they wear, instead of contenting themselves with whipping out their MasterCard as soon as they've found their size. Think of how great Astaire always managed to look, though he may in fact have been wearing a business suit, a sailor's outfit, or even one of those ridiculous ascots.

And if you think dress is not all that important except on nights out, you are sadly mistaken. "It is only the shallow people who do not judge by appearances," said Oscar Wilde, who knew a thing or two about such matters. Why, Fred Astaire looks impeccable in pajamas! His dress, his carriage, his manners all evoke that sexiest of attributes, breeding. And that's why, whether he was cast as a millionaire, a psychiatrist, or a struggling vaudevillian, Astaire always managed to convey an ambience of affluence and glamour. The Attitude, so well illustrated by his wardrobe and, of course, his dancing, was also marvelously epitomized by the tilt of his hat, the way he descended a staircase, the way he phrased a song, the way he made Ginger Rogers feel, the rose in the bud vase. No, no, they can't take that away from me.

Glamour, after all, is a state of mind. Granted, Astaire is a superb dancer. And granted, he got plenty of help in his films by way of props, sets, the costumes of his partners, to say nothing of some great scores. But for the truly ardent Astaire enthusiasts, for the hardcore, guts-to-the-wall fans, the most splendid moments in the Astaire films are the simplest ones, those in which he subtly turns the merely pedestrian gesture into the natural expression of exquisite grace: his gait when he crosses the street, the way he enters a room, how he holds his cane, the instant in a dance when he pauses and looks into his partner's eyes. Now, next time you're spending the evening in a disco, look around. Need I say more?

But my hero isn't only charming, glamorous, refined, and elegant. He is also honorable, brave, and audacious if need be, and this despite his obvious (and so endearing!) natural timidity. Fred Astaire dared! He dared to go after the girl, he dared to wear spats, he dared to call Audrey Hepburn "Funny Face," he dared to dance. He was somewhat homely, not particularly tall, much too skinny, yet he dared, dared to be a movie star. But even when he was bold, he had grace—none of this brassy vulgarity so evident in the behavior of the contemporary go-for-it set. After all, would anyone ever accuse Fred Astaire of being coarse or pushy? Certainly not. He remained modest and restrained and he still got the girl or the job. Even when he had a temporary setback, he did not throw a nasty tantrum. If Joan Fontaine was (for the moment) unresponsive, he did not turn on her like a Doberman pinscher and inform her that she was a repressed lesbian and a disgusting ballbreaker. No, not once in any of his numerous films did Astaire ever exhibit the urge to utter a primal scream. I guess no therapist had ever told Fred to Look Out for Number One. He may have sulked every once in a while, but he always remained civilized. At worst, he'd go out in the London fog and sing a little.

In fact, Astaire's boyish cheer is part of his appeal. It seems impossible not to be fond of Fred Astaire. He is inexhaustibly good-natured. (Who else could put up with Edward Everett Horton?) Even in these cynical times, his perennially winsome mien seems pleasant rather than irritating. And I speak as one who is ready to kill when a waiter says "Enjoy" as he places a plate in the vicinity of my seething bosom and clenched jaw.... The Astaire genius consists in never dancing over the line. And this is the magic one looks for, in vain, among the business-lunch/open-relationship types: good cheer without doltism, warmth without mawkishness, elegance without archness, nonchalance without indifference, and excellence devoid of arrogance. He embodied that uniquely American combination of energy and looseness, but he added to it a Continental gloss, the result being an irresistible mélange of chic and good humor. He's perfect.

All right, I know. I know the Astaire films are hokey. I know people watch them as camp artifacts, as frivolous confections filled with air. But let them eat hot dogs. As for me, I'm hooked on soufflés. I'll take it: the candelabra, the carnation in the lapel, the bashful smile, the top hat, and even "The Yam." I can't help it. Try as I might to maintain the proper contemporary disdain for sexist film themes, and as much as I may attempt to regard with mere contemptuous amusement the absurd plots with their chestnut devices of mistaken identities and the inevitability of the wedded-bliss conclusions, I can't help it, I'm sold. As far as I'm concerned, the worst part of watching Fred Astaire movies is the bilious aftermath of two solid hours of being jealous of Ginger Rogers.

Just think how much better the world would be if more people felt as I do: All personal problems would be resolved as soon as boy got girl, which would invariably occur. There'd be champagne parties every night, and all the men would be clever and wonderful dancers, and all the women would be beautiful blondes wearing dresses made of ostrich feathers. Why, there'd even be moonlight again.

THE NIGHT
THEY STARED
INTO THE GAZPACHO

O H, no," said Nick when he came into the living room and saw me and my club soda.

"Hi," I said grudgingly.

"How long have you been up?" he asked.

"Since six," I said.

"Oh, no," he said.

"Why?" I asked.

"I just woke up and I'm still in direct contact with my unconscious."

"So?"

"I'm not ready for a discussion of American culture," he announced, firmly.

"Who said anything about American culture?" I asked.

"You will," he said, "within half an hour."

"Certainly not," I said.

"You always do when you have a hangover," he said.

"I certainly don't have a hangover," I said.

"Aside from the undeniable evidence of the club soda at 9 A.M.," he said, "I can tell by your expression, the unopened newspaper, and the filled ashtray that you've spent the last three hours nursing your hangover and regretting the things you said at dinner last night."

"Nonsense," I said, picking up the *Times* and pretending to study the headlines.

"Do you want some oatmeal?"

"Certainly not."

Nick stalked off to the kitchen with a tread so heavy it seemed to be broadcast live in my skull cavity. (I happened to have been nursing a terrible hangover.) And then I heard him in the kitchen removing every pan from the cupboard to find the one he prefers to prepare oatmeal in.

Why did I have to say those things last night? I asked myself for the two hundredth time that morning.

I had assumed there would only be editors and writers and their spouses or spouse-equivalents at this dinner—not an unreasonable assumption, considering how much effort one must expend ever to meet anyone socially who's not an editor or a writer or an editor/writer's spouse or spouse-equivalent. Though every once in a while one might run into a photographer or an art director. Anyone not in journalism or publishing seems positively exotic. Imagine my amazement, then, when I arrived to discover that one of the guests was not only a lawyer, but *black*.

Carl Carlton, his name was. For once I even remembered a name when I was introduced. After all, I hadn't had dinner in the company of a black man in ages.

"I hadn't had dinner in the company of a black man in ages," I said to Nick when he came back in with his bowl of oatmeal.

"Perhaps it was unwise to mention that at dinner," he said.

"But that's what everyone else was thinking about. None of them had had dinner with a black man in ages either."

"But you were the one who talked about it. You broke the code."

"And please take your bowl back to the kitchen when you're through with the oatmeal. You always forget," I said dryly. By now I was very irritated. I knew which code I'd broken, and felt I didn't need to be reminded.

"You broke the code of polite white people never to bring up race when there's a black person around," said Nick mercilessly.

"Not directly," I pointed out. "All I said was that I was bored to death with living in the ghetto of the white upwardly mobile print-oriented."

"Which was bad enough. But then you had to bring up sex too."

"Not directly," I pointed out. "I said I missed having black women friends."

"But you added that one of the things you missed the most was black women's frankness about sexuality."

"But it's true," I said, somewhat belligerently.

Nick reached for the C section.

"I don't think we should discuss this now," he said.

"I happen to have been thinking lately about black people and sex," I said.

"Mm-hmm," he said, taking his turn at pretending to be reading the paper, which was an absurd sham since one of the things Nick has often indicated in the early morning is that he can't read while I talk.

"Because of the Bobby 'Blue' Bland concert," I continued. I knew he wanted to read the book review, but I can be merciless too.

"What Bobby 'Blue' Bland concert?"

"I went to the midnight blues show at the Beacon Theater the other night, to hear Bobby 'Blue' Bland. And there were almost no white people there."

"Mm-hmm," he said.

"And there were a lot of black girls there who were calling out the most incredible things."

"Like what?" he couldn't resist asking.

"Like yelling: 'Do it slow, Bobby. Take your time.'"

"That's not so incredible," said Nick.

"Not at a black concert, but that's the point," I said. "It was just so frank."

"Mm-hmm," said Nick.

"And about the blues..." I began.

"Don't you think it's a little early in the day for generalizing?" pleaded Nick.

"Generalizing!"

"Believe me, I can see your argument about black music unfold in all its splendor, but that's why everyone started staring at their gazpacho when you piped up last night. You were feeding the stereotype that white people think about black people in stereotype."

"Well, it's no wonder," I opined. "The white people I know don't ever get to meet any black people. There are barely any black people in journalism, for that matter, which may be one reason why there's almost nothing in the general press about black culture."

"That's why your journalism pals were upset last night. Because they went to school with black kids, and they grew up with Little Richard and the march on Selma, and they rooted for Black Power, but now it's an unusual event to have dinner with a black person."

"But, so, why not talk about it?"

"For one thing, because the first message they want to send a black person is 'Hey, I'm cool. I've got no problem here.'"

"Yeah, it's really convincing too," I muttered in my most sardonic delivery, considering it was so early in the morning I hadn't revved up yet.

"But also because there's a *modus vivendi* that depends on people not talking about it publicly, except with the utmost caution."

"Well, I think the *modus vivendi* stinks," I declared.

"Would you like some of my oatmeal?" asked Nick.

"No," I said.

"You'd feel better."

So I went back to pretending to read my part of the paper too.

In the alto section of my high-school chorus, I used to sit next to a black girl whose name was Misha. We shared a score. I was a better sight-reader but she had a truly beautiful voice. She was really great-looking, had the best cheekbones and surprising blue eyes; she was tall and slim-hipped and had breasts which, now that I think of it more than twenty years later, I still envy. When we were both fifteen, the comparison was calamitous for me.

The alto section always needed the least rehearsal, so while the conductor worked with the more neurotic sopranos, or the somewhat wispy tenor section, Misha and I talked. We talked about a lot of things, but since we were both fifteen, we talked mostly about sex. I was rather at a disadvantage because, at the time, I was still seriously pondering the subject of my troublesome virginity. Misha's uptown experience was, from my pale downtown perspective, endlessly fascinating. There was nothing unusual about this disparity: black kids were one or two years ahead of white kids on everything that really mattered then, like sex or drugs or music, until sometime later in the sixties when many of the white kids wised up some.

At any rate, too generous to be contemptuous of my inexperience, once we'd become friends Misha would recount in the most absorbing detail the events of the preceding nights.

"It was bad," she once told me, about sex with a boy she particularly loved. This was the first time I'd heard the word "bad" used for "good," and it opened vistas in my consciousness applicable to a good deal more than sex.

"He was huge," she said.

"He was?" I queried noncommittally. Since I was personally rather terrified at the idea of huge, I wasn't sure whether this was good or bad. Or, for that matter, "bad."

"We did it real slow," Misha told me. "It was sweet, it was really sweet."

Sweetness wasn't something I associated with sex either. For one thing, I was accustomed to hearing the word "sweet" used synonymously with "cute," often condescendingly. This was a new construct, interesting to bounce off of not just sex but also, say, music, beauty, mood. And even though I didn't possess the sensory knowledge to truly understand Misha's use of the word "sweet" in the context of sex, in order to begin to extrapolate its meaning I had to rid myself for the moment of what I had already been indoctrinated to associate with sex: fear, shame, barter, and nebulous romance. This other view of pleasure, honest but tantalizingly girdled in the gentle restraint of sweetness, was much more sophisticated than anything I would have come up with on my own. So after I'd heard the inflection in Misha's voice when she said "It was sweet," I started thinking. That is, there are certain things I never thought of the same way again. In fact, I'd say my brain took a turn it's never quite recovered from, fortunately for me, by the time our chorus got through with Handel's *Israel in Egypt,* the Mozart Mass in C, and Fauré's rather thinner but lovable Requiem.

But the last fascinating thing Misha told me was: "Then his mother came home, so we had to jump out of bed and put our clothes on fast. Then we quickly opened all the windows because, you know, sex smells different when you're pregnant."

I sighed.

"What?" said Nick.

"I'm depressed," I said.

"Why?" he asked.

"I was just thinking about this black girl who was my friend in high school. She had to drop out when she was fifteen. She's probably somewhere in Harlem now, bringing four kids up on welfare."

"Maybe she isn't. How do you know? Maybe she wound up going to medical school."

"Chances are she didn't," I said.

"That's true," he admitted.

"While I have three more appointments this week for gourmet dinners out in the white upwardly mobile print-oriented ghetto."

"That's why it's a lousy *modus vivendi,*" he said.

"Then why are you reproaching me for saying those things last night?" I demanded.

"I'm not," he said. "I didn't mind."

"You didn't?"

"No, I was the only white person who didn't stare into the gazpacho, which gave me the opportunity to look around the table and note that the only other person not staring into the gazpacho was Carl Carlton, who, I believe, was interested in what you were saying."

"I'll never know," I said. "The subject was changed with head-spinning rapidity."

"I think," said Nick, "he noticed that too, and didn't want to embarrass anyone."

"Really?"

"I don't know, for sure. As you say, the speed with which the subject was changed was vertiginous."

"And to *Ghostbusters* too. *Ghostbusters!* Every dinner you go to, that's what people are talking about. They'd much rather talk about movies than about anything. They'd rather talk about movies than about life. I mean, it's incredible! I can't believe they'd rather talk about movies than about *sex!*"

"They'd certainly rather talk above movies than about race, unless it's a movie about race."

"What was the last movie about race?"

"Uh," said Nick, *"Guess Who's Coming to Dinner?"*

"Oh, never mind. I don't get it."

"It's complicated," said Nick. "These particular people feel off the hook about racism, because they believe they're not racists, and because they in fact admire blacks. In many ways, they're jealous of blacks. But at the same time they know they wouldn't want to be black."

"Well, I know it's complicated."

"People are uneasy," said Nick.

"For crying out loud," I said, "it's not as if I'd brought up the size of black men's cocks or anything."

"Thank God," said Nick, picking up his newspaper again when he saw I felt better.

"Why?" I asked. "Do you know that I saw an article the other day in a national magazine about condoms that specifically mentioned that they manufacture condoms in smaller sizes for Japanese men?"

"Do you know what time it is?" asked Nick.

I looked at my watch.

"Nine-forty-five," I said.

"It's too early in the morning to discuss Japanese penises."

This annoyed me.

"It's true," I said.

"What?" he asked.

"They're huge."

"What?"

"Black men."

"Oh God," he said.

"Well," I said, "it's as good a metaphor as anything else. It all has to do with fear."

Nick folded the paper.

"The reason it's all right to write in national magazines about Japanese penises," I declared, "is not just to make people feel okay about having honky wienies, but because ultimately American whites are less afraid of yellow people than of black people."

My head was clearing; I was starting to feel more like myself.

"I win," I said.

"What?"

"It's over half an hour and I haven't used the words 'American culture' once," I pointed out.

Nick stood, and neatly centered his oatmeal-caked bowl on the coffee table.

"You know," he said as he headed out of the room, "when you get up before I do, my life is a vale of tears."

PART THREE

THE
PRICE

THE RISKS OF ROCK: STING

ONE night at dinner, I picked a piece of shrimp shell off of Sting's sweater, and it's been bothering me ever since. I don't know: was that presumptuous on my part? You'd think not. We'd already done several interviews. We were pretty friendly, considering the inherent manipulativeness of a relationship between two people who mainly talk with a tape recorder on.

In any event, that night, my tape recorder was off. And though I was sitting next to him, I was studying him only slightly, out of habit. We were at that glitzy place Mr. Chow's, having a fairly swank meal, even by rock-'n'-roll standards: Cristal champagne, for example. There were six of us at a large round table and everyone was talking a lot, except Sting, who was in one of his subdued modes. He's often pretty quiet when there's a bunch of people around, but I think he was protecting himself from the glitz too. He usually lives pretty simply, avoids the high life, if you want to call it that, eagerly embraced by most other seven-digit-income rock stars. He's not a vulgar man.

For example, his off-stage wardrobe is studiedly low-key. Well-cut clothes in soft fabrics, pale, neutral colors. However, he wears these sweaters that don't look like much to the uninitiated but which actually took six Irishwomen a year to knit. That's what he had on that night, a very handsome fuzzy item. Anyway, at one point well into the meal, I happened to notice that he had a piece of shrimp shell caught in the fuzz of his sweater. It was as an appetizer that we'd had the salt-and-pepper shrimps (or, in Mr. Chow's parlance, *crevettes sel et poivre),* and the shell must have been dangling there for some time.

So, naturally, I reached over and picked it off.

Sting looked down at his chest. Then turned to me. Then back at his chest and back at me again. He gathered his eyebrows, tilted his head, became the very picture of gruff bonhomie, and declaimed in a stentorian voice, "Why, thank you!," his pitch rising as if in a vocalise practice for Shakespearean theater.

Now, you could say he was just being playful. What's the big deal, you could say. But, trust me, it was incongruous. It didn't go with the evening, with his mood, with his sweater, with my gesture. It was such a small gesture, such a small courtesy. But I'd committed a gaffe. I'd had no idea Sting would be so startled to be touched that he would cover his response with that inappropriately delivered banter.

In my own defense I'd like to say that even if I had given prior consideration to the shrimp-shell-removal decision, I would probably still have reached over and picked it off. After all, this is the man whose declaration that he is good in bed made headlines in the American Midwest. You'd think you could pick a shrimp shell off the guy's sweater, right?

Yet, when I thought about it later, it made sense to me that the rock star who'd had to battle his way out of hundreds of halls swaying with eerily violent lust-filled teens would no longer have a normal reaction to casual physical contact from a relative stranger if it took him by surprise. It's not just on stage that the crowd roars at him but on the street, whenever he's recognized, and, in a subtler but no less alienating way, via the carefully expressed hero worship of his entourage. He gets hit on wherever he goes, first degree by the fans—for his power as a performer and for his sex appeal—and second degree by people in the entertainment industry—for his success. With the exception of a handful of people who are in the same extraordinary situation, even among his colleagues

the response he'll get whenever he walks into a social situation
is usually, at best, a pathetically transparent veneer of very,
very genial casualness over the ever-present obsequiousness.

Anyway, now I know: you don't pick a shrimp shell off a
rock star's sweater if you don't know him well. And almost
no one knows him well. His true affect will always be hidden.
When he talks to you, you can search his face for clues, for
supplemental information, but you will see only the expression he has chosen to compose for you. Sting is really talented
at this. You almost forget the composition is deliberate, because you get distracted by the profusion of colors in the
emotional palette he is able to display. There's no way of being
completely sure which are the moments when he chooses to
reveal himself truly. You can't blame him: he's got no choice
but to protect himself. And I think it suits him fine to stay a
moving target.

If you were so inclined, you could characterize Sting as the
son of an English Catholic milkman who began to play the
guitar at age nine ("I always wanted to escape"), and is now
the bass player and lead singer of one of England's most
successful rock-'n'-roll groups.

Sting is the most visible member of the Police. "His face is
our face," one of the other group members is quoted as saying.
He sings, he fronts the band, and he writes most of its material. In the seven years since its inception, the group has
sold more than twenty-five million records.

"Day by day I've been transformed," says Sting.

"Do you like the new person better?" I ask.

"I think the new person is more adaptable, and also that
I'm more appropriate to my life situation. I mean, the person
of seven years ago could not have coped with what's going
on today."

The Police are still churning out chart-topping records, but
Sting is restless. So he is spending much of his time now in
Hollywood, building a film-acting career. He's doing well,
getting good parts, good press, but he's quite aware that he's

confronting the rock-star stigma directly. Hollywood is ambivalent about rock performers. They want the drawing power
and the vestigial glamour, yet they can't help being equivocal
about these outsiders, stars who have made their name with
a dubious audience.

It's hard to be a rock-'n'-roll star in the 1980s. Who takes
you seriously? In the past, this wasn't an issue. In the fifties, rock stars were teen idols: adulation, not respect, was
what they wanted and got. Dignity was for grown-ups. In the
sixties, they were still heart-throbs, but they were taken
very seriously by an audience hungry for iconoclastic, free-
wheeling spirits. And that was good enough. In the seventies,
rock stars themselves became grown-ups and most made their
choice as to the kind of respect they desired. A decade later,
in the mercantile frenzy that has gripped the entertainment
business and the public's perception of its stars, successful
rock performers are usually perceived as rapacious business-
men, calculated weirdoes, driven dopers, or casualties of past
decades. What does it take to beat that rap? And what price
do you pay? Maybe rock-'n'-roll stardom isn't enough any
more.

"Success and money haven't made me happy," says Sting.

So Hollywood beckoned, as a new challenge and, at least,
a distraction. And, in addition to his reputation, his talent,
and his looks, in Hollywood Sting's got a powerful trump in
his consummate flexibility.

He knows when to be humble: "Acting was another dis-
covery project for me, a new plateau. I'd like to learn how to
do it. But I know that when I first came on the set, they were
saying, 'Oh God, what's this rock star going to be like?'"

He also knows when to be defiant. At the beginning of his
rock-'n'-roll career, he dyed his hair blond for a bubble-gum
commercial, and he has the effrontery to keep it that way.
"Why shouldn't I?"

Even his looks are flexible. Sitting across a table from you
in a room, he seems almost frail, vulnerable. His frame seems
fragile, slight under the soft, bulky sweaters he favors. Then
he pushes up his sleeve and you see he has an athlete's arm,

tanned and muscled. In fact, you soon discover that he exercises vigorously. He's an early riser. No cigarettes, no drugs, very little alcohol. It's the routine of a man who wants to be prepared for anything.

In his photographs, he appears in a new role each time. Sometimes he's the devilish punk rocker; sometimes the glacially handsome young man. Seemingly at will, he's the abrasive mod proletarian or the irresistibly endearing choirboy. In the course of our interviews, his very physiognomy seems to alter as his mood changes.

"I'm blessed with a very mobile face," he says in his soft, off-stage voice. "I look different every day. Some days I look really ugly and some days I look handsome. I'm not bragging, but sometimes I do look really handsome. The next day I look like a frog. But I think *that's* a blessing in a way. People can't really pin me down. In England they tried to pin on me the idea that I'm a sex symbol. And I'm not. I don't want to be. My mobility has fended that off."

"If you have many facets, isn't being a sex symbol okay too?" I ask.

"Yeah, some of it is," he says. "I can do that. I'm an actor and I can do a lot of things. I mean an actor in that all the world is a stage. It's part of my job, after singing, to be a sexual projection."

His mutability's no put-on, it's his organizing principle.

"Immobility is corruption, the lack of courage to move on," he says. He loathes the security of predictability. But he warns you that he may change his mind about even that at any time: "I have the slippers-by-the-fire fantasy." Then you discover that he loves dangerous sports, that he competes, successfully, in marathons, that he's had skiing accidents, and that one of his favorite touring memories is of a near-crash in a small plane over Venezuela. "When it was over, it was the best feeling I'd had in a long time." Naturally, he drives a motorcycle. "You can flirt with danger, you can laugh at it." And danger is also the most alluring remedy for chronic restlessness.

In England, Sting is a huge star. He's in the news almost

daily. The break-up of his marriage, the affairs, the tempestuous relationships of Police members, the audacious career moves, all is fodder for the English press. In a class-conscious society, the exploits of the conspicuously ungovernable son of the Catholic milkman are of perennial interest. Is that why he's exiled himself once more, or is it that he couldn't resist the challenge and the dangers of taking on the American entertainment world?

Clearly, America is the terrain on which Sting can get maximum mobility. There's upward, lateral, every kind of mobility here, if you've got help, luck, and talent.

Sting seldom talks about talent; he describes himself as having "a valve." "Sadness is an emotion that teaches, so it's useful. I've used my sadness, I've exploited the emotions that it's brought up. It's a gift to be able to do this. I think that most people don't have the ability or the opportunity to exploit their emotional selves. They have them, and they don't know what to do with them. They feel unhappy. And it is uncreative ... and therefore just goes inside you, and builds up and builds up. Until you become psychotic. I think that is what psychosis is. A build-up of this pressure. Whereas I have a valve. I just turn it on."

But not all emotions are amenable to the "valve": "It's not even an emotion; it's evil, guilt," says Sting, with more force than he usually exhibits. "I'm trying to lose it." If he were a member of the American middle class, he might have had psychotherapy. But "In England, therapy is for craaaazy people," he says, smiling. So Sting practices self-therapy: he reads, he crash-courses areas of learning, musical instruments, sports, creative endeavors, and, as much as possible, he uses that "valve": "I'm very much a person who creates his own crises. I think crisis is essential to creativity, it's what makes you do things you couldn't do before."

Is he saying that being in a stable situation is not conducive to producing good art?

"I'm saying it is probably conducive to producing nicely balanced work. But not the really good stuff. That comes from pain, not comfort. I think pain is essential. If you have not got pain, then you had better go and get some... or change your job."

Pain is essential. I think he's perhaps talking about the break-up of his marriage, so I say, "That's pretty bleak. Is it possible that it is freedom that is essential, even if the price is high?"

"Freedom," says Sting. "I don't know what that means."

There's a story Sting tells about his childhood. In the grim industrial town of Newcastle, where he grew up, he lived on a street of terraced houses. At the end of his street, he could see the great bow of a ship being built. Each year a ship was built, and each year, when it was completed, it would sail away. Then they'd start building a new ship.

"One of the engines of my rise was a need to escape. From my environment, from my home, from my family. I didn't want to become my father or my mother. But lately I'm coming round to the realization that I am my father. Even though I've escaped geographically and socially, I'm still a product of my parents."

"What were the attributes that you wanted to escape?" I ask.

"I don't really want to say that, because it's about my parents," Sting says. It's the only question he won't answer. "I used to blame them a lot. I was bitter. Like, why the hell am I here? I hated them and wanted to escape. But now I realize that they too are the victims of circumstances. The pain I suffered as a child and a teen-ager wasn't their fault at all. It wasn't anyone's fault. So now I'm coming round to loving them again."

He's started to doodle.

"Thinking about the ship story," I say, "what I see is not the ship but the child who is watching the ship going away, the child who's abandoned every year."

"Yes, the recurring thing," he says, pencil poised over the useless parallelograms he's been drawing. "It builds up and then it goes away. Cyclic creation and decay. It's a real primary image with me. I am a traveler more than anything."

"Does that also serve the purpose of avoiding being abandoned?" I ask.

"I suppose so," he says. "I think I probably had a terrible fear of being left. What I tend to do psychologically is leave first. It's quite a stupid thing."

We're both silent for a moment. There's only the sound of Sting's pencil scratching the pad. Maybe I went too far for a first interview, I think.

"Are you okay?" I ask.

"I've become more relaxed." He clears his throat. "I'm learning to trust you."

Really? Can Sting really trust anyone? Can he really trust me? I felt a surge of, hmm, guilt. And compassion, though I don't know why. It seems absurd to feel sorry for Sting. Yet even some of his friends do, they tell me. They don't know exactly why either. For a long time, I can't figure it out. But it's a feeling that will often recur as I sit across a table from Sting watching him doodle or stare down at his hands. I'll keep changing my mind about it. Because, of course, if you start to think any one thing about Sting, he'll keep faking you out.

Sting talks about sadness in the abstract with ease, but it's easy to tell that he doesn't want to talk much about the seven-year marriage that ended a few months ago. Yet he shows me photographs of his children. A tiny little girl and a pretty five-year-old boy.

"Is he like you?" I ask.

"He's clever" is all Sting says. And then he looks at the photograph for quite a while.

But a few moments later, he's in a different mood.

"This year is a watershed year for me," he says. He's in New York for just a few days before going off to Los Angeles to sign a contract for his role in *Dune,* or to Montserrat to mix his record, or to Switzerland to ski with his son.

"Is this a good time or a bad time for you?" I ask him.

"Both," he answers. "It's really difficult, yet I am relishing the challenges. I am really enjoying myself by fending off the nightmares and putting myself in uncomfortable positions, being away from security and safety. I prefer being an itinerant."

He points to a filled suitcase on the floor beside him. "I never unpack."

"Is there safety in transience?" I ask.

"I never want to get there. Driving to a gig is the worst time for anxiety, nausea. I always want the journey to last forever. I suppose, in my life, the journey does last forever. I think I must have been around the world about sixty times. I'm addicted to being a traveler. Jupiter in my night clothes."

Several weeks later, I get a chance to see Sting triggering his "valve," though in a small way. That night they're going to shoot the album cover for the new Police record, *Synchronicity*. In accordance with Jung's concept of the convergence of acausally related events, Sting's got a scheme that he and the other two band members, Stewart Copeland and Andy Summers, will all make up their own cover photos. None of them will know what the other two are planning. The photographer, Duane Michaels, is the only common thread. (Did he do this to avoid posing for yet another cover shot with his two colleagues? Their feuds are renowned. It's a moot point.) For his third of the cover, Sting has chosen as his environment the dinosaur exhibit at the Museum of Natural History, which has been rented for the night.

In the limo on the way over, Sting is accompanied by his roadie, a record-company art director, and me with a yellow pad. The others and I chat together, because Sting is being even quieter than usual, and I imagine that he doesn't want to be observed in a conspicuous way. Because he's usually quiet, though, when there are several people around Sting they all seem to talk more with one another than they would if he weren't there. Bank shots.

When we get to the museum, the photographer has already arrived, with his assistant. A stylist for the record company joins us. So now there are seven of us at stalking the silent, semi-dark rooms. We amble down the empty stone hallways, the umbrella the photographer's assistant carries adding an especially absurd note to our procession. Now and then we pass a guard who only nods at our approach. Sting walks at the edge of the group, silently. The guard, if he has noticed Sting, probably assumes that he's only tagging along with the group. The photographer is in charge; Sting doesn't mess with that.

Even more than his words, his demeanor speaks of the massive insecurity he must combat or utilize to perform: off stage, one doesn't encounter the brazen bare-chested lead singer of the Police, or the diabolical arriviste he portrays in his films. He speaks very quietly, his eyes evade yours, he hunches over somewhat. "He's shy," says a good friend. "People refuse to believe that, but it's true." Yet, of course, his restraint, the stillness he exudes, elicits response in a way that more flamboyant behavior wouldn't.

Finally, we reach the room of "The Late Dinosaurs." Sting stares for a while at the animals among which he will pose; he seems to make eye contact with a trachodonts. Then he quietly goes about changing for the camera. What a jackpot, I say to myself. The Late Dinosaurs room! While they're setting up, I sit down on a bench and use my yellow pad. The showcases contain Armored Dinosaurs, Flying Reptiles, Aquatic Duck-billed Dinosaurs, the particularly vicious-looking Dinosaurs with Horns, and a rather gruesome Dinosaur Mummy. I'm about to move down to the next showcase when it suddenly occurs to me to wonder why I'm not watching Sting instead. He's been in such a quiet mode that, like the others around him, I've come to try to protect him, in this case from even my own observation.

Sting is changing into the clothes he's selected for the cover shot. Suddenly I notice that the famous sex symbol puts his shirt on peculiarly, holding it close to his body in an odd way. I can't figure it out unless—unless it's to keep his chest covered. Is that possible? I look around and see that everyone else is watching him too, with what appears to be casual

interest. Then Sting buttons up his shirt, and he looks...
relieved.

Now he climbs over the chain fence into position under the
colossal trachodonts, who shares his graveled island with the
equally forbidding triceratops and tyrannosaurus. Sting stands
quietly in his black pants, white shirt, black coat, holding a
white paperback copy of *Synchronicity,* making a mild joke
now and then. "Shall I read to you all?" He reaches up and
pats the grotesque jaw. "Anybody got some sugar?"

When the photographer has finished setting up, he looks
at Sting. "Ready?" Sting runs his fingers through his hair.

The photographer bends behind his camera. Sting says,
"Ready." And then it happens: the famous cheekbones are
ejected from the face, the lips become narrow and almost
cruel, the eyebrows lift slightly, just enough. In twenty
seconds Gordon Sumners has become Sting. If he is self-
conscious, none of us present will ever know. He looks in
turn majestic or mischievous; he runs through a gamut of
expressions for the camera with the ease of an experienced
model.

He'll pose now for hours, among the Late Cretaceous dinosaurs, some of the last dinosaurs to live on earth. Then we'll
resume our positions in the strange cortege and move on to
the Early Dinosaurs room, where Sting suggests that he can
pose inside the ribcage of the stegosaurus, a mean-looking
skeleton.

Sting spots the art director and the stylist in a confab in a
corner.

"What are you whispering about?" he calls out.

The art director clears his throat. "Holly was just suggesting
you take off your shirt."

"*I will not,*" the photographer interjects. They all laugh.

Sting makes a moue.

"Is it okay?" the photographer asks him. Clearly, any photographer would think it's a good idea to have Sting bare-
chested inside the ribcage of a stegosaurus.

"Oh, all right, then," declares Sting in a pseudo-coy delivery.

Bare-chested, Sting becomes mobile again, on cue, whenever he's asked for it, the only sign of his discomfort the occasional joke. "This one's got B.O."

The art director and the photographer converse.

"How about some profile?" suggests the art director.

"Okay, we can try that," says the photographer, "but what's beautiful about his face is what he does with the eyes, and the thing with the bones."

Later the photographer says, "Maybe you're right about the profile." Sting's got a lot of angles.

Everyone else is tired. Sting still doesn't show his fatigue. Now that he's accustomed to the photographer's way of working, the latter seldom has to ask for anything. Finally, traces of tedium begin to show.

"A dinosaur song!" he declaims, while the photographer is changing rolls. Then Sting starts to hum a Gregorian-like dirge, which reverberates spookily in the big hall.

Finally, he's relaxed a bit too much. The photographer says, "No, do that fierce thing," and, again, it happens.

By then everyone except Sting and the photographer is sitting down. I'm on a bench a few feet away, writing down dinosaur names again. I look up at Sting. It's been almost an hour that he's been standing inside the stegosaurus, uncomplaining except for the jokes. Maybe from the pain of standing still with his arms raised for so long, his face now has an odd expression of, what, anger? Maybe only fatigue. No, something more disturbing, some quality he's projecting and I can't think of the name of it. He's perspiring now; his bare flesh glistens. I keep trying. Suddenly, I think of the word I've been looking for. It's, well, sexy. I'd completely forgotten. It isn't the image he's chosen to project in the course of our interviews, at least not in the overt way he has for the camera, so he'd actually made me forget. He's that convincing a performer.

As the photographer winds up, Sting is clearly near the end of his considerable resources of stamina. The jokes are becoming feebler. "Mommy, I want to get out." He shakes his head now and then.

"Your hair is cooperating," says the art director.

"You want to share this gum?" says Sting.

"There are people who would kill for that saliva," says the art director.

Sting doesn't comment.

About a month later, Sting is in town for the weekend again.

"People around you say that you don't confide in them," I tell him.

"I have about three really close friends, whom I do confide in and do trust. Apart from that, no, why should I? I think I am lucky to have three; some people have nobody to confide in. In a sense, I confide publicly, in my work. I get on stage and sing about being lonely. That is as public as you can get. For me it is a great psychological gift, to be able to get on stage and tell fifty thousand people that I feel lonely. As ridiculous as it is, surrounded by all this attention, I actually feel alone."

"Did you ever have stagefright?"

"I always get stage nerves, but I think that is essential to a good performance."

It's probably on stage that Sting uses his insecurities most effectively. In fact, much of the appeal of the Police is the combination of the band's pitilessly stripped-down instrumental sound with Sting's voice—sometimes a bittersweet plaint, sometimes a sharp, untidy wail. Modern sex appeal: not vigor but tension. Not for him the implacably rigid mien of the new crop of rock performers. If anyone wants to observe Sting's lonely restlessness, it's there in the stage mannerisms he exhibits in his trancelike state. He often jumps up and down, rubs his head, shakes his hair, alternately glares and smiles at the audience. He even sucks his thumb. But what he uses to his best advantage is his fear. "It's like skiing down a really fast slope. The steeper it is, the more exciting. The closer to the edge you get on stage, the better it is. I like the audience to take part in that. There are certain points in the set when I do nothing. There is a hole ... and the audience fills it up. You look as if you are going to fall over. You look as if you've forgotten the words. You look as if you are terrified. The audience comes around you. It's really quite a wonderful experience. Scary."

Never mind if he has to spellbind himself to believe it; somehow Sting finds the audacity or strength to assume the audience will "fill up the hole." If he has "stage nerves," as he says, it is because he has never come to take that assumption for granted. Indeed, if he did he might not be able to spellbind himself. Or the audience.

Most rock stars, if they try to do any spellbinding at all, think they need help to do it, that it's too terrifying otherwise. But Sting has rejected drugs as an option, "though I can see why others do it," he says. Instead, of all things, he reads. "When I think of Sting, I see him with his face in a book," says a friend who has come along on Police tours. For his last album, he studied Arthur Koestler, and *Ghost in the Machine* is titled after a Koestler work. Now, with *Synchronicity,* he's moved on to Jung. So these days he thinks a good deal about Jungian notions of the collective unconscious. "Music is a perfect example, because it's totally abstract," he says. "It is a very simple tonal code which taps into the collective unconscious. Why does a certain series of notes do this? People behave in an extraordinary way *en masse.* And you can use that for positive or negative purposes. To see people physically, unconsciously respond to an unconscious stimulus is very exciting."

"It sounds like a pagan ritual," I say.

"Right. I often feel like performing is some sort of shamanism. Frenzied. Sexual. It frees people for a while. I induce that by going into a trance, really, which is why I like to be almost unconscious. I don't want to meet someone's eye in the audience, because that brings you back to consciousness. And I like to be out, to appear like a man on the edge. Like a man who has pushed himself too far... That is when the audience really gets sucked in. It is a performance. If I sing a really high note, my body gets overoxygenated, and the whole hall goes back and forth. I get close to fainting. It's really exciting. I do that every night: when I sing 'Roxanne,' there's a very high note which I sing a long time. I must look as if I am going to fall over. That is really exciting to me, that dangerous feeling that you could fall. The audience responds to it. It is not safe."

Not long after this conversation I rent a videotape of *The Secret Policeman's Other Ball*, a film of an Amnesty International benefit in which he participated. Sting appears in a solo performance, just him and the guitar. This must be how the songs sound while he's composing them. Alone on the stage, he starts to sing "Roxanne." It's one of his most powerful songs, with its mournful melody and cryptic lyrics. "Roxanne, you don't have to put on the red light." Dressed in baggy pants, a loose T-shirt, an army fatigue jacket, he looks very small and still on stage by himself. Usually, Sting describes himself as an introvert in life who is an extrovert on stage, but this performance has the quality of solitary brooding, of inward tension. Now, toward the end of the song, there's the note. Not held as long as in the more exuberant Police concerts, but, unmistakably, Sting seems to turn even deeper into himself. Luckily, it's a close-up. There it is: "Roxaaaaaaanne." Stop the machine. Rewind. Start again, a couple of bars or so before the end. In slow motion you can watch Sting winding up toward his note. When he starts the note, use the pause button and freeze each frame. Watch: a tendon in Sting's neck starts to appear, his eyes close tight, there's a throb in his temple. He reaches the end of his note. In the frozen frame you see...what? Maybe it's the child who's just watched the ship leave. Maybe it's the seventeen-year-old kid whose best friend just died. Maybe it's the star who left his wife and children this year. Who knows? If you're looking for the real man, and this is it, what he's showing is somewhere among fear and pain and tenderness. Or is it thrill? Is it grief or ecstasy? Maybe it's only a great performance, and what you see is what you want to see. Even when Sting thinks he's not protecting himself. After all, it's only a note. Push play. The song ends. Sting opens his eyes. The audience applauds.

What's a modern hero? Someone who uses everything. Why not a performer, a child-man, petulant, whimsical, generous, ambitious, vulnerable, real tough, pained but undaunted, someone with only one name (and a preposterous one at that: "Yes, I'm going to keep it; people will get used to it"). So it's not as Gordon Sumner but as Sting that he's had the defiance to appear as a bigger-than-life character who struggles in modern arenas to prove, over and over again, that he can take it. His childhood and adolescence were studies in alienation. Now constantly surrounded by admirers, he's one of the most isolated men you'll ever meet ("I'd be isolated anywhere; I'd be isolated if I was working in a shop"). A kinsman of Joyce's Stephen Dedalus: he'll exile himself from everyone and everything and then use the torment of exile to create. Create what? Himself. That's how modern he is. But there's something in it for the rest of us. A Daedalus for our decade. Why shouldn't we have our own myths? We need them. And if star quality is the ability to make people bond, to fascinate, then Sting's got wings.

Yet he constantly changes his mind, or seems to, as to his ratio of luck and aptitude. He's not insolent as a rule, though he often exhibits an alluringly playful impertinence. The word "arrogant" occurs almost as often as the word "charming" in the press about him, but in the course of our interviews he's peculiarly humble. Of course, some of this is the specious humility of the star who can afford it: "It was luck"; "I have been fortunate"; "I'm very privileged." Specious because, even though it may be sincere, it seems obligatory: it's what we expect of our stars. But there is also an unmistakably genuine, consistent self-deprecation that is all the more poignant because it is almost invariably exhibited in a statement that incorporates his desire to shed it. Sting makes an art of ambivalence.

"When you talk about luck," I say to him, "it's as though you're talking about your career as something you didn't earn or deserve."

"The fact that I can sing is an accident of genetics," Sting replies.

"And do you pay a preposterous price for that?" I ask.

"It is preposterous in that, because I can do that, then people ask me questions, serious questions, about life, philosophy. Who am I? I'm just a guy with a good voice. Yet, why not? Why shouldn't you take me seriously? I do feel very guilty about it. I suppose I have to get over that."

"Can you?" I ask.

"I don't know," he says. "I'm trying."

Will he be able to transfer his performance talent to film? The ingredients seem to be there. He's almost unequivocally ambitious, impressively industrious. His natural exhibitionism is both tempered and enhanced by unending discipline. And whatever his insecurities may be, he seems always able to externalize them by expressing himself. He's a consummate performer. His musical career can only help him.

A first class rock-'n'-roll star has many of the qualities of a fine actor: he has to be able to perform and project, hold an audience with his gaze and with his physical equipment, the power of his personality. He has to be brave.

"The problem is getting the same adrenaline rush that you get from fifteen thousand people, getting the same amount from one director. He is the audience at first. You have to work for him. It's difficult. When you go on stage you feel low, and suddenly you're plugged into a socket and you explode. Doing that for one person, a camera, and some technicians is quite difficult: exploding in front of them. I suppose the analogy is masturbation. How do you masturbate in front of people? It's hard, difficult, embarrassing. It's a dangerous situation to put myself in. I can really fall flat on my face. I enjoy that risk-taking. I enjoy just going back to square one. It's a relief. Because I feel, if I can do this, if I can succeed in this, then it means I do have talent. And I can do anything. If I apply myself."

"He's not crippled with self-doubt," a Hollywood insider

muses. "He doesn't make you like him. He doesn't court you. He is not solicitous. He's more interesting than that. It's not arrogance, it's the self-confidence of someone who has created himself. It's not the usual bravado of rock-'n'-roll people. It's the smugness of the truly, truly hip."

Will Sting be successful?

"Yes. He's talented, not self-destructive, and very methodical. He has picked the right people to work with. He's been impressive in the way he's gone after a movie career. The only thing that may limit him is his own taste, if he always wants to play the dark prince. How many times can you play the dark prince? He's terrific at it, and maybe he can keep doing it over and over again. Or maybe after he's played the dark prince four times it will be sufficient and he will look for something else. Maybe it is just a myth he's operating with now."

Sting's acquaintances and friends seem no less perplexed by him than the Hollywood executives he's been encountering.

The people around Sting describe him as attentive, perspicacious, generous, but very withdrawn. "He will come in and be very charming and then the 'No Vacancy' sign is up." "Aloof," "almost reclusive," and, time and again, "guarded." "He's always on his guard, especially when he is being flamboyant," says a close woman friend. "He's very good at playing that role. When he walks into a party, he will realize that he is the center of attention and he will act out his part. He's aware that there's a job behind being a star. Yet when you get him alone, he suddenly becomes very intellectual, and very quiet. He listens to what you have to say and wants to know why you think that. But it's very hard to give warmth to him and have him give it back."

"He's developed an aura, which scares people," says Police manager Miles Copeland. "A mystique has been built up around the band, which has made people afraid to talk to them. Each individual in the Police, and Sting in particular, has had an incredible amount of attention heaped on him, and they've handled it very well. They are still sane, which isn't so easy. You are an open target for everything, there is an incredible amount of pressure. And it is so easy to be a raving bastard and get away with it. The fact that these guys have not done that is a real tribute to them."

"Are you susceptible to his charm?" I ask.

"It's something that is valuable. The fact that he is charming, as the others in the group are as well, is something I've used to our advantage. When I send them in to do a radio interview, I know that when they walk out the people at that scene are going to like that group. They're liked. That means that people will work harder to promote and sell our records. It's an obvious ingredient in Sting's success: people like him."

It seems to me that charm is also a very intimate gift of one's self. What resources Sting must have to stay perpetually seductive, and how isolating that must be. No wonder he occasionally has to put up the "No Vacancy" sign. Perhaps that's why he can sometimes be so playful and the next moment become remote, almost stern. Perhaps that's why he writes songs with titles like "Don't Stand So Close to Me." Perhaps that's why he's so fond of danger, of traveling, of staying a moving target. Perhaps that's why he learned to escape into a trance state when he needs to. But does the trance state really get left behind at the stage door? Is he crazy? No, I don't think so. Not any more than a rock star has to be.

I was thinking of all this at the end of my last talk with Sting. He was leaving New York the next day. He was tired. I could tell he was depressed. I was looking at him and wondering, again, how someone with such powerful stage presence can look so fragile off stage. Yet when we'd talked about life on tour, Sting had told me about being on stage: "I feel more at home there than I do during the rest of the day. It's an hour of frenzy and twenty-three hours of boredom and inertia."

But I wasn't sure whether to believe him: he'd warned me

early on that he lies, that he hates to be predictable. "I change my mind a lot," he'd explained. "All the time. My defense is, at least it shows I'm thinking."

Now, we were winding up our final interview. I'd already turned off the tape recorder. He was talked out. He'd been, as usual, impeccably cooperative and courteous, but it seemed to me that he was approaching psychic overload and wanted to get back to the synthesizer in the next room of the friend's apartment where he was spending the weekend.

We'd been talking about love. "Have you been loved a lot in your life?" I'd asked him. "Yes," he had answered. "Often too much." Then he had told me of a girlfriend's suicide, twelve years ago, when he was nineteen. "I spent a long time flailing myself about it," he'd said.

The room had grown quite dark, though it was only mid-afternoon. Sting was seated across from me, at a plain round wooden table, wearing a loose, soft sweater. He was looking down at his hands. There was an electric light on, but the low wattage only made him look frailer, more vulnerable, blond and gentle. We were both silent for a bit. Then I turned the tape recorder back on.

"I have a strange thing to tell you," I said. "I feel bad for you."

He remained silent for a while. Then:

"You fell for it," he finally said.

"What?" I asked. He hadn't moved, not even his eyes. He was still looking down at his hands. He'd spoken so low I thought I had misheard.

"You fell for it. I suppose I've been trying to leave you the impression of a kind of gypsy, so that you'd feel a bit sorry for me. And yet you shouldn't be. I've had an extraordinary life, more than most humans on this planet even dream about. I am privileged beyond belief. I have a job that is demanding and satisfying. I've found love affairs that are wonderful. I have two wonderful kids. I am just trying to deal with it. It's dealing with that luck that's hard. I feel guilty about having such a good life. That's probably why I live like this." He gestured to the comfortable but unadorned room.

"I wouldn't really fit into a millionaire's life. I wouldn't feel comfortable in a massive hotel room with jacuzzis and women flying around. There's more balance here. All this luck has been heaped on me. I have to balance it out."

But why does luck have to be balanced out?

I didn't ask him. I felt bad for him, so I didn't want him to have to answer more questions. Certainly not about the inextricable connection between reward and punishment, or escape and imprisonment, or adoration and isolation. And, in any event, whether or not he can emotionally reconcile his ambivalences, he's able to make them work for him artistically. Maybe it's part of his talent to talk himself into making it look easy, even to himself.

WHAT HAPPENS
=== TO ===
PRETTY GIRLS

AT THE SHOOT:

Eight-fifty-five. I've arrived early. Only the hairdresser is here.

"You're doing a story about us?" says the hairdresser. "Fabulous!"

"I'm going to several shoots," I tell him, "to make up a composite."

"What a wonderful idea. You'll see, it'll be great today. The photographer is so talented. And the girl is adorable."

"Oh, really?" I say.

"Oh, yes. She's fabulous."

If this weren't such a sad story, it would be funny to relate how nervous people in the fashion industry get when you interview them about the modeling business. The shifting glances, the anxious hands. These poor people, they know you're going to question them about nightlife, sex, and (oh, no, not again) drugs. Though they love talking to the press, this kind of interview isn't their idea of a good time. They hate straight talk. They prefer the comfortable cadences of hype, superlatives, and verbal excess that have come to be second nature to them. Great, fabulous, wonderful, marvelous, adorable—that's the currency they feel comfortable with.

So, of course, when you're questioning them about very young models, they fidget in their seats as soon as they hear questions about nightlife and drugs. And when they see what you're getting at, their answers are all prepared: *It's been exaggerated. I'm sure it goes on, but not among the girls I know. It used to go on, but now it's different.* Some tell the truth, most lie. You promise them that you won't use their names, but still they lie. They're used to it; they do it well. But then they give you, invariably, some version of this statement: "There's a lot of gossip about our business, but the great models aren't like that. And they have wonderful careers." And they mean it too. They stop playing with their pencils and look in your eyes when they say that. The only trouble is that the "great models" they're talking about, by which they mean the very few who have long-standing careers in the business, are—optimistically—one out of a thousand, and that the casualties, the thousands from Kansas City and Saratoga who shine for a few months or a year and then are never heard from again, the little candles who do not make it through the night, those girls are often fourteen, fifteen, sixteen years old.

"Everybody wants to know about the drugs," says a makeup artist, "but I hate to talk about that, because there are so many nice people working in the business. A lot of the girls are really hardworking, nice people. It's not fair."

Well, that's true. Many of these fourteen-, fifteen-, sixteen-year-old modeling stars who are now working hard every day of the year to pull in their several hundred thousand dollars a year are nice girls. Many of them don't touch drugs or alcohol. There's a new breed of gym-going models who stay away from the discos and the freaky stuff. And, for all one knows, many of them take drugs and are still nice girls. But the saddest part of this story is that it has very little to do with drugs.

What happens to all these nice girls, to all but the handful who manage to survive? Where do all the pretty little girls from Kansas City and Saratoga go when they're through in the modeling business? Nobody seems to know, though there is a consensus that these girls probably can't go home again. "The smart ones become actresses or go into some other aspect of the fashion business," an agent tells me. Yes, the smart ones. But what about the others. "They get a rich boyfriend?" a makeup artist speculates. "For all I know, they become stewardesses," a fashion editor snidely suggests.

But when I repeat this remark to a model, she answers, without irony, "Oh, no, we spend much too much time on planes to want to become stewardesses."

"You must have had some friends in the business who are no longer working," I tell the model. "Where did they go?"

"Gee, I don't know what happens to them," she says. "You know, people just kind of disappear. I don't know. A lot of them make a lot of money. Maybe they buy houses some-where. They really just disappear. I think a lot of girls must go to Europe when they're older."

"Older?" I ask.

"Yeah, you know, twenty or something."

These days a model is old in her twenties. Naturally, the fashion-business people will give you exceptions: Isabella Rosselini, Cheryl Tiegs, Lauren Hutton. ("Look at Lauren Hutton—she's been around forever, and she's still absolutely *fabulous*.") But you'll hear the same names over and over again. The truth is, there are only a few names. You can't even say that for every Brooke Shields there are a thousand eighteen-year-old has-beens. Because there's only one Brooke Shields. It was a big story, several years ago, that many of the star models were girls in their teens. But no one in or out of the industry seemed to wonder what would happen to these children a year or two down the line. Perhaps it was assumed that once these kids became stars they would have careers of normal lengths—maybe ten years, fifteen if they were lucky, hardworking, and had the right looks. But it hasn't turned out that way. "They burn out so quickly, it's unbelievable," says a magazine editor. "Sometimes in a matter of months. We're going for younger and younger girls, looking for that special quality of vitality, that freshness. But something happens to them in the process that robs them of that very freshness that made us single them out in the first place."

It's almost as though, just as primitive people believe, the soul is somehow stolen by the camera.

AT THE SHOOT:

Nine-fifteen. The photographer and his assistant have arrived. The fashion editor, her assistant, the hairdresser, the makeup artist are there. The model arrives, a slender blond girl dressed in jeans and a sleeveless T-shirt. Her name is Valeria (*née* Susan Jackson in Wilmington, Delaware). She's fifteen years old.

"Hi," says Valeria.

"Hi," the others chorus.

"You look cute," says the photographer.

"You cut your hair," says the editor.

"Yeah," says the model, smiling. She sits down at the dressing table.

"Who did it?" asks the hairdresser, running his hand through her hair.

"André, the other day, at a shooting I did for French *Vogue*. I was so scared about how it would turn out."

"It's great," says the hairdresser.

"Adorable," says the makeup artist.

"You did the right thing, it's gorgeous," says the photographer.

"I'm so happy," says Valeria. "I was so scared."

"I love it," says the editor.

"Gorgeous," says the photographer.

"Divine," says the hairdresser.

Of course, there's nothing new about young women coming to New York and getting chewed up by the harsh realities of the glamour professions. What's remarkable about this particular phenomenon, aside from the extreme youth of the casualties, is that the worst victims are the ones who do become "stars"—as stardom is thought of in the fashion business. "She couldn't take the pressure" is the phrase used about the sixteen-year-old who goes over the edge.

"It's true that these days you really do have overnight successes," says an insider. "It's like in everything else: trends in the fashion-photography field have been succeeding each other at an accelerated rate in the last few years. A model used to have to work up to being a star. The instant 'discoveries' were mostly legends. But now, if the right girl walks into the right place at the right time, she really can be a hit overnight."

The photographers, the makeup artists, the hairdressers, the editors, the agents can usually tell you the prestigious cover the girl did just before it happened. Just before she tried to commit suicide and her father came to bring her home. Just before she was found flipped out on a bathroom floor in an Upper East Side bachelor apartment. Just before she became so out of it at the shoot that she was sent home and the photographer swore he'd never use her again. And then they're just another anecdote, all the girls with only one name.

The inexperienced models who haven't had to struggle for their acceptance usually aren't aware of just how expendable they are. "You have to understand," says an unusually frank magazine editor, "that these girls are *props*. They're props not only for the clothes but also to show the work of all the people who use them as props: the hair and makeup people, the photographers, the magazine people, or the advertising people." And the Look these people wish to convey changes continually: the girl with plump rosy cheeks who was a huge hit when the Gym Look was in will be cast off without a second thought when the Look turns to sultry young beauties.

Moreover, in the last couple of years the criteria for selecting types of models have shifted drastically from the "perfect" all-American-girl standards of past decades. Quirky, "imperfect" looks are now sought after: small eyes, heavy eyebrows, anything goes. Undoubtedly, it is no coincidence that this should have happened concurrently with the influx of very young models. Anything is forgivable, and even appealing, on a very fresh young face and body. But by the same token, these are faces that one tires of more quickly. A model can become overexposed in a matter of months. "Most of the agencies will send the girl on all the bookings they can get for her," says an agent. "It's big money, especially if the model gets a lucrative exclusive-commercial deal. She can pull in half a million dollars a year if she works all the time." But there aren't that many women anyone wants to look at that much. All of a sudden people say, "I don't want to have to look at that face one more time."

And the girl, of course, doesn't know what hit her. She feels like a star, has been shown every evidence that she is indeed a star. She's rich. She's famous. She's sought after in her milieu. All she has to do to remind herself of her stardom is to open her portfolio. "They're so young that they don't really have any identity of their own yet," says an agent. "They come into the business quite innocent, and then they begin to believe the image of themselves that they see in the pages of the magazines."

"I can't stand having to work with these little girls who've done one cover and think they're stars," says an editor. "Oh, of course I do it if we're dying to have that face. And I put up with all the crap they pull at the shooting. Going into the bathroom to snort, throwing tantrums—I'll put up with anything to get a good session. But it drives me crazy when they behave unprofessionally. They think they're stars and they forget that this is a business."

"This is a business" is a phrase I heard again and again from fashion-industry members. It's a kind of caveat: don't forget it's work to create glamour for the reader, to arrest the glance of the consumer. It's hard work. But the readers aren't the only ones susceptible to the fantasies created by the models.

"Last week my booker called and said, 'You're going to Jamaica,'" a model tells me. "So, just like that, I got on a plane, and the next day I was on the beach." She smiles with that very seductive sweetness so many of these young girls have. She makes me smile too.

"Did you have fun?" I ask.

"Oh, it was wonderful. The people were so interesting. I had such a good time. And the clothes were just beautiful.

White clothes on the beach. And the sun was beautiful. And the wind on the sand. I knew I was really good, I could have just kept going forever. There was just such a wonderful... mood. It was like a dream."

"Aren't you terribly tired at the end of an eight-hour shoot?" I ask another model.

"Oh, no," she says. "Well, maybe I am, but, you know, I don't even feel it. Everyone is so nice to me, it really doesn't feel like working."

AT THE SHOOT:

Ten-thirty. The makeup artist is finishing up. The photographer and his assistant are out in the studio setting up, but the rest of the shoot personnel are crowded in the dressing room, chatting while they observe the metamorphosis of the adolescent girl. The makeup person is applying the last of the nail polish.

"How's this?" he asks.

"Oh, I love it," says the fashion editor.

"Yeah, I love these purplish reds," says the hairdresser.

The model looks at her fingers. "I like it," she says.

"It makes your hands look real pretty," says the makeup artist.

The photographer peers into the room and examines the model's face. "The makeup looks gorgeous," he says. "You're gorgeous."

The problems of coping with sudden success usually aren't characterized by anything as dramatic as a suicide or a nervous breakdown. But, inevitably, the girl's personality evolves in some way, and often that evolution is a type of dissolution.

Perhaps in part because of the demanding hours of the work itself, the social life that frequently accompanies it, and the common para-anorexic diets, the dissolution can simply take the form of constant fatigue. The model becomes unreliable. And then, unless she is a very big star indeed, there seems not to be very much sympathy for such a model among the people with whom she works. "No, I don't feel sorry for them. Do you know how much money they make? These girls know what they're doing," says a photographer. "Don't make the mistake of thinking they're children. They may look like children, but these days a sixteen-year-old is very sophisticated. Believe me, a lot of these models are very shrewd. I have no respect for them when they behave unprofessionally."

The best shoots are executed in the spirit of a friendly collaborative effort. When a model becomes a liability, the professionals who are obliged to work with her quickly grow resentful. "Very often in these quick successes the girl soon becomes intolerable. She starts acting like a star. She's out all night partying and shows up late for work, with her face all swollen, her hair dirty, her nails not done. She becomes demanding about who she'll work with. She throws tantrums on the set," says a hairdresser. "No one wants to work with girls like that. They don't realize that."

If the girl is marginal, unreliability and bad temperament will be sufficient to get her blacklisted. If she has a great appeal on camera, however, she will hang on for a while. But this is a short-term reprieve. Because, ironically, the camera reflects the girl's personality. And the naïve charm that made the girl successful in the first place cannot be faked by an inept actress.

"But *how* do they burn out so quickly? What is it that happens to them physically?" I ask a makeup artist, one of the best in the industry.

"They get that tough, bitchy look," he says.

And then they're ruined. You can't fix that with makeup.

AT THE SHOOT:

Eleven o'clock. The photo session is starting. The photographer has taken several Polaroids of Valeria in her first outfit: a tank top and wide-legged shorts. Everyone has clustered around the photographer to look at the Polaroids.

"Oh, it's great," says the editor.

"I love those grays," says the hairdresser.

"The stool is great," says the makeup artist.

"Yeah," says Valeria.

"And the legs! The legs are great!" says the editor.

"Fabulous," says the photographer.

Valeria smiles.

"Maybe we'll use the other earrings, though," says the editor.

"The big ones?" asks Valeria. "Oooh."

"There," says the editor, clipping them onto Valeria's earlobes. "How's that?"

"Much better, *much* better," says the photographer. "Fabulous."

"I just love these," says the editor.

"Yes, they're much more of a statement," says the editor's assistant.

"Yeah," says Valeria.

"I don't know how to describe what I do in front of the camera. You create something inside your head and then you let it show. It's a lot like love," says a model.

Somewhat more articulately, photographers speak of good models' extraordinary receptivity during the photo session, their pliability and responsiveness, their ability to project mood. But if, for the model, the process is "a lot like love," it seems obvious that an adolescent girl will not have the mature distance to separate the photo session from life. Being pampered and petted by the hair and makeup people functions as a prelude to the often overt intimacy and warmth of the photo session itself. And even when the photographer is a woman or a male homosexual, there is about the photo-session process an unmistakable aura of eroticism. Undoubtedly, the photo session is a form of seduction.

"Do you think your relationship with the model is, on a certain level, sexual?" I ask a photographer.

"Of course," he says. "In fact, it's very consciously sexual. There's always kidding around, telling naughty stories to each other. With the models I work well with, there's a kind of sexual familiarity. I think it helps to get them to be very warm, and friendly, and fearless. And that's reflected in the pictures."

And also reflected in the pictures, of course, is the young woman's sexuality.

"But it's always been true," says a photographer. "Any time you capitalize on the fact that a woman is a female, it's a sort of pornography. Any perfume ad is pornography. Any time you reveal the curves of a woman's breasts and crotch it's pornography. And I think there's nothing wrong with it, though people should admit it's pornography."

Yes, it's always been true. It's just that, coincidentally, it's now *child* pornography. And even if erotic seduction has always been a subtext of fashion photography, it has never been as overt as in recent years. So, while much sensational copy has been written regarding the actual sex life of the models, the affairs in quick succession, the drug-and-sex connection, the kinky nights spent in trios, the most profound exploitation of adolescent sexuality occurs in the photo studio and on the printed page.

"I think there's nothing wrong with child pornography either," says the photographer. "Except for the children. The girl knows what's going on. Oh, she doesn't know from big dicks or anything, but she knows what's going down at the session. And there's a lot of nudity too these days. The girl knows that all the little boys in her class look at the pictures and jerk off. That they've seen *her thing*. She knows. And that's got to have an effect on her. She knows people want to fuck her. And, come on, it's a normal fantasy to want to fuck a fourteen-year-old. Everybody's got that fantasy. They just don't admit it. But the girl knows."

AT THE SHOOT:

Twelve-fifteen. The session has begun. There will be short breaks for lunch and while the girl changes outfits, but the shoot will continue until nightfall. The photographer works in bursts of several minutes each. In between shots, the hairdresser and the makeup artist make adjustments. Valeria stands still while they work on her, not even stretching. There isn't a woman alive who will observe this scene without visualizing this image from childhood: a beautiful doll is being groomed, adorned, and caressed. When the photographer's camera is reloaded and he is ready to shoot again, Valeria returns to the stool. During the session, everyone is silent except for the photographer. No one moves except Valeria, who only shifts slightly according to his directions. Grouped behind the photographer, the others watch.

"Chin up slightly?" says the photographer. "Beautiful. Hold it! A little more. Beautiful, beautiful. Face to the right a little? Gorgeous. Hold it! A little more in the shoulder. Yes. Hold it! Now push away from the toe. Yes, yes, yes, yes. Gorgeous. Hold it! Yes. Beautiful. Chin out a little bit? Beautiful. Hold it! Hold it! Gorgeous."

"It doesn't feel like working." "It's a lot like love." For the teenage girl, the physical pampering, the verbal caresses are indeed a form of love. The rest of life seems pale beside it. It makes sense, then, that the girl would try to search for that warmth outside of the photo studio. Tonight, after a nap, Valeria will get dressed up to go dancing. "Studio 54 is really something if you're from Nowhereville, U.S.A." At the discotheque, the small-town girl will meet up with her entourage. "You look fabulous." "I saw the cover, it's great." "Valeria, you look beautiful." Valeria feels beautiful. Flattery, narcissism, manipulation, exploitation, these are abstractions she's not equipped to think about. They have nothing to do with what she feels. Valeria feels beautiful. Valeria feels... loved. Tonight.

"I'm glad we had this conversation," a successful agent with years of experience in the field tells me at the end of an interview, "because this is something we don't think about much. We're too busy, you see. We're so frantic in this business."

"Yes, I can imagine," I say.

"You have to understand, this *is* a business," the agent tells me.

Here we go again, I tell myself. But she continues: "But it's the business of making dreams. And people need dreams, you know."

I look at my tape recorder running and I tell myself: Not this old line. But then I look up at the woman's face and I see that she's sincere. It's kind of shocking, this romantic theory from this tough and successful businesswoman. But it's not another glib bit of hype, she really means it.

Later, when I think about her remark, I realize that she's telling the truth. People do need dreams. So, yes, it's sad that these young girls are sometimes confused by dream and reality, and are then ruined by the dream-making. But the suicides, the addictions, these are only the flamboyant and exceptional extremes of the process. For the most part, what these children lose is only their youth.

And the girls who stay in Saratoga and Kansas City, they too will someday lose their freshness and their sexual innocence. When they've become secretaries and bookkeepers, their youth and adolescent charm will vanish in a perhaps more timely, more natural, but ultimately no less inexorable death than that of their sisters in New York. So perhaps the saddest part of this story is not the prematurely lost youth of the young dream-makers, but that in our culture, our dreams are so elaborate and desperately needed that we do not care that they are bought at such a brutal price. In their innocence, young girls may reason (if, indeed, they reason at all) that it's a fair trade-off: youth in exchange for wealth and fame and love. And the people around them in the fashion industry consummate the transaction: it's their job, and they reap their own rewards. But we, more cynically, allow them to do so, and for such a small reward to ourselves: that almost negligible *frisson* of interest, just before we turn the page.

KLAUS KINSKI

GUESS I'll have to call it the "thing." I can't think of a name for it. During one of our conversations, I tried to pin Klaus Kinski down for a name and he reminded me of the fairy tales in which people died when they found out a forbidden name. "But anyway," he said, "there can be no word to express this thing, this secret. Because this secret which is not actually a secret, it is very simple but it includes, includes, endless, endless, almost everything, you know. The thinking about it and being conscious of all this means at the same moment changing everything, like in nature, changing and changing and changing, endless, always, never-ending movement, you see."

I don't know whether I'll be able to explain the "thing" to you in this article, though I believe that I myself understand it perfectly after spending some time with Klaus Kinski. It is not so much any specific thing he said, any one word that he uttered, as it is the accumulation of many words, images, metaphors, examples that he used, also gestures, facial expression, tone, the settings in which we talked, and, above all, the moods he can generate when all of those are combined.

Kinski has a unique mode of speech, often elliptical: he himself calls it "telegraph style." Sometimes his meaning is clear only by inference, by a leap of the mind from an image to an ostensibly unconnected idea. But in talking to him I soon understood how skillful he is, by instinct, at leading one to the leap. I realize now that Klaus Kinski could have talked to me in this seemingly inexact manner about the quantum theory, and I would have learned a great deal of physics. In fact, in a way, this is exactly what he talked to me about: the emission and absorption of energy in nature. And I, as a rule stubbornly rational, came to feel that imagery was not only more eloquent, but also more convincing, than intellectualization. This was my first important lesson about what it is the "actor" does.

So most of the time when we talked together, we referred to it as "this thing."

I know, though, that other people would have names for the thing. Some might call it talent, because it is the energy out of which artists create. But some might dismiss it as nonsense or would simply call it insanity. In fact, it is the pain of the exposed, hypersensitive psyche. To try to convey its essence to me, Kinski sometimes also called it the force, or the power, or nakedness, or receptivity, or the incarnation of all that is alive. Sometimes he used the phrase "participating in the universe." In the East, there is a tradition of seeking this merging. Indeed, Kinski admits that certain of the states he sometimes enters resemble meditation and embody some of the tenets of yoga. "But," as he puts it, "I don't need anybody to tell me how to be alive."

The next thing he said was "Faster!" or, rather, he yelled "FASTER!," which made my heart leap for the hundredth time that afternoon, since I had only just learned how to drive and also have a terrible fear of heights, and we were at the time heading toward the ocean on what I considered to be a precipitous mountain road.

"Can't you see there is someone behind us? Why do you go so SLOW! Just GO!!!"

"But I'm going to drive over the cliff," I protested.

"No, no. Look, you have much room. Let him pass. I can't bear this, to have these people stick on other cars' ass. Why won't they pass? It is unbearable. Stop. STOP!"

"Okay," I said, and lurched a few feet closer to what I thought was certain death.

"Just let him pass," he said. "It's true, for you it would be easy to go over the cliff here."

"I knew you'd be irritated by my driving," I muttered.

"Irritated!" he exclaimed. "I HATE it!"

But he was being good-natured, in his own way. By then I'd become accustomed to his sometimes yelling. Tricks of the print medium cannot, capital letters cannot convey the intensity of Kinski's voice when it rises, as it often does. And in the several long telephone conversations we'd had before I came to see him in northern California, I'd been somewhat frightened by it, at least at first, when I thought it was directed at me. "Why should I do any interviews? It is all SHIT," Kinski would crescendo. "Why me? Because I am what they call an actor? It is me or someone else, a murderer, or a conductor, anybody, anybody, anything, that can be *consumed*. They consume everything, art, executions, hamburgers, Jesus Christ. It is all supermarket talk. It is consumer SHIT to fill up their pages."

"Well, that's true," I had to admit before I hastened to point out that this would be different, that our talks would not have to be structured like routine interviews, that he would have freedom....

"Freedom!" he interrupted, as he almost always does. "FREE-DOM! That's what every shitty ruler promises you before he takes you over!"

"Well, it might be fun for you to..."

"Fun?" repeated Kinski, in a suddenly weary voice, faintly, as though he'd turned away from the phone. "There is no *fun*."

Later, when I knew him better, I understood that it was the imprecision of the catch-all banality that had arrested him. But also, I had reminded him of how little "fun" there was to be had in the fulfillment of his professional obligations.

"I am like a wild animal, who is behind bars. I need air! I need space!" he said. It sounded almost like a plea.

"I'm sorry," I said. "I don't mean to..."

"No, don't be sorry," he said impatiently, but not unkindly. "Don't be sorry, okay?"

You can witness Klaus Kinski have a mood swing within a minute, within a *sentence*, as his mind conveys him from an infuriating image to a soothing one to a humorous one. If you watch his face while he speaks, you will see it become a mask of ire, his glance menacing as he spits out words of contempt and outrage. Then suddenly, there'll be a smile of such gentleness that something will constrict in your chest. It's impossible not to respond.

He's so close to the surface, I had thought to myself in the course of those telephone conversations. But after I'd spent some time with him, I sometimes felt there was no surface at all. And that's often how I think of him now that I am back home: exposed, pulsating consciousness, as fragile as a human organ taken away from the protective case of the body. I think that's why he has isolated himself. Why, in between films, he lives alone, in the cabin in the middle of his forty acres of forest in northern California. Only his eight-year-old son, Nanhoï, comes for the weekend, twice a month or whenever his mother lets him stay longer. "I love him," says Klaus Kinski of his little boy, "more than anything in the whole universe."

But Kinski often goes for weeks without speaking to another human being, severing his contact with the outside world. He reads no newspaper. He watches no television: "I climbed up to the roof and smashed down the antenna," he explained to me. He keeps few possessions. When he has finished reading a book, he uses it to start a fire in the hearth that is his sole source of heat. He cuts his own hair, he grows his own vegetables, so that he does not have to drive into town. The animals in the forest do not threaten him as do people and their societies, nor do the storms, the wind, the trees. In the cabin, surrounded by vegetation through which there is no path save that made by the passage of his own body, and in his forest, he is safe. Except from the thing.

It was when he was about five years old that Kinski first remembers feeling this thing. He says he can recall looking at a dog or at a tree or at a whore on the streets of Berlin and hurling his own consciousness into creatures or even inanimate objects, not pretending to be, but *becoming* the dog or the tree or the whore. "Incarnating" is what he came to call it later, not playing a role. Being, not acting. He detests the word "entertainer." "What does that mean, this word 'entertainer'? Entertain what? Who?"

Though he is sometimes forced to use it himself, because there is no other one, he also hates the word "actor," and mocks the European critics who have called him "the greatest actor of the twentieth century," or "the only genius among us, the only prince of the grace of God."

In any event, he loathes all critics, and usually refers to them as "the masturbators."

He loathes most directors too.

"Do you think other people, directors, for example, understand this thing we have been talking about?" I asked him once.

"Directors in general understand shit," he answered.

It is now part of his legend that he has turned down roles from Fellini, Pasolini, Ken Russell, Steven Spielberg, and many more, the reason usually given being that he hadn't been offered enough money. "I make movies for money," Kinski asserts, "exclusively for money." And so most of the several hundred films in which he has appeared would be described, by any standards, as trash; others as some of the greatest of any time. But Kinski says it is his terrible destiny to be an "actor" and therefore to appear in movies, and that there is not much difference between the trash and the so-called art films. Almost always, he says, the latter are merely pretentious and, what's worse, pay less. "So I sell myself, for the highest price. Exactly like a prostitute. There is no difference." Kinski hates pretentious trash much more than the many so-called Spaghetti Westerns he has made, which brought him a large audience and, as he puts it bluntly, the most money. Of course he turned down Ken Russell and all the others. Why, he asks, should he work with someone like Fellini, who will pay him less and who treats actors like marionettes?

He is somewhat less harsh when he speaks of Werner Herzog, the German filmmaker whose work has given Kinski the

most breadth in displaying his ability to "incarnate." And
though he was already widely known in Europe for his stage
and film work, it is his roles in the Herzog films that are now,
in Europe and in this country, invariably joined with his name:
Aguirre, the Wrath of God, Nosferatu, Woyzek, and *Fitzcarraldo.*

Both men have been quoted as saying that they work together by a kind of telepathy. Herzog, says Kinski, gives him
no instructions. "In all of my scenes," says Kinski, "I am the
one who does it." But their fights are famed and they are said
to have occasionally come to blows on the set. There is a
notorious anecdote of an altercation Kinski and Herzog had
during the filming of their first movie together, *Aguirre.* They
had already spent several months in the Peruvian jungle when,
in the course of an argument, Kinski is said to have announced
he was leaving. Herzog has been quoted many times in the
ensuing years as claiming to have then pulled out a gun and
said, "Before you reach the bend in the river, there will be
eight bullets in your head. The last bullet will be for me."
Kinski comments: "This story is so shitty! Because he didn't
even have a gun to pull. Besides, there is no gun with *nine*
bullets! And *I* was the only one who had a rifle."

In the decade and a half since they started working together, the two men have sometimes not spoken for years.
But then Herzog will telephone Kinski in the middle of the
night, and ask him to meet him in yet another strange part
of the world, for yet another strange cinematic enterprise, and
Kinski will agree. "He is a less big asshole than the others,"
says Kinski, which in his parlance is a high compliment for
a director.

And Herzog, though he once diagnosed Kinski as a paranoid
schizophrenic, has more recently suggested that it is all the
others who are crazy. "He has an exacerbated sensibility,
inconceivable for the rest of us." There Herzog is also talking
about the "thing." And, in fact, Herzog has a name for the
thing. He calls it an "instinctive formulation" and says that
what Kinski has is genius.

It is in Herzog's films that Kinski is most tormented by this thing, which, in devouring him, allows him to create, or rather, not to create but to convey an extraordinarily organic identification. The torment is not conjured on the set, as in method acting ("Completely worthless shit" is his assessment of method or any other acting school), but lived through as soon as he reads the part, during the shooting period, and long after the film is completed. Kinski appropriates another's feelings, his furor, his pain, as he dons his costume. "It is not just putting on a costume. It becomes like a skin. You sweat their sweat, you suffer their suffering." During the filming of *Woyzek*, he often spent the night weeping in his trailer. When he was Nosferatu, Kinski came to hide from his own face, feeling that a hideous past was written upon it, so that he could not bear to look at himself in a mirror.

I asked Kinski once what he thought of when he first read the script of *Aguirre, the Wrath of God*. "I didn't think anything. I just was Aguirre," he said. "It was as if you say 'Oh, yeah.' Like you remember, you remember the fifteenth century, you remember yourself in the fifteenth century." For years afterward, he was plagued by back problems, because he had so distorted his spine for the humpbacked, off-centered, crablike demeanor of the Spanish conquistador. "This was not a 'tic' I decided on to be Aguirre," says Kinski. "I did not even decide. I *was* this cripple."

These films therefore imprison him; he becomes the slave of the "thing." "Sometimes," he says, "my heart hurts so much I beat it with my fists. I try to run. But you cannot run away from this. You cannot run from it. Wherever you run, it waits for you. Even when you think you have escaped it, it is there, where you have run to. It waits for you, to ambush you. It is like those vines called lianas, those tropical creepers that grow around you and strangle you. You cut off one branch, but there is another that grows. You leap over the wall of one ghetto, and you find yourself in another ghetto." That's why, he says, the good films imprison as much as the bad ones: "It is only a different kind of cage." The image of the cage often recurs in Kinski's speech.

In the articles that have appeared about him, there is a

much-repeated quote of his: "I am like a wild animal born in captivity, in a zoo. But where a beast would have claws, I was born with talent." In recent years, these articles seldom omit the word "legend." The Kinski legend is that of the masterful but fractious, embattled, anarchist artist, who does not seek prestige and shuns respectability. He rejects awards: "If they're not changeable in cash money," he explains. "It is the Nobel Prize I want," he says, laughing. "It's worth four hundred thousand dollars."

"You can call it," he tells me, "my consciousness of using my talent like a whore uses her body: to pay the price."

His autobiography, which has not yet been published in this country but was a best seller in Germany and in France, was variously declared to be "ordurious" and "pornographic" and deemed "the work of a magician," "atrociously lucid," and compared to Rimbaud, Céline, and Henry Miller. The book is a powerful howl of pain and eroticism. The account of his childhood in Berlin between the wars is not for the queasy in its vivid re-creation of hunger, cold, and filth, of a family of six sleeping on a maggot-filled mattress in a heatless room, of stealing to eat, of the state institution when there was no chance of eating, of incestuous sexuality. The sensuality of the adolescent and adult Kinski exhibited in this book is not for the queasy either: explosive, compulsive, unrelenting, strangely combining brutality and tenderness, his erotic sensibility is articulated in the most defiant detail in the pages of this book. "Don't you dare to judge me!" its author seems to be saying.

And just as he recounts the intolerable misery of that childhood with no self-pity and no self-justification, so he recounts his desertion from the German army, his subsequent incarceration in the British prisoner-of-war camp where homosexual favors were traded for a cigarette and where he first went on stage, aptly enough as prisoner performing for prisoners, to divert them for a moment from their imprisonment, and then the years spent sleeping in the parks and on the pavements of the capitals of Europe, the winters when he shared the hoboes' street stoves, hands and feet protected by rags, sleeping on subway grates for their intermittent wafts of warmth. But during the day the young actor worked on his diction and began to perform in Shakespeare, Ibsen, Cocteau, and in his own adaptations of Dostoevski.

Then came the spectators to the cabarets of Berlin where Kinski, barefooted, recited Villon's poetry and collected money afterward, in his hat. From there it seems like a natural trajectory to the one-man "recitals" that lasted as long as four hours, and for which Kinski filled the biggest sports arenas of Europe with standing-room-only crowds. By that time, movie offers had begun to proliferate. Kinski turned down some forty of them because the roles, he felt, did not have enough scope.

Then there was an about-face, typical of Kinski's aversion to the trappings of a prestigious career. Headed for a distinguished image as a fine and celebrated artiste, he said, as he would now put it, "Fuck YOU!," and began to accept any offer that was made him, solely on the basis of salary. "I realized it didn't matter," he says. "It was all the same. So I went to work for money, only for money. Many people do not believe me when I tell them this, or they think this is disgusting. But it is true. I could not do what I wanted anyway in this fucking ghetto, and I wanted money, because I had never had any. And I learned that people do almost everything for it."

Then came the years of sumptuous profligacy, of palazzos in Rome, of caviar diets and huge domestic staffs, of Ferraris and Rolls-Royces given away when Kinski decided he no longer liked their color or the way a door closed. By then he was living in Italy, where he was a top box-office draw and began doing "guest appearances," working on a film for a few days, one day, a few hours, which enabled producers to feature his name on the marquees and brought him the cash he constantly needed to support his extravagances.

But now his pattern of deserting what he had been able to conquer was established: adulated in Italy, where he had lived for a decade, he then left everything behind and moved to France. But he only stayed there for a few years, long enough to become a star of the French cinema, though with *Aguirre* he had already conquered the French public. Herzog, asserts

Kinski stubbornly, as though challenging one to question his motivations for working on those films, pays him a very great deal of money.

Then he moved, most incongruously it seemed to me, but perhaps not, to California. And this is where, with some difficulty, I contacted him.

It was *Aguirre, the Wrath of God* that first interested me in Kinski, though "interested" is an inadequate word for the eerie mélange of attraction and fear with which one responds to that character. But it was his book that then fascinated me, both as a reader and as a writer. Though I had read the book in the mid-seventies, there were many scenes I had not forgotten a decade later. It wasn't only because of the strangeness of this man's life itself, filled with unlikely, bizarre events, permeated with passionate sexuality; it was the explosiveness of the very prose style; the violence of the projection of the self.

There was one scene especially that remained vivid in my mind. Some time after World War II, Kinski was locked up in Wittenau, a lunatic asylum outside of Berlin. The events leading up to his incarceration are not completely clear in the book, but apparently he threw a shoe at the director of the hospital where he was recovering from jaundice and exhaustion, and was then immediately committed to Wittenau. His own doctor said nothing in his defense. She was a woman with whom Kinski had a liaison, but at the time he was also regularly going to bed with her sister, and her sister's daughter. By this point in the book, none of it seems surprising.

Before this doctor finally acted in his behalf, Kinski spent about six weeks at Wittenau, and his description of the common room where the insane and the sane who were going insane slept, ate, screamed, and waited is hallucinatorily alive.

As Kinski describes it, journal-style, he does not know when and how he will get out, and he is suffering from intolerable headaches, for which he receives no medication. Despite all of his efforts to present a bland, unthreatening façade to the guards, to avoid any incident that might prevent his release, he has moments of weakness.

"I think I've surmounted the worst of it, but it's not so easy," he writes. "When I approach the barred window, hoping to glimpse a fragment of sky, the guard orders me to stand back. I turn away and cry. A one-legged patient whispers to me:

"'Don't cry. If you cry, it means you're not healthy.'"

And so it was his hatred that kept him sane, he says. "Above all, don't give in to despair!" he would tell himself. Not to despair, or even sadness, which diminishes hatred, or to scorn, which weakens it.

This is what I found most compelling about Kinski: his ability both to experience and to deny despair. He seemed to me like a man at the end of his rope, who screams "Fuck you!" to the rope. This is why I wanted to meet him and write about him. Unless the job really is "consumer shit," an interview found and written only to fill pages (and perhaps even then), every journalist hopes to take, to steal, something for himself or herself from an encounter with a subject. A journey into someone else's mind is like traveling to a foreign place: the traveling itself is exciting or instructive or perhaps useful, but also there may be some artifacts of a foreign sensibility that you can acquire, something you can bring back with you when you leave, that's yours to keep. What I wanted for myself from Klaus Kinski was some of his power and his rage.

But Kinski was now a nearly total recluse, I was told, living alone in the cabin in the forest, refusing interviews, limiting all contact to a minimum. So I wasn't surprised when my request for an interview conveyed through routine channels was summarily rejected. I continued to pursue him, however. Finally, I asked a mutual acquaintance to intercede for me.

I don't know why Kinski called me the first time. I think that probably it was a call designed to be a polite refusal, as a favor to the person who had spoken to him in my behalf. As to why he continued to talk to me, perhaps it was because I did not argue with his initial indictment of celebrity journalism, nor did I defend the merits of the press. Indeed, why should I have? I agreed with him. In fact, I agreed with most everything he said, though I found it curiously expressed, and saw no need to argue with him at all, including as to why he should allow me to invade his privacy for my article. "Why should I do this?" he asked. "Because it is important to you?" I had to agree, this wasn't a reason. And perhaps because I didn't argue, Kinski then proceeded to explain to me that it wasn't me personally or even the press that infuriated him, that the press was merely another structure in the ghetto that also includes filmmaking and most of the organized, regimenting categories of thought and behavior of a society he perceives as a prison. And once he started talking to me, perhaps because he knew I was really listening, or perhaps only because he had started talking, he continued. Indeed, his conversational style is as instinctive, and as spontaneous, as any "artistic" improvisation. He will range from subject to subject seamlessly. At first, his monologues seem almost to wander at random because of his digressions, his strange transitions and associations, but then one begins to detect a pattern which perhaps most resembles a very fine jazz improvisation, in which a musician explores a theme from which he often detours, the detour then becoming an adjunct to the theme itself, which is always returned to. It is a highly personalized way of addressing any subject, especially in combination with his sometimes curious syntax and his bursts of invective.

"You have to protect yourself, your body, your being," he told me once. "You cannot treat it badly, you have to keep it, not only to keep it, but to make it, sensitive, as sensitive as possible. Since I was born I have been like this, till today. Nothing changed. Even more, even worse. Once about twenty-five years ago I was in an apartment or somebody gave me a room to live in, I don't know what, and next door they put on the radio, so I struck the wall with my fist, but they did not put the radio down, so I took a tool and banged until I made a hole through the wall." Kinski suddenly laughs. "It was like a comedy movie," he says. Then, as suddenly, he becomes stern again. "I didn't laugh then," he says. "And then I left, of course, the apartment, because they didn't let me live there any more. When I come back here from the airport—most of the time when I travel I leave my car at the airport, even some weeks, cost me some hundreds of dollars, I don't care—but once I took a taxi. I hate those, what do you call them, limousines, so ugly. They stink and their drivers have been driving dead people to the cemeteries. I hate those. Okay, I took a taxi, and now this guy had a radio on. First of all, he had this thing EE—AAAH-UGGHH-OO-UGGH—ACHHHHHHGGG, these machines, how can somebody all day long hear this? He must be already deaf. I don't know what. And then I say, Do you need this? I say, this machine? And he looked at me, like maybe I am crazy or whatever. I say, I just come from Tokyo, Hong Kong, long flight, I am exhausted. I said, Look, just half an hour. Do I have to listen to that crap? Can you turn the radio off? And he was even willing. He turned around, and he said, But it's the news. I say, I don't need this. I say, I don't want to, I have never listened to it, never in my life, I said, okay? I am almost on the border. I need to stop. I have to get out of your car. And he switched it off, but saying, as though he was really surprised, and almost sorry for me: How can you know what's going on? There, you see. THIS IS EXACTLY WHAT I DON'T WANT TO KNOW!!!!" Kinski laughed again. "He was so surprised. He is in a prison forever, thinking he needs to know what is going on. You know, this sort of shades on top of the cell bars, so that the prisoner cannot see what's going on outside? So, he needs the *news*. He was nice enough to switch it off, and I didn't continue this talk, otherwise I would have said: DO YOU THINK I DON'T KNOW WHAT IS GOING ON? I KNOW, I KNOW YOUR TRASH OF HELL! WHAT'S THE DIFFERENCE TODAY? WHO IS EXECUTED TODAY? WHO HAS CROOKED WHO TODAY? WHO IS THIS ONE AND WHO IS THIS ONE? WHO SHOT HIMSELF IN THE HEAD TODAY? WHAT ELSE? THE BOX OFFICE? WHATEVER, WHATEVER THE FUCK YOU WANT TO TELL ME TODAY, I DON'T WANT TO KNOW IT, NOTHING OF IT." Kinski paused. "I mean, I could have told him, it was not the point, because he was just harmless, and he was at least nice enough to switch it off."

I came to appreciate Kinski's explosions of anger at the media, at the entertainment industry, at the girl behind the McDonald's counter who says "Next!" and expects you to respond in the same rhythm ("I will NEVER be 'next!'"), at

sluggish telephone operators, at governments, at lines in the
bank, at traffic signs ("There is a sign that says 'Right Lane
Must Exit'; right lane MUST exit! MUST! And I say to myself,
MUST? Fuck YOU!"), at all the words and structures of our
society that limit and regiment the individual. Actually, I found
that, no matter what mood I'd been in when I answered the
phone, I always felt much better afterward. "Why should these
conversations feel cathartic for me?" I wondered. And it occurred to me that it was because Klaus Kinski so easily expressed the anger I myself feel but am unable to articulate
directly, and sometimes am even too inhibited to allow myself
to experience. It wasn't just the words or the examples he
used, though these were often colorful; it was his conviction,
his tone and his delivery, his projection. And it happened every
time, whether I expected it or not, whether I was prepared
to analyze it, intellectualize it, explicate it to myself for the
purposes of my article. It was a visceral reaction. This too was
for me an important lesson about what it is the "actor" does.

Of course, I had no control over these conversations, which
Kinski conducted entirely according to his fancy. And at that
point I hesitated to ask any direct questions. He would simply
hang up, I knew, if I chanced to offend him. I'll wait, I told
myself, until I am in California. Even after he had agreed to
my visit, however, one of his phrases nagged me with doubt
as to how willing he might turn out to be to cooperate with
an interviewer:

"It's not who a person is that is important," he had told me,
"it is what goes through a person."

"Well, it's both, no?" I had said, somewhat uncertain of
what he meant by what goes "through" a person.

"Yes, okay, both," he had replied, as if to humor me, or to
dismiss an irrelevant distinction.

What goes *through* a person? This turn of phrase worried
me. Was it lyrical? Was it mystical? Would he be as cryptic
face to face?

Well, I consoled myself, I'll have more control over our
conversations once I'm in California.

But, of course, in California it was no different. It is out of the question for Kinski to be controlled by anyone, let alone a journalist. He simply talked to me about whatever he had decided was suitable, or, rather, wherever he had been led by mood or instinct. It's true that one of the conditions of our meeting had been my promise that our talks would be unstructured and could ramble freely, that they would not have to take the form of routine interviews. But I had underestimated Klaus Kinski's disregard—indeed, unawareness—of structures and conventions, journalistic and otherwise. He followed none of the rules of the interview situation. Not one, not even the most basic. "I don't want to talk too much about myself," he would suddenly declare, notwithstanding the fact that I'd come several thousand miles to hear him talk about himself, and launch into an anecdote about Eleonora Duse, or Van Gogh, or Paganini, a synopsis of a Dostoevski short story, or a long disquisition about a Holbein painting or about Jesus Christ in his grave, which he had for his own reasons decided was germane to our discussion. He refused to sit in a quiet room with a tape recorder, so that all of our conversations took place in cars, at the beach, in noisy restaurants. Actually, he didn't "refuse" anything: I never had a chance to ask him. He would simply announce our schedule for the day. On some days, he would call me at my motel room to tell me that he couldn't talk at all, that it was impossible for him to see me. He'd been tortured through the night by insomnia, or by one of his terrible nightmares. "I am completely destroyed," he would tell me. I found myself curiously unresentful. After all, if predictability was what I wanted, I told myself, I could go interview a statistician. And I soon realized it was almost always hopeless to ask him any direct questions: if he didn't interrupt them, he argued with their wording or with their relevance, or simply would digress, no explanation given, to another topic.

The odd thing is that I came to be content to let him meander as he chose. His way of expressing himself, I now realized, wasn't cryptic after all, if one was willing to be receptive. I began to understand that his digressions were often telling, and to realize that most of my questions would be useless. I saw that any attempt to "conduct" an interview would only antagonize him.

Despite my initial frustration, after some thought it came to seem logical to me that Kinski would not be "conducted" in this situation either, and I began to enjoy often remaining silent and not having to "conduct" anything. Even this, however, would occasionally make him suspicious. He would pause, perhaps because he had come to a natural punctuation in his own discourse: "You," he would say, "you don't talk," and he would request a question. But usually, before I'd gotten a full interrogative sentence out, he'd be off again, because a single word in some dependent clause had reminded him of some idea he wanted to explore or dispute.

"What? What is it you want to say?" Kinski queried when he saw me open my mouth several times.

"There was something you mentioned the other day," I began, "about how money is freedom...."

"I never said that," he assured me.

"You did," I replied. "You said..."

"No, no. I never said money *is* freedom! I said money *buys* freedom. BUYS! What does that mean, money is freedom? This is ridiculous: money is freedom. It means nothing. What do you think, that a dollar in a savings account is freedom? Maybe you have understood nothing I have said. You are trying to make me sound like an American average citizen."

Making Klaus Kinski seem like an average American citizen would probably be as easy as getting a lion into a three-piece suit, but I knew better by then than to try to insist on a locution. His arguments to my questions were often semantic. Kinski hates words, he resents having to use them to express himself, he finds them untrustworthy, limiting, confining, reductive.

"Experiencing the ocean is an experience of liberty," he told me as an example. "When you talk about the ocean, is it liberty? Even looking at the ocean is not liberty. It is like a wounded bird looking at the sky and saying, Why are my wings broken? Or even worse: putting a bird cage near the window so that the bird can see the sky. But of course it's much better to look than not to, even if it hurts. But words! You cannot talk long about the sea. When you are on the sea, then you cannot say anything any more. You become part of it, you grow in it. Things are going on that you cannot name any more. You know that you are part of it and then you cannot talk about it any more. There are a hundred thousand books about the sea that will not tell you what the sea is. Words are not enough."

"But sometimes," I felt compelled to say in defense of my own medium, "you can put them together to evoke a certain feeling."

"But this is a consolation for cripples," said Kinski. "Yes, sometimes spontaneously bringing words out can be outscreams. Outscreams of joy or pain, or whatever you want. Or sometimes you can describe. But you aren't *there*. When you are there, you *are*. With words you *aren't*. It is true what Rimbaud said once, it's absolutely true, I proved it. He said if you think a book is strong enough, try it at the ocean, in the wind, at the waves. If the book can resist the ocean, the elements, then it exists. Otherwise, throw it away."

I thought this over. Frankly, by now I was having a good time thinking over this sort of stuff. I still had occasional bursts of anxiety as to whether any of it added up to an article, but by then, for my own reasons, I'd become too interested in the "thing" to make any attempts to try to steer Kinski in other directions. And, in any event, he wouldn't have allowed it, since he had decided soon after my arrival that the "thing" should be the theme of my article. "This is the essence, the fundament of what it is that they call the 'actor,'" he told me. "Otherwise, why write about me? Anyway, if you write about this, you write about me. It is the same."

The night I arrived we'd had a conversation driving in from the airport and at a Vietnamese restaurant, though this talk had been in my view somewhat desultory, and without a tape recorder. This was before I understood that all of our conversations would be desultory, and most without a tape recorder. But overnight Kinski thought about some of the subjects we had discussed, and it came to his mind, he told me the next day, that this, this thing, should be the subject of my article about him. We were speaking on the phone. It was one of those days when Kinski called to say he couldn't see me. However, he then proceeded to talk to me on the phone for about four hours. I know it was about four hours because it was as I was turning over my third ninety-minute tape that I realized my tape recorder wasn't working.

Afterward I tried to write out some of the things he had told me when he started explaining this thing to me. He'd given me examples, images that he thought I would grasp. It was comparable, by analogy, to the power of Kung Fu, he had told me. He had mentioned Bruce Lee, for example, and how it is possible to observe that the concentration, the energy connected into by the Kung Fu artist begins long before the point of impact, the lethal kick, and continues afterward. He talked to me also about how this thing that enables you to create is the thing that makes you suffer, suffer so much that you hate your fate, which has driven you to it. Because it is not a choice, he told me, to do this. You start doing it, and then you cannot stop, and the more you do it, the more it makes you suffer. And you cannot get rid of it, once you have felt it. You cannot kill it, no matter how much you hate it for making you suffer. You try to kill it, but it is like the snake with a hundred heads: there is always another head.

But this is only part of what he told me, and I hadn't a chance of reconstructing the scores of images, metaphors, and examples he had given me or, more important, his manner of expressing them. It was the best single explanation he ever gave me. I knew this even then, after we hung up and I played the tape back and listened to the droning buzz of the faulty connection that drowned out most of his words. I knew I would never get this from him again, and that I couldn't even ask him. He had already told me, in the most violent terms, how he felt if a director asked him for another take when he had already, according to his judgment, or rather, his instinct, done the take. "Those assholes!" he had expostulated. "ASSHOLES! Do you ask a car crash for another take? Do you ask a volcano for another take? Do you ask the storm for another take?"

So *I* certainly wasn't going to ask him for another take. ... Though by then it was more out of respect for his principles than fear of his anger. I wasn't afraid of him any more, because I'd learned that the anger was not directed at me, or, for that matter, usually at anyone in particular. "It's not the people I am talking about, you understand?" he had told me. "It's what people create when they make a society. Sometimes I feel sorry for the people." Also, I'd observed that his angry diatribes were often intended to be humorous. Besides, beneath the anger there was often only a certain gruffness, and beneath the gruffness was often whimsy, and even great gentleness, though that gentleness could be glimpsed only occasionally, according to whatever mysterious dictates made his distrust of his interlocutor wax and wane.

That was that, I figured, for my "power and rage" theory of what I could bring back from Klaus Kinski's world. But, I told myself, when I see him tomorrow I'll at least ask him about anger; I knew by now, though, that I'd almost certainly not get a straight answer to such a question. What would he come up with, I wondered, to dispel another of my assumptions about interviews, or, indeed, to disrupt one of my fundamental assumptions about human interactions in general? Because usually, in my opinion, what you discover in the course of an intimacy, even a journalistic intimacy, is, under the veneer of adaptation, a person's pain and fear. But Kinski wears pain, fear, alienation on the outside, expresses them openly, even casually. Inside is ... what?

"It's idiotic to analyze" is one of Kinski's favorite dicta. "This is a waste of time. The greatest philosophers, they will teach you nothing unless you know it already. There are things you must know *here*." He pointed to his heart. "Here," he pointed to his head, "is distractions, lies, everything gets deformed. If you say to me, 'Explain to me the storm,' I will say, 'Shut up so you can hear the storm.' It's like there is an old Chinese philosopher who says ... A story of China is nothing new, when you think about it, but is forever new because we never understand anything. But there is a story, a very famous old story from China, in which a philosopher says: When you point your finger at the moon, don't get concentrated on the finger. You will miss all the glory of the moon."

But none of this was much consolation to me the day I sat in my uncannily ugly California motel room staring at the tape that had only the buzz on it. Well, I thought, I can't ask him to do another take, but maybe I can get him to repeat some of these things. You see, I still hadn't completely gotten it: there would never be any repetition.

The next day, however, I was in high spirits, despite a harrowing ride on the highway (my first ever), when I finally reached the little town where he'd given me an appointment. "From there, we will go to the ocean," he had announced on the phone that morning. He had seemed in a better mood too.

Fortunately, I had allotted two hours for what I'd been told was a half-hour ride, so I was a few minutes early despite all the time taken by my seemingly endless wandering in the incomprehensible maze of California roads, not the least part of which had been spent going around in circles because of those infuriating "Right Lane Must Turn Right"/"Left Lane Must Turn Left" signs. I had sometimes attempted to tell myself "Must? Fuck you!" like Klaus Kinski, but whenever I tried this, other drivers would honk at me, even when it had nothing to do with them, from across an intersection! One woman driver kept her hand on her horn for a full minute when I executed what I was convinced was a perfectly harmless, albeit, I admit, illegal, U-turn, even though I was a hundred feet away from her. This taught me a thing or two about how people will react when you don't follow the rules by which they themselves are willing to be bound. This has nothing to do with traffic safety, you understand. But it led me to some thoughts about the price Klaus Kinski pays for his defiance of as many rules as he can manage to disobey, because of his preference for this thing that makes him un-willing to take for granted any of the regulations societies have established to codify experience and behavior. In a civ-

ilization that is increasingly complex, mechanistic, technological, and organized, the battle for the individual self becomes
even more difficult. The compulsion to locate the self becomes
stronger as civilization becomes more constricting, and methods of staying "self-alive" (merged with the external world)
must sometimes be violent and are of necessity passionate.
Maybe my interest in the source of Klaus Kinski's power and
rage isn't so foolish after all, I speculated in my parked car.

This is the sort of stuff I was mulling over when he arrived
at our meeting place. There was something wrong with his
car, he told me; we would use mine. I started to get out of
my side, expecting him to drive. "No, no," he said. "You will
drive." I'd warned him that my driving was still somewhat
uncertain. But he wouldn't drive a piece of shit like this, he
told me, casting an indescribably scornful glance at my rented
Ford Escort. And in any event, he told me, he won't drive a
car other people have driven. The latter did not surprise me
so much, for he had already told me that he won't read a copy
of a book anyone else has read, and that one of the reasons
he hates old houses and hotel rooms is that he can sense the
lingering presence of its former occupants. Still, it was with
dread that I got back into the driver's seat, turned on the
ignition, inched from my parking space toward the road, and
then stopped to see if any other cars were coming.

"Further! Further!" complained Kinski, who had obviously
made a quick assessment of my driving skills and had con-
cluded that I could use some coaching. "How can you see
anything? You must go on the road. Now, just go! GO!"

I floored the accelerator and drove off in a flurry of gravel.
If this made me even more nervous, it seemed to affect Kinski
not a bit. In fact, he now simply sat back, though it did seem
to me that he maintained a high degree of, shall we say,
alertness throughout our ride. I suddenly remembered a passage in his book where he describes driving his Ferrari on
the Italian highway at over a hundred miles an hour, closing
his eyes, and counting to ten. If he could take that, I guess
he can take this too, I thought.

At the first red light, I got out my tape recorder, set it against the windshield, and turned it on. But I soon abandoned hope of getting him to repeat anything he had said the day before. He began right where he'd left off.

"What I was telling you yesterday," he said, "this is why the ultimate acting is to destroy yourself."

"I wanted to ask you..." I said.

"The more I think about it," he told me, "the more it makes sense to me. You are too far on the left. Look how much space you have on my side. An article including everything that we said, so it's not just talking about somebody that is what you call an actor. You cannot separate it."

"I wanted to ask you a question," I said.

"What?" he said, for once.

"About anger," I said. "I wanted to ask you..."

"Why are you cluttering up your article?" he said. "This has nothing to do with what we have been talking about."

"You know," I said, casting a quick glance toward my tape recorder to see if the meter needle was moving, and of course drifting into the next lane. "You know," I said, "I have been thinking about this, and you are taking my article over, exactly like you take over your scenes in Werner Herzog's movies."

"Where are you going?" said Kinski.

"Sorry," I said, and careened back into my own lane.

"Of course," he said. "It's obvious that you should write about this. You cannot write in a story everything about me."

"Well," I said, because I know very well I have a tendency to clutter up my articles, "you may be right."

"Of course," he said.

We headed toward the mountains. The road became sinuous as we climbed.

"Why are you so worried?" asked Kinski.

"I'm not worried," I said.

"You look worried," he said. "Why? This is what you need. This is what is important to know. This is the essence, this thing. This is what journalists were trying to get out of me for twenty years. And I never thought of it in this way before, but last night, because of our conversation, I thought: This is what is essential, this is the fundament. It is obvious that this is what you must write. Don't keep mixing in these other things."

"But..." I started saying.

"It only confuses," he said. "What are you doing? You are too far on the left again."

"But you need a framework," I said. "You need..."

"A framework! What is this, a framework? You don't need a framework. They told you you need this. You don't need this. You need a painting, not a frame. You are going too slow. Just go."

"Well..." I started saying, but then I gasped, suddenly jolted backward because Kinski, having decided the car was too sluggish on the steep road, had without warning shifted down.

"That's better," he said, as we picked up speed.

By the time I recovered, I'd lost my train of thought.

"Of course, when I say I thought of this last night," he continued, "it is not a question of the moment. It is just that I don't talk about this. It was because of your questions."

(I had some doubts about this, but kept them to myself.)

"Because, when I am alone, I do not talk to myself. But, anyway, it is not a question of the moment. It is a question of years and years. What I discovered is, the farther you go, the more you become the victim of it. At first I felt it coming up in myself, just really physically growing in myself, and happening, but it was a jungle, so I couldn't distinguish things so much. I knew there were in myself the souls of millions of people who lived centuries ago, not just people, but animals, plants, the elements, things, even, *matter,* that all of these exist in me, and I felt this. Okay, this pushed and pushed and pushed. Okay, that was the beginning.... And through the years it became clearer and clearer, this thing; it started to separate itself. I could make it come when I had to concentrate on, let's say, a person I had to become: this thing became stronger, and took more of me. In this moment, I let it do it, because I wanted, I *had* to be this person. And as I was led to doing it, there was then no way back. And the more I tried to do it, the more I hated it. But there was no way back any more; it was always going farther and farther and farther.

Until one day, when I was walking through the streets of
Paris, I started crying, because I could look at a man, a woman,
a dog, anything, and *receive* them, anything, everything; there
was no difference between physical and psychological. I felt
like I was breaking out, breaking up, receiving everything,
every moment, even things I did not see. There is no turning
back from this once you have gone that far. You cannot get
back. But this danger is the power you have. It is this same
power that lets you hold an audience when you are on a stage.
Then it is a concentration, the same concentration that in
Kung Fu is used for the kick that kills, or to break a table
with your hand. It means that you are sure of the power, and
that you relinquish yourself to it."

Kinski paused. "Where are you going, anyway?"

"I'm just stopping for a minute," I said, and turned over my
tape. To tell you the truth, I was glad to stop for a moment.
I was now in the throes of a full-fledged paroxysm of acro-
phobia, with the added frustration that my fear of taking my
eyes off the road for even a second prevented me from looking
at Kinski, who was gesticulating in the seat next to mine.

"Is that fucking thing still on?" Kinski gestured with contempt toward my tape recorder. "You don't need this."

"Do you think there are other ways of feeling this thing?"
I asked.

"What kind of a question is this? What do you want, a list?
I am not a list-maker," he said.

"Sex, for example?"

"Sex! I hate this word. What does that mean, this word,
'sex'? Or the expression 'making love'? I have never understood those words. Eroticism, this is something else. But eroticism is everywhere, in a tree, in a stone. A stone is alive. A
wild animal, in a jungle."

"I read that you spent much time in the jungle during the
filming of *Aguirre* and *Fitzcarraldo*."

"It's true," he said. "Often I would walk deep into the jungle
by myself. You feel then that you become part of it. You don't
have to go far. You can sit there and soon you become part
of it, part of its vibration, physically part of the sounds of the

jungle, part of the animals. You participate in the jungle, in the trees, in the birds, in the panthers, even in the snakes."

"Weren't you afraid?"

"No, not afraid. Alert. It is an alertness that gives you energy, life."

I thought of the kind of state one might experience in a wild jungle and pondered the idea that Klaus Kinski would feel comfortable there.

"Do you ever," I risked asking, "feel peace?"

"Peace?" he said. "Everyone has a different meaning for that word. I don't know what that word means to you. So I cannot answer your question."

I started the car again.

"I am dying of hunger," he said. "Go this way."

He'd seen a sign that said "Food Service."

I bore left and found, with some relief, that we were now on a long, flat road. My acrophobic spasm subsided, and I stepped on the gas.

"What does that mean, Food *Service*? Is this food? I don't understand their signs. Why are you going so fast?"

"I thought it was okay, here," I said.

"No, no, it is very dangerous, this road, you cannot see what is coming."

I slowed down.

"It should not be necessary to explain things," said Kinski. "But you can say it another way. I avoid the other way, but I could say, okay, the madness is waiting for me. Some other person would say, okay, I am afraid to get mad, for years and years and years, and I see the madness, how it's waiting and waiting, and I am going to fight it. I don't name it this way, because I don't want to accept it this way. I wouldn't have suffered day and night for so long, okay, for so long, more and more and more. I don't know... maybe it comes from this fucking occupation that they call 'art.' I don't know what the meaning of that is. And they call me 'actor,' and I know this is shit, okay, because it just means that some idiot, absolutely imbecilic cretin illiterate director can say what he wants to me, even harm me. So I say to him, FUCK OFF! Or I go home, or whatever. And then they say, He is mad, he just happened to have been an artist. These people who do not see the terrible things, and therefore do not see the beautiful things either. But I cannot dump, *dump* this thing. They think you can dump all this and be an actor. Then they say, 'Good job.' Do you say 'Good job' to an earthquake? But this is all shit, the directors, the critics. What is going on in myself belongs to me, and *I* have to find out what it is. Stop. We are here. STOP! No, you missed it. That was the road. Now we have to go back."

We went to a little fast-food place at the beach, an absurd gray structure that had been weathered to look quaint against the background of the ocean. I watched him stand at a counter and eat a chili dog, using plastic knife and fork. "These beans are disgusting," he said. "They are hard. Look at this sign, 'Homemade.' What does this mean, 'home'? Does it mean that the beans are even more disgusting than others? I don't understand their signs. I don't WANT to understand their signs. This 'Homemade,' it's supposed to tell you these disgusting beans are good. These fucking signs! Signs everywhere that lie."

Then we walked along the beach. Or, rather, Kinski paced back and forth on the beach, while I traipsed along behind him, with my useless tape recorder: there was a howling, violent wind, which whipped our hair and our clothes and which I knew would make this tape inaudible too.

It was cold that day, already autumn. We couldn't see the horizon; the gray of the ocean somehow merged into that of the sky. Even the sand seemed gray in that light. Behind us were more grays, those of the cliffs, and then the brown of the mountains. It was the only time I saw Klaus Kinski not dressed in white: he had a bright red windbreaker on, the only splash of passionate color in the mist, in the grays and browns.

We paced, back and forth, back and forth, back and forth. Kinski talked and I listened until I started shivering in the relentless wind.

"Let's go back," he said.

We sat for a while in the parked car. He opened the window, for air, or perhaps to hear the gulls crying, or the sound of the wind, which he likes so much. But it seemed almost silent now, away from the beach. There was a stillness. We sat quietly for a moment.

"Why do I continue making movies?" he said, in reply to a question I'd asked hours earlier, and to which I no longer expected an answer. "Making movies is better than cleaning toilets," he said. "And, besides, I am used to kicks."

I think he meant kicks in the Kung Fu sense: not taking them, that is, but giving them, connecting with the force that generates a point of impact.

"Do some roles leave you cold?" I ventured to ask, since he seemed more willing than usual to answer questions.

"In a way, everything concerning a movie leaves me cold, and everything involves me. For a smaller one, you just give a smaller kick."

I remained silent then, thinking of *Woyzek* or *Aguirre* and made-for-TV movies.

"I don't know. Why have I had this life? If I knew, I wouldn't have done it. Do you know what I mean? You cannot even say, I cannot even tell myself, 'Why did I do it?' I shouldn't have done it. It's ridiculous."

"It wasn't a choice?"

"It wasn't my choice."

He sighed.

"So it means," he continued, "the only thing I can say is, okay, shit! Just like, like saying 'shit' to yourself. You say 'SHIT' ten times, and you hurt yourself. You say 'SHIT.' Nobody is there. You just say 'SHIT.' So I could tell myself, Oh, shit, why, WHY, why did all that happen to me? Why was I not a bird on the ocean? You know? Instead of this, you know? This I could say, but just to myself. SHIT! It doesn't even make sense after a while when you say 'shit' from morning to evening, but there was a time when I could not stop. It was like a tic. I said 'shit,' all the time. SHIT!!!"

For the first time in his presence, I felt afraid, not of him but of the furor of that younger self he was reincarnating now in the small, cramped space we sat in, yet another cage to be filled with that power and rage, which I finally understood to be his furor at his own fate. And I saw the same vein stand out on his forehead that I had seen on Aguirre's and the same intensity in the set of his jaw: it was not the rage of help-lessness, it was the rage of defiance.

Kinski opened his eyes, which had been clamped shut, and then looked away, at the ocean. In the car, the silence now seemed new. Well, it wasn't a silence. There was still the wind, the sound of a seagull's wings flapping. It only seemed like a new silence to me because I had watched a man say "FUCK YOU" to his own pain.

Kinski stared steadfastly at the ocean.

"I don't know," he said.

"Why do you live alone?" I asked.

"I didn't choose solitude" was all he answered. It was un-usually brief, for him.

"Because in your book," I said, "you seemed capable of such love."

"Yes," he said. "Love is the salvation." He sighed again. "I didn't choose to be alone. But... I cannot explain this. I could be with a woman in a bed, for weeks even, and it would seem to me like three seconds. Or three hundred years. You know, then, there is no time sense, because of things that are going on in you. I don't know, there is no explanation of this. But every time, even with someone I... But whenever I was with a woman, I always sort of want another one. So there was always another one. I can't explain this, but it means that these women, they were not sharing my solitude. I wanted to stay with somebody but I couldn't, it wasn't possible, be-cause of this thing moving in myself. I had to learn this. I didn't want to be alone, but I had to learn that the dimensions of my feelings are too violent. I had to learn this. It is what I was just telling you before. Why? Why am I like this? It is the same as: Why wasn't I born a fisherman? This is not a choice. There is not a why. Look at this bird there. Why does he fly to the left? Why?"

We watched as the gull flew out of our sight, toward the

mountains. A few hundred feet off, on the road leading away from the beach, a truck pulled up, and some men got out, carrying electric drills, hammers. They set to work, and now the sounds of the pneumatic drill and the jackhammer reached the car.

"Look at them!" exclaimed Kinski. "They are not happy if they don't hammer. They hammer, they hammer, it is unbearable. That is why you have to go away. It is not a solution, but you have to go away, to protect your feeling of life, where people won't shock you and hurt you. They hammer everywhere! Everywhere they can possibly hammer! They hammer in your brain! Hell, these idiots, they come with their hammer, where people are sitting, to hammer, to hammer, to hammer! Let's go."

I started the car, mercifully without stalling it, and drove away. We headed back toward the towns, and I got more driving tips from Klaus Kinski, and we talked some more, about the thing. But I'm not going to say any more here about the thing. If I haven't managed to make you understand it by now, that is perhaps because I am not able to convey it. Or perhaps because you don't want to hear about it and, as Kinski says, the philosopher will teach you nothing you don't know already. But I think you do know this thing: you have felt it when you watched a great performer on the stage, or on the screen. And, as Kinski says, this thing is also the power a sculptor uses with his fingers, a painter with his brush, a virtuoso musician with his violin, and, as even he admits, a writer with his words, though perhaps, among writers, it is the poet who is closest to this thing. Of course, these people may have their own ways of thinking about this thing, though perhaps less passionate and mystically expressed than Kinski's, and perhaps they even have names for it. But I think it doesn't matter what name you give it, or whether you give it a name at all, if you have felt this thing.

And you must have, it's not so difficult, if you have ever stood outside, alone, at night, when there were many stars in the sky. Or if you have spent any time out, far out, on the ocean.

We've had other conversations since, but it is at the ocean that I remember Klaus Kinski best. And when I think of that afternoon, and of Kinski gesturing against the sky, I remember what he had told me about Rimbaud, how he said that, to test a book, one must take it to the sea, to find out whether it will still seem strong among the elements.

Even on that stormy day, Klaus Kinski's vitality was as eloquent and powerful to me as any of the elements, perhaps because he seemed to belong among them, and his passion transcended the pedestrian idiocy of the artificially aged fast-food place near by, of the clots of chattering tourists who occasionally crossed our path, and of the journalist who stumbled after him with a futile tape recorder. Even though many of his words were torn from his mouth by the sea breezes, and hurled toward the ocean or the mountains, or buried in the sand, Klaus Kinski led me to grasp, with what I felt was perfect clarity, the definition of an ineffable force of nature, because he seemed to be both a part and an expression of it, even though now, when I listen to my tape, there are only fragments of speech, meaningless all by themselves, and what I can hear, mostly, is only the screaming of the wind, and the detonation of the waves. This is the most important lesson I learned about what it is, ultimately, the "actor" does.

PART FOUR

EVERYONE SHE KNOWS SEEMS SO RESTLESS

LADIES NIGHTS

For nearly two years, five of us have gathered together for an evening every once in a while. The group—though it isn't a formal group—is composed of five women journalists, editors, and writers. We meet because we like one another, and we call those gatherings Ladies Nights.

We began by meeting once a week. Every Thursday night was Ladies Night, and we would settle upon a different restaurant, where we would invariably make up the rowdiest table, to the great amusement of the waiters, whom we addressed with a kind of cheerful familiarity that only women in groups can afford to exhibit to strange men. But the meals always seemed too soon over, and we grew tired of traipsing about the city in the cold in search of appropriate bars where we could finish the evening. We began to meet at one another's houses. Some of the dinners are elegantly prepared, others are somewhat comical. But, then, women in their early thirties who place more importance in their work than in any other aspect of their lives aren't always reliable in the home-entertainment department. In any event, whatever the quality of the cuisine, these evenings always seem like parties, the women looking festive, and as graceful and attentive to one another as if they were guests at a formal dinner.

It had been my idea to organize these dinners. The women were my friends, whom I had brought together, and in the beginning it seemed natural for everyone to rely on me to arrange for our meetings. But after several months I began to feel burdened by the considerable logistical problems of getting five women whose lives were crammed with activity to gather in one place at the same time once a week. Our schedule had become too cumbersome, too often interrupted by one of us leaving town on assignment, a bad cold, the imperatives of a new love affair. When I announced at large, reluctantly, that I was giving up trying to negotiate our scheduling problems, I assumed this would be the end of those evenings, that Ladies Nights would become a sweet, vague shadow in my memory, a lark from the end of the seventies.

But none of us, as it turned out, had had her fill yet of whatever it was that made those evenings at once so pleasurable and so astonishingly comfortable. We all kept copies of a funny Polaroid taken in my living room near Christmas of that year. Whenever I go to one of these women's apartments, I see tucked in a mirror or leaning against a lamp on a desk the photograph of the five of us clustered together, tall and laughing, the image somehow as poignant and melancholy as a memory from childhood.

So now we meet at irregular intervals. Every few weeks, or every couple of months, one of us asks, "When are we getting together again?," and we gather with the high spirits of a reunion of old and good friends.

What is it I like so much about these Ladies Nights? The contrasts, for one thing. Beth's poise and Marianne's diffidence. Erica's dry asides and Hilary's uncouth humor. Everyone boisterous and yet ladylike. The openness tempered by good manners. This is no encounter group. We are gentle with one another, side-stepping raw areas. Nor is it a support group. If we comfort one another, it is indirectly, by the pleasure we take in one another's company and the high degree of interest with which we listen to one another speak.

None of us needs these Ladies Nights. They are a luxury, a pause stolen from the maniacal rhythm of the rest of our lives. We expect no results from these evenings, no approval or advice. None of us needs or wants group therapy. As it is, we get too many opportunities in the course of our careers for self-examination. In any event, we are too different from one another to serve as mirrors for each other. Nor do we want psychodramas: we get enough confrontation and reward in our work. We may often feel fragile, but we've learned we're pretty tough and that we can't afford to forget it.

We are all women who have learned so well to talk like men when necessary, and even to seem to think like men, that it has become habitual to us. On Ladies Nights, we speak out of all sides of our mouths, jumbling the several lives each of us carefully compartmentalizes in the course of the day. We can be dainty and aggressive. We dress with care for one another, but we lean back in our chairs and gesture with uninhibited exuberance. We drink a little too much and laugh a great deal. The talk sometimes rises to such an enthusiastic pitch that several of us are yelling at once. We gallop through the evening's conversation, devouring an incongruous assortment of topics like a band of locusts. We attack each subject with an analytic specificity and a knack for generalization which give away our training as journalists, but we move from one idea to another by *non sequitur* in a peculiarly feminine organization of conversational dynamics.

One night last week, when I was keeping track, we opened with the usual journalism gossip and lamentation, and before we had finished our dessert or our fifth bottle of red wine, we had also meandered through discussions of the recent election, the anatomy of the Reagan staff, the differences between Eastern and Western preppie sensibilities, the image of Design Research as an icon of the sixties, Porthault linen, Bloomingdale's as an environment, the influence of the gay subculture's aesthetics, the way men cry, the origin of studded denim apparel; one of us also recounted in some detail the events leading up to the loss of her virginity at the age of twenty-one to the first subject she ever profiled.

Part of what I like so much about those Ladies Nights is the combination of the frankness with which we talk and all that is unspoken. There is a lot on our minds that we don't speak about. But there is a kind of strength in our mutual experience, even when nothing is said, when no one has brought up her fight with her boyfriend or her humiliation at work that day.

That's why, when the subject of crying came up the other night, I didn't mention that I had listened to Erica weep on the telephone the day before. A psychiatrist I interviewed once told me that anyone can make a diagnosis of depression in about a minute. "There's nothing remarkable in detecting certain kinds of pathology," he said. When I called Erica that day, some almost imperceptible alteration in her voice when she answered made me ask, "What's wrong?" "Oh, I don't know," she said, her voice quavering. And then she started crying.

"Did something happen?" I asked.

"I don't know what's wrong with me," she managed to get out. "Overwork, I guess."

"Yeah," I said. "I get that sometimes." Though I know it's not overwork. I don't know what it is either.

By now she couldn't talk.

"Do you want to call me back later?" I asked.

"Yes," she said, and hung up.

Half an hour later, she rang again.

"Hello?" I said.

"Bendel's?" she said.

I laughed, and a little while later we were in a taxi headed downtown.

I got a little woolen hat, a blue one. Erica bought two of them, one blue, one sea-green, a sweater, a pair of boots, and three pairs of shoes: two weeks' salary. "Phew, I feel much better," she announced. "And we can still make it to Saks."

"Oh, no!" I said.

"It's almost the end of the month," she said, "and I'm still not up to my American Express limit."

"Erica..." I started.

"Don't," she said. "Just don't. Please."

So I didn't, though I knew that a month from now, or around the time the credit-card bills arrived, Erica would be telling me with a mixture of wrath and despair that she'd accepted yet another assignment, or two, or three, from some glossy magazines to write articles she didn't want to write, on subjects she wasn't interested in. The same hundred pages of her perennially unfinished novel would be back in the same drawer. The same justifications would be on her lips when she'd have to face an irate editor at the newspaper where she works. "So I was a little late again," she complains to me. "Big deal."

But I know it is a big deal to her, not just to be late but to be always too tired to do a good enough job at her column. Yet when Erica's on deadline, I often get a call at one or two in the morning. "What do you say?" she'll ask, and I know she wants to meet for a drink so she can escape her typewriter.

Not loath to escape my own typewriter, or the hours spent reproaching myself for not being at the typewriter, I often meet her at an all-night restaurant in the neighborhood where we both live. It's over those late-night drinks, while Erica is finishing her fourth pack of cigarettes of the day, that we've become friends. We drink and talk until they stop serving liquor, and sometimes we stay even longer, and have coffee and eggs, and talk some more. I like talking and drinking with her into the small hours, but then I know that afterward I'll go home and not waste a moment in becoming horizontal. Erica, at five or six in the morning, will sit down and write a thousand words.

She knows what she's doing. "The only reason to give any thought at all to the subject of self-destruction," she once informed me, "is to figure out more ingenious methods of accomplishing it."

Whom does she call to ask "What do you say?" when I'm not home or not up to going out?

"I saw Tom last night," she'll sometimes tell me. Or Dick or Harry. Or whoever. I've never figured out how Erica can meet so many men in a city where women are perpetually complaining that there are no available men around. But, then, she's both clever and very pretty. She's red-headed and remarkably blue-eyed and has that milky-white skin often described as luminous.

"How was it?" I'll say.

"He's a jerk," she'll tell me.

She always says that. I always laugh. I think she says it partly to make me laugh, partly to make herself laugh, but there's a level on which she means it. I've never known her not to be exasperated at the men she spends a night with for being jerks. Usually it's only one night, though I've known Erica to have longer affairs, which are invariably occasions for her to stay furious and condescending on a full-time basis.

"His politics!" she'll exclaim. Or his work habits, speech mannerisms, apartment, clothes, or sexuality.

"That's it," she once told me about a man she'd been seeing for a while and whom I happened to have liked. "Last night I met his ex-wife. What a dog!"

"You're kidding," I said.

"No," said Erica. "A terrible dog."

"No," I said. "I don't mean the wife. You're kidding if you're telling me that's it and you're going to break up with him because his ex-wife is a dog."

"These things matter," said Erica in her archest tone. "Everyone can make a mistake, but this was really *beyond the pale*."

"You must wait for it," I said. "You were just waiting for something to be wrong."

"Well, of course," said Erica. "I have to keep busy somehow. I mean, his *conversation!*"

I don't know whether or not she's really kidding. Herself, that is. I don't prod too much, because I know Erica can't bear to exhibit her vulnerabilities. That's why I was so surprised yesterday, when I heard her crying on the phone.

I'd seen her cry once before, though. It was one of those nights when we were out particularly late. There was no one else in the restaurant, just us and a tired waiter. Outside, it was dawn. Erica's face, now that some morning light came in, looked haggard. There were cruel, bluish smears under her eyes. She'd been uncharacteristically silent, sipping yet another Scotch and soda.

"You look tired," I said. My affection for her must have

shown in my voice. She looked up and smiled.

"I'm always tired," she said. "Always tired."

"Do you have to do any more work tonight?" I asked.

She looked at her watch. "Today," she corrected me. It was past six o'clock. "No. Not today. In about an hour, I'm going over to my mother's house. She'll be back from the hospital."

"Your mother's been in the hospital?" I repeated, surprised. Erica never spoke of her family. I knew only that her parents were divorced and her mother lived in town. I'd assumed Erica seldom saw her.

"Yeah," she said. "She's always up early when she's had her stomach pumped."

I said nothing.

Erica took another sip of her drink. "That's my mother's occupation," she said. "Suicide. Like me, though, she fails at everything she does."

"You don't fail at everything you do," I said, thinking of her very considerable professional achievements.

"Well," said Erica, and she laughed a little, "I try."

"Do you?" I asked.

"Oh, I don't know," she said. "I can't believe I have to go to my mother's again for another one of these sessions."

"It must be hard," I said.

"Almost all my life, I've had these post–stomach-pumping sessions with my mother. When I was a kid, she used to do it every time my father left, and that would get him back. Some relative would call him, and he'd come back. When I was old enough, I was the one who'd call him. 'Daddy,' I'd say, 'Mom's done it again.'"

Erica started crying. Not sobbing, but tears suddenly swam over her lower lids.

"But then," she said, "he stopped leaving a number. So then she'd do it and there'd be only me. That's how I got started in journalism, you know. In college. That was the first time I didn't go back home for one of these swell morning-afters. I got a call from the hospital and I just said, 'I'm on deadline and I can't make it this morning.' Plus, when my father called I'd have something to tell him aside from 'Mom's done it again.' You know, my writing is the only thing he's ever shown any interest in. From the first time my byline ever appeared in print, he suddenly became a little interested in me. He calls me a few times a year and says, 'I've been reading your stuff, kid, great going!' You know, just because his stupid suburban friends and his horrendous suburban wife see my name, *his* name, in print, that suddenly makes him interested in me. What a jerk. What a *jerk* he is."

I passed Erica my handkerchief and she wiped her face.

"I look like a wreck, don't I?" she said.

"No," I said. "I always love the way you look."

"Well, then, you're a jerk too," she said. "Just as I suspected." She smiled. "Thank God, the only man I'll have to see this morning is my mother's doorman."

"You're very beautiful, you know. Do you know that?" I said.

Her smile went. "Don't say that. Don't say that, all right?" she said.

I could tell she meant it. "Okay," I said.

She looked at her watch again.

"Oh God," she said. "Let's go."

A few hours later, my phone rang.

"Bendel's?" said Erica.

"You must be kidding," I said, still mostly asleep.

"No," she said. "I'm absolutely not kidding. It's a great new day. Time to go shopping."

I don't mean to imply that the architecture of Erica's personality has its sole foundation in her conflicting emotions concerning her father. But, in any event, if this was one of the primary forces in the shaping of her character, she is certainly not unique in that regard. There isn't one among these five women who hasn't long ago recognized that her father was a crucial generator of personality traits, whether she was in search or in spite of his love. It is a psychocultural cliché that we learned to live with so long ago that it has become moot in the context of our daily preoccupations, just like our equivocal emotions about power and celebrity, the fear of aging, loneliness. An unspeakable terror of failure. This is the tricky stuff of the psyche we take for granted when we meet, but that aliments a conversation about Bloomingdale's just as much as one about crying, in a peculiar way I don't fully understand. Perhaps this is how women bond.

When we talk about crying, therefore, just as we do about Bloomingdale's, we pool our observations for the sake of diversion more than anything else. The dirty emotional laundry is tossed onto the dinner table not for catharsis but for entertainment. And there is no need to acknowledge that both are accomplished. Cries from the heart become amusing anecdotes. We don't pity. We take another sip of wine, lean forward, and smile.

"So finally, one night, I told him it was over for good, and he cried," said Erica, concluding the story about the profile subject.

"I hate it when men cry," I said, for comic relief.

"I think it's interesting," said Erica.

"You've seen men *cry!*" exclaimed Hilary, who has a trick of making her voice rise for humorous emphasis.

"I think they should hold it in and repress it," I said.

"How did you get them to cry?" asked Hilary. "I don't understand it. No man has ever cried over *me*. I mean, God *forbid!* They only *laugh* at *me!*"

It is difficult to imagine how anyone could resist laughing at Hilary, whose utterances are invariably designed to provoke laughter, without regard to subject matter. Hilary is always on; ultra-American, ultra-pop, she is a product of television culture. Indeed, being her friend and privy to the logistics of her life is like becoming a front-row spectator at the taping of a high-quality sitcom: one empathizes and provides the laugh track. No matter how deeply she may be touched by anything, Hilary always seems to articulate her life in punch-lines.

"I was the hair on the hamburger," she announces after a party where she felt she couldn't make contact with anyone.

"She's such a cash register!" she opines about a mutual acquaintance we both find rather calculating.

"So I told him he couldn't go on treating me like this. I

mean, *please,* gimme a break with this bathos, these lies, and these broken dates. If he wants to stay with his wife, that's fine with me, but I have to have *gifts* and *attention.* I'm a baby-blue light!" she fairly yells into the telephone in the course of one of our frequent conversations.

Hilary has a loud, detonating voice, perpetually inflected: angry, disgusted, questioning, exuberant. In a crowded room, her catch-all "Oh my *God!*" or "You *said* it!," alternately thrilled and contemptuous, will cut through any hubbub. Not that one could miss Hilary even in a crowded room. All of last year, she wore nothing but jogging clothes, blue, red, or bright green, accompanied by the most dashing running shoes money can buy and an inevitable visor on her head. This constituted her *toilette* no matter what the occasion or the venue, and one became accustomed to seeing expressions of disbelief when walking into a smart restaurant with Hilary. Arrivals and departures are equally flamboyant, since her preferred mode of transportation is the limo. Hilary can afford to have expensive tastes: her father, who made a large fortune in the entertainment business, amply supplements her journalist's income. But she has bursts of egalitarian behavior. She's been known, for example, to take a wealthy friend's houseboy to the theater, "because," she explains, "I could trust him not to bore me with intelligent chitchat between acts."

This season, however, Hilary threw out the jogging wardrobe and, as she puts it, has "gotten her visual together." Her visual the other evening consisted of bright yellow cowboy boots, pink tights, a low-cut violet leotard, and a speckled punk fifties jacket, while on her nose (fixed at her father's expense some years ago) sat a pair of mother-of-pearl Lina Wertmüller sunglasses. Actually, the glasses are a hold-over: she was already wearing them last year with the jogging suits, and she has a nervous habit of continually shifting these preposterous glasses from her nose to the top of her head and back again. Nearly six feet tall, carrying her long thin frame with an easy glide, she looks like a cross between Supergirl and a Fiorucci cherub.

One evening recently, she was denied entrance to the Palm Court at the Plaza because of her attire.

"Can you imagine!" she booms. "I was kept out of the *Palm* Court by a dinosaur in an antique *bow tie* who looked like a panelist on the '$1.98 Beauty Show.' My *God!* That's going straight into my article."

Hilary's life and her articles have been inextricably intertwined since she began her career in journalism at the age of nineteen, right out of finishing school, working for underground papers while living in a Park Avenue apartment. "Basically, I hate to write," she says, "but I fall in love with cultural scenes, and writing about them gives me an excuse to participate."

Essentially, Hilary is a sixties casualty, still looking for action. In the last decade, she has "participated" in an array of phenomena that have included the fashion scene, the art scene, the jazz scene, the Acapulco scene, the Hollywood scene, the underground scene, the straight reporting scene, and the television scene. Each of her romances with one of these environments has left its traces and added yet another facet to her multiplicitous sensibility. Because she once went on tour as an Ikette to write an article about Ike and Tina Turner, she still occasionally lapses into black slang. From her bout of fascination with occultism and her association with a stream of louche readers, psychics, and astrologers, she has retained a reluctance to initiate any project while Mercury is in retrograde. Since the planet Mercury retrogrades three times a year for periods of two and a half to three weeks, she is often out of circulation. While her acquaintances wonder at Hilary's mysterious disappearances and canceled appointments, she is "safely" at home for days at a time, in bed, watching daytime television.

Sent to cover the Olympics, she became a fervent athlete as a result of having observed Nadia Comaneci at close hand. Following the action with a slew of other sports-related articles, she became a bona-fide member of the jock scene, rising before six every day to run, spending her afternoons at a professional gym, and initiating a rigorous training program (though one's not quite sure what she's training *for*) while chumming with athletes and coaches.

In the past year or so, though she has remained basically loyal to the jock ethos, she has eased up somewhat (as evidenced by the abandonment of running suits and visors) in order to devote more time and effort to her new and increasingly consuming interest in the health field. She still makes the occasional reference to aerobics and Nautilus equipment, but these days her conversation is mainly studded with talk of holistic medicine, Nathan Pritikin, blood-sugar levels, and high colonics. She has managed to wangle an astounding number of assignments from an odd lot of magazines, which have provided her with the funds and the pretext to visit an untold number of spas, clinics, medical centers, and intensive diet programs covering the breadth of the United States. At each of these places she undergoes a battery of tests and emerges with a new scheme for improving her energy level, a new diet, and a new malady fortuitously detected by her most recent medical acquaintances. So far this year, Hilary has announced with conviction that she suffers from hypoglycemia, walking pneumonia, an exceedingly rare form of the herpes virus, pregnancy, an allergy to dairy products, and countless debilitating episodes of acid indigestion. The movement of her bowels has become the subject of intense observation and great concern. Of a given evening, she arrives (by limo) at my apartment brandishing a paper bag that I know to contain a family-size bottle of Maalox, pushes her Lina Wertmüller glasses back on her head, kisses me hello, and informs me that she can stay only ten minutes because she has to get up at dawn tomorrow and have her thyroid tested.

Last year, her buddies were the guys down at the gym. This year, her dates all have names ending with the letters M.D. Gynecologists, nutritionists, proctologists, and ear, nose, and throat specialists all are candidates for Hilary's attention this season, and each is the harbinger of a new ailment. She called me this summer from the Cooper Clinic in Texas. "Well, I must tell you that Houston is a complete write-off. Houston is a *major* bore. Houston is just *too* Air Force," she announced. "But I'm in a great mood anyway: tonight I have a date with the Teddy Kennedy of cardiologists." Naturally, when she got back to New York, her first act was to arrange for a stress test.

No doubt, hypochondria is a construct for Hilary, just as all of her other "scenes" were. They are constructs not merely with which to gather material for stories, entertain herself, and extrapolate a view of the world, but, most important, to serve as foils for her profound disorientation and self-involvement, and the ensuing, unavoidable isolation from which she suffers. A vast, heart-crushing solitude emanates from her one-liners about her not infrequent attacks of depression, almost always expressed in metaphors for suffocation: "Today's bad. I have a paper bag over my head"; "I've got to snap out of this. I'm under water this afternoon"; "I don't know what's the matter with me. I feel like I'm trying to breathe through Saran Wrap."

I wonder what Hilary's next scene will be. She's been expressing interest lately in New York's cosmopolitan milieu, so her friends are hoping she'll soon abandon her clinics in favor of the bars in the United Nations area. Certainly there's an article there, but, then, there is an almost infinite number of articles Hilary could do. Almost. Once she said to me, "You know, if I ever have a baby, I'll have to do it as an assignment. I bet I could get some women's magazine to send me to do a piece on the Lamaze system of childbirth...."

But that's one assignment I think Hilary may never seek. Nor, chances are, will she ever write the definitive feature on the At-Home Scene. With uncanny consistency, the men she sees are transients, or living in other cities, or, often, married men. I pointed this out to her once and it seemed to shock her, as though she had never considered it. "You know, it's true. I guess I don't let anybody get too close to me," she said. For once, no punchline. Perhaps no one has ever made Hilary feel like a baby-blue light. But then she brought her glasses back on her nose. "But, you know," she said, "I did almost get married twice."

"Really?" I said.

"Absolutely, but no cigar. Once when I was very young, but he was too short. I got tired of feeling like an Amazon whenever I was with him. The other time was with that director I lived with in Malibu. But he was too old. I was twenty-two, he was fifty-five. It was ridiculous, but I came close. My parents even flew out there. They were really nice about it, but I realized it was hopeless. We were sitting there at lunch and my mother kept going to the bathroom a lot while my father choked on his ratatouille. I mean, *please!* By the way, have you got any Excedrin here? Well, anyway, you know, sometimes I dream about marriage, but in my heart of hearts, I know it's not *me*. I value my own bathroom too much. I mean, having to *look* at someone else's stuff in *my* medicine cabinet. *Oh my God!*"

"I've never even seen a man cry," said Hilary last Ladies Night, "except my father."

"Why was he crying?" asked Erica.

"Anger, of course," said Hilary. "What else?"

"What a horrible spectacle," I said. "Though the worst is seeing your mother cry."

The other women chorused their assent.

"I can't take that," said Marianne. "I always start crying with her."

"I think it's worse," I said, "because women cry more out of sadness than anger."

"Oh, I cry out of anger," said Marianne.

"*Me too!*" said Hilary emphatically.

"But I won't cry in front of men," said Marianne.

"Me neither," said Hilary.

"I'll get nail marks in the palms of my hands, but I won't cry in front of a man," said Marianne.

I wonder how often Marianne has nail marks in the palms of her hands. Every once in a while when I try to call her at the magazine where she is a senior editor, the receptionist tells me that she is not in the office today. When I reach Marianne at home, she answers the phone with a comatose voice. "I have a bad cold," she used to tell me before I knew her well enough to understand that there was no point in asking because she would only lie.

I still don't know what she does on those days of the muffled voice. Probably she is crying, or sleeping. Perhaps both. Perhaps she is eating: eating all day, eating... how? Ravenously? Slowly but continually? I don't know. When I see her for dinner, she eats very little, in small bites, meticulously. But I imagine it must take a great deal of eating to reach and maintain a weight of over two hundred pounds.

What else does Marianne do in her secret life, on the moody days when she stays home alone and removes the masks of the vivacious, effective woman? She dreams, I think. She fantasizes of those men who will never love her, of the lives she will never live because she has placed herself, as she puts it, *hors de combat*. And her fantasy life, vast, elaborate, hermetic, seals her off from exposure as effectively as the carapace of her flesh.

Marianne reminds me of the Russian dolls that fit one inside another, matreshkas. The painted smile on the outermost, largest doll is happy and mild. As the inner dolls descend in size, the smile starts to seem fixed and weird, the features strangely cheerless. Marianne lives in layers, hiding her fantasies and her alienation in some inner cavity of her being where no one can penetrate.

As a journalist, by way of armor, Marianne wears her preoccupation with stuff. Stuff: design, objects, products, things to buy are her turf. Merchandise, or "merch," as people in that circle call it, the finding, the handling, writing of it, is her most effective protection. At the magazine where she works, she is legitimized by her expertise with regard to stuff, safe in a traditional woman's area, not in competition with those after bigger journalistic game. Her unusually sharp mind safely hidden, in the cutthroat ambience of the magazine world Marianne threatens no one. Marianne laughs a lot, a hearty, fat-person's laugh, and her colleagues and superiors laugh with her because her appearance and function do not lead them to believe that she has to be taken seriously. Equipped with an intelligence and a sensitivity that should enable her to attack successfully any area she chose, she has placed herself *hors de combat* in the professional fray as radically as in her personal life.

In any event, the stuff fills the lacunae in that personal life. When Marianne has lunch with a man whom she finds attractive, it is because she is editing an article he has written on the latest in office furnishings. When she goes to a party, most likely it is one she has organized for her magazine to get photographs for a home-entertainment issue. If she takes a trip to the Caribbean, it is to prepare an island shopping guide. Marianne's days are filled with an unending shopping spree.

"I learned to shop when I was around eighteen," she told me once. "I wanted to travel, you see, and I had no one to travel with. But it was uncomfortable by myself. I felt I had no place in those societies. If you're traveling alone, you have to find a role for yourself. You can start going to museums and you have the role of an art connoisseur, or you can go to restaurants and play the role of a gastronome. I chose the role of shopper. The minute you go into a store, you're a consumer. You don't even have to buy anything. And there are thousands of stores. It gives you a reason to be somewhere. Just like journalism."

Becoming friends with Marianne is a difficult process, even when one meets her under circumstances that ought to lead casually to a friendly relationship. She must be pursued, persistently sought after. She avoids intimacy: "I just have a cold." She turns down invitations: "I need a lot of time alone." It takes a long time to cross all the gates she has constructed and arrive at the mercurial woman hidden inside the good egg, retreating behind her seeming self-sufficiency. But even when one knows her well enough to perceive her frame of mind, she skulks. If she's blue and one tries to console her, she resorts to offensive humor: "What are you, a missionary?"

And even when, at last, she trusts one's affection enough to reveal the extent of her moodiness, it's a mistake to believe that one's found the fundamental person. Sometimes I feel I know Marianne only by intuition. I think the essential Marianne cowers, out of sight to all and perhaps even to herself, the Marianne who is tiny and dainty, a secret bloom hidden in her dreamy cocoon at the center of all of the outer layers.

"I'm in love!" she called to say about a year ago.

"You are! With whom?" I asked.

"Edmond Tomichek!" she announced, as though the name should mean something to me.

"Who?" I said.

"*The* Edmond Tomichek, who wrote *The Corrugated Eye*, the bible on postmodern design!"

"Oh," I said.

"He called today to suggest an article. He sounds wonderful. I'm in love."

I laughed, because I thought it was meant as a joke. I continued to be amused over the next week or so when Marianne would tell me that Edmond Tomichek had called again, that he had the most wonderful idea for an article, that he knew everything there was to know about design, that he had the most exquisite taste. "A design expert," I'd say. "He's the perfect man for you, Marianne."

But Marianne wasn't joking. She was in love. And Edmond Tomichek continued to call. Soon their conversations were no longer about the article he was writing for her, but extended to more general talks about their common interests. Once or twice a week, Marianne would tell me that Edmond had called, that they had talked for an hour, two hours. "He's so sweet," she'd sigh.

Had Edmond Tomichek fallen in love with Marianne's voice? The tone of those conversations seemed to hover on the flirtatious. Edmond Tomichek and Marianne began to exchange notes and, finally, stuff. A messenger would arrive at Marianne's office with an envelope containing a nineteenth-century advertising card that Edmond had thought would please her. She would send him a patent-medicine bottle for his collection. Tin containers, turn-of-the-century matchboxes, antique postcards, and books on old New York were exchanged by mail and messenger. Never in person.

One day Marianne told me that Edmond had finished the

article she had assigned him. It was a Saturday. Since he was over deadline, he had called and offered to bring it himself to her home that afternoon.

"I told him I wouldn't be home and to leave it with the doorman," she told me later.

"But, Marianne, don't you want to meet him?" I asked.

"No," she said. "I don't want to have to see the look on his face when he sees me."

It was no longer funny. Marianne's moods began to vary wildly according to the frequency and substance of her telephone conversations with Edmond Tomichek. For eight months.

Finally, one night, she said to me, "I did it."

"Did what?" I asked.

"I made an appointment with him for tomorrow," she told me. Her tone was so bland over the telephone line that I could almost visualize how pale she must be. "I can't take it any more, I had to do it."

"Well, that's great," I said, trying to disguise my own fear for her. "Look, the worst that can happen is that you've made a very good friend," I nervously added hypocritically, knowing full well that this was not the worst that could happen. She was silent for a moment.

"You know," she finally said, "I've never been first with anyone. Not anyone, ever. Not even for a weekend."

We didn't talk much more that evening. The next day, I had no call from Marianne. Finally, I telephoned her office. "She's not in today," said the receptionist.

"No, I'm fine, I was just catching up on my sleep," said Marianne groggily when she answered her phone at home. It was the late afternoon.

"Well, how did it go?" I asked.

"What?"

"Your meeting with Edmond."

"Oh. Fine."

I didn't say anything. I didn't know what to say. I knew Marianne must have seen that look on Edmond Tomichek's face. What could I say?

"Yeah, it was okay. We were both pretty nervous, but we had a pleasant chat. It was fine."

That was months ago. Now Marianne only mentions Edmond Tomichek's name occasionally. I gather that they still speak on the telephone sporadically, since he still writes for her magazine, and sometimes they even meet for lunch.

"I still think he's awfully nice," she said to me the other night.

"Do you not feel any rancor?" I asked.

"No. Because I don't think I'd be where I am now if it weren't for him. Well, maybe I'm wrong. Maybe I was ready anyway. I don't know."

I don't know either, and I figured it doesn't matter. Ready or not, the week after Marianne "fell in love" with Edmond Tomichek she went on a diet. And she began to walk to work; she who couldn't stride down a single block without getting out of breath. When she started to lose weight, she took up swimming. Sometimes she'd get dizzy after a few laps and quickly climb out of the water to black out by the side of the pool. She would come to Ladies Nights carrying her own broiled chicken wrapped in a piece of tin foil. She'd seldom speak about her diet, but the layers of flesh began to disappear.

Now, nearly a year since she began, she has lost seventy pounds. And last week, as she was finishing the preparation of her magazine's annual Christmas-gift issue, she said casually, "You know, it's certain that I can do this sort of thing very well, but sometimes I wonder what the point is. It certainly doesn't absorb me. Lately I've been thinking I'd like to work on some articles of a less concrete nature. I'm kind of toying with the idea of trying out something less tangible: there's something that really fascinates me about urban life."

If Marianne continues to lose weight at her present rate, by next spring she will be "normal." Can she do it? And if she does, will she find the weapons with which to gain territory and defend it when she is, at last, part of the combat? Can she, for the first time in her life, in her mid-thirties, survive without the camouflage, the armor, the outer dolls?

The other evening, she was the last to arrive at the Ladies

Night. She was breathless, having rushed over from the pool, her hair was still a bit damp, and she carried her little packet wrapped in tin foil. All the other women exclaimed at her appearance.

"Marianne, you look wonderful!"

"You look great!"

"I love your blouse!"

No one mentioned her startling loss of weight since our last meeting.

And when she mentioned the occasional nail marks in the palms of her hands, no one had to ask her what she meant.

"*Nail* marks!" yelled Hilary. "I'll stuff my guts into my eyeballs before I let any man see me cry...."

"I won't give them the satisfaction," said Marianne, folding her napkin.

"Have you ever cried *with* a man?" asked Hilary.

"No," three of us answered.

"I have," said Beth.

"You have?" said Hilary. "Where you were both the sobber and the sobbee?"

"Oh, I've had real sobbing sessions with men," said Beth.

"What a horrible thought," I muttered.

"No, it's terrific," said Beth. "It usually happens because of an important realization about the relationship. It's a watershed. It's a moment when you can start again clean."

"There's no such thing as starting again clean," I opined. "And, in any event, I don't want to see any men cry under any circumstances."

"Why?" asked Erica. "It's such good material."

"They don't know how to. They've been so programmed not to that you can see it doing violence to their nature. It's too painful and too dramatic to bear. Women cry much more naturally."

"They only cry much more quietly," said Marianne.

"I can't stand to see that much pain," I finally said.

"It's true. It is frightening," said Beth, "but it's better than the kind of emotional dishonesty that goes on when there's a pretense that everything's fine."

The male friends we have in common who know about our Ladies Nights are very curious about those evenings. "What goes on? What do you talk about?" I'm often asked. But when I answer truthfully, they seem somehow dissatisfied. What I find oddest of all is the consistency with which they will make jokes that are meant to be offensive: "Well, did you settle the Kotex versus Tampax controversy last night?" a friend will say. I respond good-naturedly, but I find that kind of humor odd. It occurs to me that perhaps it is generated by discomfort.

I don't mean to say that I think there isn't anything funny about five women getting together. There is, of course, but that's part of what we like about those evenings. It was Beth who first dubbed them "Ladies Nights," and the phrase immediately caught on with all of us, in acknowledgment of our being amused by the idea of these female reunions. Perhaps we are able to think these evenings are funny because we are comfortable with the roles we have created for ourselves in a man's world. Perhaps it is because we are not quite comfortable enough. But in any event, the distinction between that sort of humor and the sort exhibited by a male colleague who'll quip, "Is there anything left to say about lingerie when you girls get through?" seems to me broad enough that it should be discerned by the men we associate with. And it seems all the more strange because these are men who would never permit themselves that sort of remark about any of us individually. Perhaps they don't know how to handle the unusual phenomenon of being excluded. Perhaps they are envious, or simply mystified.

I've noticed that the men who seem most curious are those who know Beth. Everyone is fascinated by Beth. "I'm still figuring her out," a man who had been her lover for over a year once told me. "I don't get Beth" is a remark I've often heard. "She's so puzzling." "She's disconcerting." "She's a chameleon."

Not that the conundrum stops anyone from being attracted to Beth. On the contrary, she has extraordinary, powerful allure. She is that rare woman to whom everyone is drawn, the kind of woman with whom all men fall in love, at least a little.

Often a great deal. One of our mutual friends tells me that something about Beth always makes him remember high school. I think it's because she reminds him of the most popular girl in school, the kind who had what they used to call a great personality, and who was so pretty and so blond and looked so unapproachable to anyone outside her charmed circle that it seemed unthinkable that you could ever get close to her.

Even Beth's beauty is elusive, however. Scrutinized dispassionately, her features are irregular, her chin a bit too weak, her face slightly too round under the cascade of golden hair. But she has a radiance that makes her stunning. I think we all find Beth beautiful because her looks are animated by her intelligence and her sensuality.

And, certainly, one is attracted to her because she has an aura of what was once referred to as "breeding." It is class in the strict sense, the lofty, ineffable appeal of generations' worth of patrician Boston stock. Perhaps it is precisely this quality that makes her playfulness so disorienting. Dressed as though she were planning to model for a Peck and Peck ad, she will casually utter a profanity so scatological that it would seem shocking coming from the mouth of an ex-convict. She has an air of impeccable decorum, but she will often eat and drink with the appetites of a Cossack, blithely picking with her fingers at the remains of everyone else's meal when she has wolfed down her own. At first glance she seems unattainable, aloof, cerebral, but she is the most tactile person I know, and I've seen her on occasion throw her arms around someone she has only met once or twice by way of saying good night, sincerely assuring him or her that this was one of the most wonderful evenings that she has ever spent. She wears her propriety like a cardigan sweater, to be put on or taken off at will.

On a dare, once, at a celebratory dinner at Lutèce, Beth removed her bra, sliding it, millimeter by millimeter, down the long tight sleeves of her silk Mary McFadden dress, while the assembled guests watched, knife and fork in hand, hilarious. "It seemed so natural at the time," she told me the next day, "though it was pretty shocking to find my bra in my pocketbook this morning." Looking like the picture of the well-bred schoolgirl, with the poise of a politician's wife, Beth can drink enough in an evening to put those of us foolish enough to follow her lead into an inebriated stupor. And while the rest of us go home to be ill, one is somehow convinced, as Beth saunters to her cab, that she will read this month's *Harper's* before she retires.

She is the product of privilege, but Beth's political sympathies are with the left. Bred in a bastion of conservative ideology, she chose a career in journalism, an outsider's profession. These days, she is an editor for a liberal publication, and it always amuses me to go see her at her office, where her co-workers idle in and out, speaking fast and gesticulating wildly, wearing jeans and deformed sweaters, while she sits, calm, fastidiously dressed, in front of a meticulously tidy desk. I am all the more amused because I know that, undoubtedly, the drawers of that splendidly soigné desk are stuffed with six months' worth of papers she hasn't gotten around to dealing with, and that, in all likelihood, she is not wearing any underwear under her discreet gray toile slacks, because she hadn't found the time to take care of her laundry in the past few weeks.

I imagine a visualization of Beth's sensibility would resemble those geological charts of the earth's strata, each a different color and texture, one pastel tier giving way to another, linear, created in the dimension of time rather than generated by any unifying principle. Considering her age and history, one might suppose that these unintegrated strata are merely the inevitable result of the cultural hodgepodge that characterizes many of us who became adolescents in the sixties. But most of us have by now found a *modus vivendi* that resolves our split loyalties between our parents' world and the one we once hoped to create, accepting one option or another or, if we are lucky, combining them somehow. But it's not sufficient, in Beth's case, to say that she was a kid from a good Boston family who went to college in California and became a member of the radical left. The attitudes of the prep school and those of the Berkeley Commune seem to exist side by side, never eradicating each other, never combining. They are compartmentalized, discrete fragments of a personality held together by Beth's fear of the unknown woman she would be if she let go of any part of the package.

Ultimately, Beth's most dramatic duality is not the good-girl/bad-girl split, but the contrast between her extraordinary intellectual lucidity and her paralyzing confusion, her implacable anxiety. It isn't until one has gotten to know her quite well that one is forced to the realization that this very successful editor with the quick, agile mind is in fact pathologically disorganized.

The practical aspects of Beth's life are in a perpetual mess. If she makes a date for a drink, one can never be completely sure she'll show. If at dinner she pays for her part of the meal with a check, chances are good the check will bounce. Despite her substantial salary, she is always in debt to her friends, her landlady, and a variety of banks. She seems incapable of turning down an invitation to a party even though she already has another date, or a request from a writer for a meeting even though her day is already overbooked. Her undependability is notorious among her acquaintances. Totally out of control, her obligations pile up inexorably, to the point where they become impossible to deal with. What Beth does then is to disappear. Literally. She simply leaves New York, the absurdly filled agenda neatly centered on her desk, the piles of laundry in her apartment, the kited checks on their way to the bank, and gets on a train, any train, to go and spend a few days in the country.

Of course, one can't handle an overload of emotional obligations in quite the same way, and there Beth is left to shuffle endlessly, like a rabbit stuck in a warren of its own making from which there is no issue. Yet she cannot seem to prevent herself from making emotional commitments she cannot handle. "I don't know why I'm compelled to always be nice to everyone," she told me in the course of one of her frequent—and usually ineffectual—phases of taking stock. "Maybe it's because of this horrible habit I have of always caring much more about what other people think of me than what I think of myself. It's as though I can only see myself as reflected by other people. I judge myself by how they judge me. I can tell if someone thinks I look nice or that I'm talking smart or that I'm making a good impression, and then I think so too." So Beth will promise anything. It's as though her image had become her impetus, and because she is sharp enough to perceive that she evokes in those around her the impression of the Most Popular Girl in School, she continues to act out the part of the zippy cheerleader, forced to secretly juggle on the side all those aspects of her personality that do not jibe with the simplistic expectations she feels compelled to fulfill.

This is the lie that pervades nearly all of her relationships. Beth effaces herself in the company of men, always allowing her male companions center stage in the presence of others. She accomplishes this traditionally feminine deceit so gracefully and with such naturalness (odd in this postliberation era) that most of the men she sees are never aware of it at all. I have witnessed the phenomenon many times, yet it is so habitual for Beth that even I tend to ignore it. One evening, however, when we were in the midst of a serious conversation with two men we know well, my glance accidentally met Beth's across the table. We looked into each other's eyes for an instant, and then she put down her glass, raised her hand slightly, and *waved* to me. I burst into laughter, to the bewilderment of our companions, who interrupted their talk and turned to look at us. I couldn't stop laughing. Beth only smiled. Our friends resumed their conversation.

Even I don't always know when Beth is "absent." I take precautions. If I telephone her to discuss anything of importance, I always make sure to ask first, "Is this a convenient time?" Otherwise, I know, whether or not she is working on a rush job or has someone waiting for her in her office, she will not ask me to postpone our talk. Instead, I will notice after a while that her remarks are very slightly strained, that she is not completely responsive, that she sounds somehow distant.

What must it be like for the men who have affairs with

Beth, who do not know that they should ask, "Is this a convenient time?" "It's horrible," she says. "I just become more and more passive. And I'm all the more frustrated because I get away with that kind of emotional dishonesty. And by the time this starts happening, I'm in too deep to confront the problems. So I just let things slide until the day when I start feeling so closed in that I break out in a cold sweat. So then I just run, run for a couple of days, until I have my bearings and my independence again."

Often, Beth will spring awake at 4 A.M., exhausted but unable to go back to sleep. Her mind will race painfully, churning over all of her unfulfilled promises, all of the emotional appointments she cannot keep. She lies in bed, helplessly, and her apprehension, monstrous and unquenchable, extends to all of her life, her career, her future. Every detail of the preceding day is examined and excoriated, every fault is probed and prodded like an abscessed limb, every situation analyzed with devastating clarity, her intelligence at the mercy of her anxiety. And all through most of that day, the golden girl whom so many people envy is always late, always harried, fighting back dread, inviting demands she can never satisfy, setting up structures she will only sabotage. She smiles and she seems merry and she makes five more appointments for the next week and at dinner that night she will have too many glasses of wine because she is so terrified of waking up at dawn again and once more facing the chaos of her universe.

"But why are you so anxious?" I ask her. "What is it you dread so much?"

"I'm scared," she tells me, "that I'm going to be found out. I'm haunted with the fear that everyone is going to see through me, that I've gotten by all my life on false pretenses and that I'm going to be exposed for what I really am. I've always felt in some part of my mind as though I've gotten jobs or head starts in things because people found me pretty or charming, and I'm obsessed with the fear that they're going to discover that I'm not what I sell myself as, what they bought me for, that I don't have the potential they thought they saw in me.

And then everything will fall apart. It's as if my whole existence is based on some house of cards that could collapse at any time. That if I took one wrong step too many I'd screw up my work and lose my job at the same time my loans came through and my boyfriend would walk out on me. I have an image of my life as being based on a precarious assemblage. One of the reasons I'm attractive to people is my job, and without that job I would be significantly less attractive, and yet my success at work is based on my being attractive. All of these things are leaning against each other in some uncanny balance, and if you pulled one of them away, the whole thing would collapse. And you know what makes me most anxious of all? I don't even know where I'm headed with all this. I have no image of myself ten years from now. I don't know if I'll still be working for this kind of paper or be part of a large corporation. I don't know whether the kind of work I'm doing now will have any meaning then. I don't know if I'll have a husband and children or if I'll be alone. Or whether any of the choices I am making now with regard to all these things will make any sense ten years from now. The future is completely uncharted. Now, *that's* anxiety-provoking."

But it is seldom that we dwell on the nature of Beth's anxiety, or mine. More often, in the course of our almost daily telephone conversations, we spend our time brainstorming tactics for dealing with specific problems.

All five of us, in fact, are perpetually strategizing, reorganizing our attack, altering our approach.

"I must become less self-indulgent," I say to Beth, "so that I don't feel guilty all the time."

"I've decided to stop being so nice to everyone," she will tell me. "I've got to become tougher."

"I have to force myself to stop analyzing everything constantly," I tell Marianne one evening.

"All right," she says on another occasion. "I promise I'll stop with the self-deprecating jokes."

"I really have to spend less time on the phone," I tell Erica in the course of a telephone conversation. "It's eating up all my time."

"Maybe I should cut down on the drinking," she says to me as she accompanies me back to my house after a walk. "How about calling me every day to sing me a tolerance song or something?"

"I've got to cut out spending so much time daydreaming," I tell Hilary.

"My problem is that I've met Mr. Right and he is me," Hilary confides. "But maybe I should rethink my approach. I have *got* to get myself together."

But not on Ladies Nights. On Ladies Nights, we talk about whether journalism is a writer's or an editor's medium, the fear of cancer, and the quality of that season's theater. And if I sometimes look around the table and think to myself how my friends, so sweet, so pretty, and so smart, have so much need to be brave, I keep my thoughts to myself.

MYSELF

It was a good touch in *An Unmarried Woman* when the husband cried because *he* was leaving *her*. I think men often cry as a way of getting out of coping.

ERICA

On the contrary. It's an ideal way of controlling a situation when all else fails.

MARIANNE

Like a power play?

BETH

I think it's because they're in a desperate state.

HILARY

Well, what else is new? Who isn't desperate?

BETH

It's true, everyone cries out of despair. But women do cry differently. They can just have tears well up from strong emotion.

MARIANNE

Women can cry out of pure melancholy.

BETH

But that's what they cry about too.

MYSELF

I always want to cry when I see the marathon runners coming in.

There is a chorus of assent.

MARIANNE

It's true, but that has nothing to do with whether you're a male or a female.

MYSELF

Yes it does. Men repress...

HILARY

Oh, I cry over that.

MYSELF

But you're a girl!

MARIANNE

I cry at parades.

ERICA

Why?

MARIANNE

At military parades. I don't know why. Longing for the simplicity of the past, maybe.

BETH

No, that's not why I cry.

HILARY

Me neither. I cry because of the pageantry.

MARIANNE

Yes, me too. Something about it makes me sad.

BETH

Yes, I cry over the pageantry and because I don't have enough of it in my life.

HILARY

You *said* it! Isn't this thing great, and *where* am *I*!

MYSELF

Haven't you ever cried after making love?

HILARY

Oh, I have, and I think it's because I feel like such a jerk. I mean, the spectacle of it! Here you've gone and forgotten yourself enough to feel like an "A" for a little while. Ridiculous. You're just a "B," kiddo. Get back to reality!

BETH

I've cried after making love when I felt that something was really over. Pulling back into somebody and afterwards...

HILARY

And then you have to face how screwed up it really is.

BETH

What it was and what could have been, what should be possible.

ERICA

And never is.

MARIANNE

Nostalgia for what didn't happen.

MYSELF

Do you remember the piece in the *Times* about tears?

HILARY

What, what piece?

MYSELF

An article about tears. They've discovered that different occasions generate tears with different chemical compositions. For example, if you cry from the cold, the tears have a different composition than the tears you cry from sorrow or anger.

BETH

Apparently, crying releases a kind of natural lithium in your body.

MYSELF

Natural opiates.

HILARY

Natural salts.

BETH

So when you cry, whatever happens when you're crying also releases whatever the hormone is that is like natural lithium. If I really sob, then after I'm through I can just go to sleep.

HILARY

Right.

MARIANNE

Me too.

MYSELF

Not me.

ERICA

Me neither.

HILARY

I can remember being thirteen and crying all the time. Do you still cry a lot?

BETH

Rarely. I think, too rarely now. But I did when I was growing up. I cried a lot until I was twenty-two or -three.

MARIANNE

My father used to be able to make me cry.

Chorus of appreciative groans.

MYSELF

They really could manipulate one's emotions.

BETH

My father could look at me in a certain way and I would start crying.

ERICA

Mine didn't even have to look.

MYSELF

These days I only cry out of rage.

HILARY

Rage?

MYSELF

Yes, the rage of humiliation.

HILARY

Humiliation for *sure*. Humiliation is definitely a big item when it's crying time.

MARIANNE

It's the worst.

BETH

I cry very little now, but I think that it must be that I'm fatigued.

MYSELF

Or maybe you're just not as humiliated as you used to be.

HILARY

Do you cry a lot, Erica?

ERICA

When?

HILARY

These days? Lately?

ERICA

No. Nothing's worth having to redo my eye makeup.

We laugh.

MARIANNE

An editor once made me cry.

We all exchange stories of having cried because of editors.

MYSELF

If they only knew.

ERICA

Oh, please. They know! They like it.

MYSELF

I don't know if they know.

HILARY

Like it! They love it! My theory is that torturing writers is
their form of sex. In fact, it's probably their *only* form of sex.
Who'd want to go to bed with these creeps?

MARIANNE

Hey, hold it!

BETH

Yeah!

HILARY

You go to bed with them?

BETH

No. Well, I mean, I didn't when I was a writer. But you might
remember there are two editors present.

ERICA

Oh, we're not talking about you. It's usually men anyway.

HILARY

Not so. There are plenty of women editors who are horrors.

MARIANNE

It's true, though, it's usually the men editors who have more
power.

BETH

They're not all creeps, though. Writers never look at it from the other side.

HILARY

All right, they're not all creeps. But you only need one or two creeps a year to make you wish that instead of being a journalist you were safely locked up in some nice place in the country, weaving baskets and playing volleyball with the other patients.

ERICA

At the Home for the Very, Very Nervous.

BETH

Isn't that a Mel Brooks line?

ERICA

Okay, I stole it.

MARIANNE

High Anxiety. I loved that movie.

HILARY

You know, Mel Brooks would be a good story.

ERICA

It's been done.

MARIANNE

Or Gene Wilder.

HILARY

Gene Wilder's a good story. Maybe for...

MYSELF

Someone should tell them.

BETH

Who?

MYSELF

Editors.

ERICA

Oh, please, it'll only add to their enjoyment.

HILARY

Who wants to give them a better sex life?

BETH

Why don't you write about it, I mean, not just the creeps, but about editor-writer relationships?

MYSELF

Too complicated, I think.

MARIANNE

That's perfect for you, you'll have something hefty to be anxious about for at least several months.

MYSELF

Anyway, I'm not sure people want to hear much more about writers. They've heard too much already.

BETH

That may be true, I think.

MYSELF

Maybe I should write about you guys, about these dinners.

Another chorus of groans.

MYSELF

What do you think?

ERICA

Can't you ever experience *anything* without writing about it?

HILARY

Of course not! That's our problem. Why else stay in this miserable business?

MYSELF

I'll change the names.

MARIANNE

It's a good story.

BETH

Yes, it *is* a good story.

ERICA

I don't know if I want my story told.

MYSELF

If you don't like it, I'll change it. You can all have copy approval, and if you don't like your character, Erica, I'll make all the particulars different so that any resemblance to you living or dead will be purely coincidental.

HILARY

Just do me one favor.

MYSELF

What?

HILARY

Just say I'm thin, okay?

MYSELF

Okay.

HILARY

Thank *God!* Just be sure to *specifically* mention it.

BETH

But you *are* thin.

HILARY

Oh, sure! You know, my breasts have gotten so big that when I'm out walking, they walk *next* to me. I feel like they're my pets or something. I mean, when I go out, I have to walk them on a leash!

BETH

I have to start running again.

ERICA

I'm sick of the gym.

MARIANNE

Why don't you try swimming?

MYSELF

It's too horrible to get undressed in the winter.

BETH

I hate the winter.

HILARY

Oh, please, I could *cry!*

ERICA

You know, actually, I did cry yesterday. I don't even know why.

MARIANNE

Didn't you just finish an article? A lot of that is fatigue crying.

HILARY

The worst is when you're crying only because you're feeling sorry for yourself. It's three o'clock in the morning and I can't get anybody on the phone. I'm all alone. Why do I exist?

We all laugh.

MYSELF

And you'll be alone forever....

HILARY

That's right, and I'll be alone for the rest of my life, crying.

MARIANNE

And you'll never have a good time again....

BETH

And you'll never have a baby....

HILARY

And you're getting old....

ERICA

And nobody cares....

HILARY

Nobody in the world.

MARIANNE

And there's no one to wake up next to.

HILARY

That's right. Your pillow is sopping with tears and the other one is untouched by human hair.

MYSELF

It doesn't matter if there's someone to wake up next to. If someone's there and you want to cry, you just leave him in the bedroom and go to the living room, shut the door and cry, all alone.

BETH

More alone.

HILARY

That's right. Exactly. It's even worse when there's somebody in your bed who couldn't care less and you have to go into the goddamn living room.

ERICA

And it's usually cold in there too.

MYSELF

And you have to cry quietly, to boot.

BETH

And afterward you can't go back into the bedroom because you don't want him to see your puffed-up face.

HILARY

Absolutely! The very worst cry in the world is the three-o'clock-in-the-morning humiliation cry when there's an insensitive dolt in your own bed and you can't even call one of your friends on the phone, and you just sit there like a jerk in your own living room.

BETH

And then you usually hate the way the room looks too. You wish you could get rid of all the horrible furniture you own.

MARIANNE

I'm having mine redone.

HILARY

What?

MARIANNE

My living room.

MYSELF

You are? What are you going to do with it?

MARIANNE

Well, I think I'll go down to Pierre Deux for some curtains. I saw a material there the other day that's a kind of small print with little rose sprigs.

ERICA

I must get a slipcover for my couch.

BETH

I like those Laura Ashley prints.

HILARY

Laura Ashley! Laura Ashley! Are you kidding! What do you think this is, *1972!*

ERICA

Would you pass the wine?

MARIANNE

No, Pierre Deux is much classier. I saw a pattern there that was...

A
Soldier's
Life

THE first time I saw Sofía, she was leaning on an AK-47 semi-automatic rifle and laughing. With her Sandinista uniform she wore a black T-shirt, and it occurred to me that she would have seemed stylish in any fashionable living room of New York or Los Angeles, now that the combat look is in. I would later come to know the sound of her laughter well, and to realize how often it rang when she was uneasy. But that afternoon I only saw the attractive woman in uniform speaking with ease to the group of visitors. She was the only one of the soldiers present who could speak English, so it was she who answered the questions of the Americans and Canadians who had driven to this village near the Honduran border to see for themselves what the front was like. The town was called Pantasma.

"Yes, all the peasants are armed," she was saying. "Everybody here is armed." And she laughed.

The Americans were interested in details. "How many bullets do you carry?"

"Right now only two hundred," she said, "because we're short. So we have to fight very carefully." She laughed again.

But sometimes her glance shifted to the hills where, a two-hour walk away, her friends were patrolling, and she would light another cigarette with her small, nervous fingers.

She had very short hair, and with her Nicaraguan army uniform she wore the black T-shirt and no bra. She had small, high breasts. On her belt she carried her cap and a canteen and a small knapsack. Everything had an American label. It was American equipment, she told us, captured from the *contras*.

"They're poor fighters," she told us. "Fifteen Sandinistas can take on forty *contras*."

"How is it," asked a lady in our group, "how is it being a woman soldier?"

"When you have a gun, you fight," said Sofía. "It's your life. And besides, for nothing would I fall into their hands alive."

She explained that she was in the area to do political work. "But there is no divorce between political or ideological work and the military. We carry a weapon anyway, and fight when the chance is given. To do political work you have to defend your life, because if you go up in those mountains you may be ambushed any minute. So in order to get anywhere you have to open your way with *this*." She held up her rifle. "And *then* you talk." She laughed.

She spoke casually with the Americans. She almost seemed to be bantering. Yet later I realized that, twice, she had mentioned that she would kill herself before allowing herself to be captured by the *contras*. Then she'd change the subject, though: it wasn't what she wanted to talk about with us. She understood her audience. As I was saying, she'd have an easy time of it at a smart party anywhere, because of her charm, her sense of humor, her cool, her looks. Even dressed as she was. But about her being braless, what came to mind was an incident I had read of: Not long ago the body of a woman captured by the *contras* had been found in the area, about ten days after her death. She'd been raped many times, the last time with a bayonet. And her breasts hung from a tree, alongside her severed hands.

But that's another story. Only a part of Sofía's story. She really was in a good mood that day. She told me later it was always a boost to the spirits to come down from the mountains to the little town of Pantasma. "We call it a town to call it something, you know. There's no electricity, no running water, there's almost nothing. But we'd walk down there every week or two. You'd meet your friends from other brigades and hear the news. Sometimes there'd be a letter from home, or candies, or chocolate, or something. And you could be sure you'd have a mattress to sleep on." So Pantasma was a treat for her. And maybe she liked talking with the Americans, and practicing her softly accented English.

"Did you do other work before you came here?" someone asked.

"Yes," she said. "I had a job, in Managua."

"What did you do?"

"I was a journalist."

Sofía Montenegro had been a writer and an editor at *Barricada,* the Sandinista newspaper. But there was no time then to wonder why the international news editor of Nicaragua's largest-circulation daily was now a soldier in the valley of Pantasma. We had to start the long trip back to Managua. Although we had an armed escort, we had been informed that we should not travel in the countryside at night. Sofía showed us around the town: just nasty shacks on a dirt road, like blisters under a ruthless sun; two horses standing, saddled, at the general store; a roofless schoolhouse; the detritus of a thousand years of solitude. It would have been dismal enough in any case, but a few months earlier it had been devastated by a surprise *contra* attack. Five hundred men had entered the town, which they knew was defended only by some twenty armed civilians. Forty-seven peasants had died resisting the attack, defending their storehouses, their new cooperatives, and a handful of tractors, the first tractors they'd ever had. The tractors had been destroyed. The cooperative was a pile of ashes. The little bank had also been set on fire, once the farmers' savings had been pocketed by the *contras*. Now the shacks were bullet-ridden, those that hadn't burned. The sawmill, once the area's chief employer, was now reduced to a few scorched planks of wood scattered in the overgrown grass.

"Do you expect another attack?"

"Yes."

Finally, we visited the orphanage where the children of the

men and women who had been killed in the attack were now housed. It was unbearable.

On the hill of the orphanage, we said good-bye to Sofía and the other soldiers. There was the constant sound of children crying. Once in a while a ragged toddler would amble toward us. Then Sofía would shift her rifle to the other side and caress the child.

We started heading out. I was just behind when someone from our group spoke to her in private.

"We're very proud of the job you're doing here," he said to her.

"Sometimes," said Sofía, looking down at the charred earth, "I miss my house in Managua."

As we drove off, she waved, smiling. Then I saw her turn away. She too had to be back before dark, where her friends waited on the mountain.

Back in New York, I became obsessed by Nicaragua, to the dismay of most of my friends and acquaintances.

"It was the most interesting thing I've ever seen," I'd say.

"I guess you had to be there," one of my friends joked.

"This is a country being run by people our age," I'd say. "It's as if we won. The head of state is a thirty-seven-year-old poet. It's called the revolution of poets."

"What about the right-wing death squads?"

"You're confusing it with El Salvador," I'd say, over and over again. "In Nicaragua they don't even have a death penalty. In fact, at bullfights they don't kill the bulls."

"Oh my God, you got est-ed out by Nicaragua," a friend declared.

I grew increasingly exasperated, and the biggest problem was that I was in a bad position to argue. The truth is, my own reaction was as surprising to me as it was to my friends. I'd gotten faked out in Central America: I'd gone to Nicaragua for fun.

I'd wanted to see a revolution. I'd wanted it for my collection

of experiences. I was bored in New York. Frankly, I would
have gone to Beirut, or to Chad. I had a bad case of cultural
cabin fever. New York was careers, therapy, relationships,
gourmet cuisine, and the sex lives of celebrities. The Third
World was action, grit, men with hats, passion. This was
where new societies were being constructed. As it happens,
I was particularly interested in Nicaragua, and I'd been trying
to follow the story for several years. But press accounts seemed
impenetrable, filled as they were with references to a history
I didn't know, names of towns I couldn't keep track of, Latin
names I could never remember, incomprehensible initials,
and queasy-making Spanish words like *commandante* and
junta. All I really knew for sure was the outline of the story:
that a four-year-old revolution that had overthrown a U.S.-
supported dictatorship was now struggling for its survival.

So when, one evening, a friend told me he was leaving
for Managua the next day and asked if I wanted to come, I
said yes.

"Are you sure?" he asked.

"It has to be fascinating. A young revolution. An idealistic
revolution. Maybe the last modern revolution."

"It's true," said my friend. "All future revolutions will be
postmodern."

I was in a great mood as I packed. What do you wear to a
revolution?

Your heart, as it turns out. Faked out by Central America.
I'd gone to observe other people's passion, not my own. But
after a few days of proper 1980s skepticism, I was unable to
resist the emotional wallop of the revolution of poets.

It had seemed more romantic to me than anything that
years of living in New York had equipped me to believe existed
any more. It was impossible to resist once you realized how
passionate this society was, how beautiful the country was
even in the midst of its pitiful poverty, once you glimpsed the
sensuality and capacity for reverie of its people. As for the
politics, the image of powerful warmongering Nicaraguans
hadn't held up too well in this tiny, rural place. In the towns,
the inhabitants, fearful of an American invasion, had dug

trenches in the earth, a few feet deep. *Trenches*. Against American weapons. In one little town, an old peasant who had helped to dig had assured me, with considerable pride, "This will protect us even against a nuclear bomb."

"You were brainwashed by the Sandinistas," one man I know bluntly asserted when I came back to New York. "It's more complicated than anything you can understand in one short trip."

"It's easy to think that from here," I argued. "And even the liberal press keeps telling you everyone is right and wrong. But when you see the effects of poverty and violence, everything becomes simpler. Go tell a woman whose lover has been killed with a weapon purchased with your tax money that everything's complicated."

"You're twenty years too late," he said, not unkindly. "We've been burned too many times."

"I'm not saying I'm qualified to judge the Sandinistas," I said. "It's not my culture. But it's not Ronald Reagan's or Jeane Kirkpatrick's either. Why are they qualified?"

It had been years since I'd argued so much. What was most infuriating was arguing for the right to argue. Some of my friends thought this was funny.

"Are you going to turn into a retro-hippie and walk around with a backpack being a revolution freak?"

It was a *style* problem I had. Talking earnestly about Central American politics was completely uncool. Earnestness of any kind, in fact, was as passé as bell-bottom jeans, eating sunflower-seed shells to get high, or sitting around in your room playing the guitar along with Byrds records.

"Are you now going to spend your summers picking cotton somewhere in the Third World?"

"You know, your problem," I stewed, "is that you can't reconcile your desire for comfort with your politics. The two aren't necessarily incompatible."

But I knew it was a bad sign that I was allowing myself to become so upset. In fact, there's no doubt that the degree of my discomfort at my friends' reaction was a measure of how serious the problem was. In a way, I felt guilty about feeling guilty. I was as much a victim of the radical-chic backlash syndrome as they were: it was embarrassing to exhibit this kind of emotion, especially if you had some privilege and wanted to keep it. I was breaking the rule of silence among the people who had spent their political passion in the sixties and who still basically hold the same views but have long ago given up any notion of acting on their principles. Except in the most cavalier terms, politics is barely a polite subject of conversation any more. It's not that these people don't despise Reagan and his ilk, you understand. The infuriating irony is that they despise these politicians so much that they'll have nothing to do with the entire mess.

"The lessons of the seventies and eighties," a sixties activist declared to me, "have been that nothing you do makes any difference."

"What about Vietnam?" I said.

"Listen, the war in Vietnam ended because ultimately corporate America decided it didn't make much sense. In the end, electoral action in this country is completely futile when it's corporations who run things."

"The alienation of man is realized and expressed in the relationship in which man stands to other men," I said.

"Is that yours?" he asked.

"No," I said. "Marx."

"Jesus," he said.

Most people were evenly divided between those who thought I should lighten up and those who wanted to lecture me about the Sandinistas. But there were other problems. Not to put too fine a point upon it, the people of Central America are, well, Hispanics.

"I can't take their brutality. I don't like their culture or their art," one particularly frank person I know declared. "They *want* to kill each other. They're savages."

"I wish you had met some of the people I met in Nicaragua," I said.

When, a month later, I returned to Nicaragua, Sofía Montenegro was no longer in Pantasma. She'd gotten a case of nearly
fatal amebic dysentery, I was told. They'd sent her home to
Managua, where she was recuperating.

"Yes," she said on the phone when I finally reached her,
"I've been sick. But I'm much better now." Her voice was
very small. Yes, she said, she was up and about now, and was
willing to come and talk to me next day at my hotel.

She was late, but she came, and sat down in a straight-
backed chair, polite and tense. It was almost shocking to see
her in a soft plaid shirt, well-fitting black pants, rather smart
sandals. She looked smaller out of uniform, but, then, she'd
lost a lot of weight. Her face was less full now, more Indian-
looking. Her hair was longer. Most incongruously, she wore
eye shadow, light blue and glistening, well applied. But under
her eyes there were deeper shadows, and her skin was sallow,
beat up.

She had just come from a meeting, she said. She was willing
to share my tepid coffee. "I live on coffee."

"Were you relieved to come back from Pantasma? Were you
too sick to feel relieved?"

"Well, I was so sick I thought I was going to die, and I
thought, 'Oh shit, I won't die of a bullet but of lousy diarrhea.'"
But then she said, "No, I was disappointed. Because of the
work we were doing. There's the solidarity you develop with
people you work with. The others remain. You know, you feel
like shit, because they are alone. There was a strong bond
that was born out of the situation. I feel almost like a traitor
to become sick."

She'd had anemia to begin with, which had worsened with
the dysentery, and also ulcers, open wounds in her intestines,
which were infected each time she drank the water from the
infected rivers when they were in the mountains. By the time
her brigade came down from the mountains to the town of
Pantasma, she had to go to the latrine every fifteen minutes
or so. For several days, she shivered with fever on her mattress. Finally, she was sent home.

"Did you have to do a lot of walking?"

"Yeah, every day. Every fucking day." But her expression belied the complaint. She laughed and lit another cigarette.

The days began at around five, when the sun rose. It had seemed to her, in the beginning, almost like a vacation. She hadn't been in the country in a long time, though as a child she'd been sent to spend the summers on a coffee plantation that belonged to her family. The mountains above Pantasma, at first, had reminded her of the farm where she'd milked cows and swum and run up and down the hills and played cowboys and Indians. "We were the good guys, like John Wayne. To tell you how much things have changed, now I see children play Sandinistas and *guardias*, but they have terrible fights, because everyone wants to be a Sandinista. Nobody wants to be a *guardia*."

The *guardias* were the National Guard, the army established and trained by United States Marines in the early thirties. The Marines had occupied Nicaragua for much of the early part of the century. They were a particularly brutal occupying army. At the head of the National Guard, the Americans installed a certain Anastasio Somoza, of whom Franklin Roosevelt said, "He may be a son of a bitch, but he's our son of a bitch." His family would rule Nicaragua for forty-five years, the longest and one of the most despotic, most corrupt dictatorships in Latin American history.

Shortly after he came to power, Somoza arranged for the assassination of Augusto Sandino, a rebel hero whose name became the byword of the men and women who formed an underground to overthrow the regime. It was the first Somoza's grandson whom the revolutionaries vanquished in 1979. At the time, Somoza and the *somocistas* controlled most of the economy and owned more than 50 percent of the arable land. His army, the same National Guard, still trained and supervised by the United States, fought against the revolutionaries with extraordinary zeal and ferocity. Toward the end of the revolutionary war, for example, in the town of León, the *guardias* entered houses and pulled out all the males, including the ones in their early teens. The men were made to kneel in rows with their hands over their heads, and then shot. Those who had their young in their arms were killed with their children. The older children were lined up against the walls of their houses and machine-gunned. Afterward, to add order to law, the *guardias* made the people clean up the debris and also pile the bodies on the sidewalk, to be set on fire.

When the revolution triumphed, it was joyful despite its sorrows: 40,000 dead out of a population of close to 3,000,000; 100,000 wounded; much of the cities destroyed; 200,000 families homeless; 750,000 dependent on food assistance; 40,000 orphans. Even so, most of the people were jubilant: the man they called the Last Marine was gone. His final gesture was to flee with the nation's treasury. Other supporters of the regime would leave too—the rich, the National Guard, the privileged professionals, the government. They left Nicaragua with no administrative infrastructure, bloody and bankrupt. That's why the average age in the Nicaraguan government is now twenty-eight: someone had to do it. So the kids who had been guerrillas and poets set aside their rifles and their notebooks and became Minister of Health, or Chief of Police. There was great popular support for the new government's initiative: hundreds of thousands of people participated in the rebuilding of the cities, a vaccination drive, a literacy campaign. A revolution was being institutionalized. The Sandinistas began working out a new justice system, and one of the most lenient penal systems in the world. And there was to be no death penalty. On this the FSLN, the Sandinista party, insisted, despite a good deal of popular will for revenge. No death penalty, even for the *guardias*.

So it was these same *guardias* who became the nucleus of the counterrevolutionary armies. *Contras*. The CIA and the Defense Department did not have to be coaxed to provide military and financial aid to the *contras*.

It was they who roamed the mountains above Pantasma, looking to ambush the Sandinistas.

"Were you frightened all the time?" I asked Sofía.

"Strangely enough, not," she said.

Life was simpler again, in the mountains. They slept in the bushes. "Or in a small peasant house. Wherever the night took you." They traveled in small groups usually, five to ten men and women. Some were soldiers of the regular Nicaraguan army who'd grown up in the area and knew the mountain roads, which rivers to drink from, where the best shelters were. Others, like Sofía, were from the cities, members of the FSLN.

When they awoke, if it wasn't too cold and if they had time, they went to the river to wash. The women joked together when they waded naked in the river, slipping awkwardly on the rocky river bed. Afterward, they prepared coffee, or bought food from a nearby hut. Then they planned the day. They tried to cover, each day, an area of twenty kilometers. Their job was to go from house to house to speak, one family at a time, to as many of the 20,000 peasants living in the area as possible.

"Did you volunteer?"

"I was chosen. It's taken as a distinction, a stimulus. It's to keep the link between all members of the FSLN with the reality of the country: if you are an intellectual, never to forget what the situation of the peasantry is and the conditions in which they live, never lose the idea of what we are working for. Always remember reality."

There was often an hour's walk between houses, sometimes more. "We could collect their opinions, their problems. What are their needs for health, food; what is the need for building roads in order to sell their products. And we would talk to them about the FSLN. We tried to explain the political problems in the area, the difficulties, the projects of the revolution. Also, we explained the military situation, the necessity of defense."

"Were they receptive?"

"Yes, but the peasant has another mentality, another structure. You have to go to his world. First you have to learn the words, and for that you have to live like them. And then you can start talking about the land, the cows, agriculture, the relation of the moon and the rains, many things. Then you can talk.

"Probably they do not understand the most abstract concepts, for example of defense. Or why they were attacked. The links of the *contras* with the bourgeoisie, the rich of other countries, and the link to the hegemony that the United States wants to make in Central America, that is difficult, this link. But they understand it by heart; they know that this country has been invaded by the Americans many times. That, they know. But *contra* propaganda confuses them, because the isolation is so great."

I'd heard that Sofía had been sent to head the local FSLN brigade as part of a trouble-shooting effort in the region to combat ambivalence or hostility toward the Sandinistas. In the aftermath of the October attack, reprisals against suspected informants by enraged FSLN workers had worsened the situation. There had been trials, defections on both sides, anger and confusion. Now the area was being bombarded with *contra* propaganda. Those farmers who had radios, for example, could receive programs from powerful stations based in Honduras. The *contras* had access to the funds and technological expertise to broadcast at that elevation.

As for Sofía and the Sandinistas, on a good day they could get to eight houses. "But you have to walk fast."

On bad days, they trekked slowly up or down the mountain paths, tense and alert for ambushes.

"There is insecurity when you don't know the territory. But then you become accustomed to the mountain, you learn how to recognize noises, the noises of the night and the noises of the day, of a human foot and of an animal foot, and which animal. Then you begin to feel under control, and it becomes less frightening." Sofía laughed. "To tell you the truth, for me the most difficult thing was the shitting in the bushes.

"It's quite uncomfortable. I mean, in a way you become a sort of savage. It's very elemental. You feel very elemental, very dirty, very animal with a human brain."

She shifted in her chair.

"Yet, each time you see you can cope with a situation. Sometimes I thought: I can never do it. I can never do this thing. But then you realize that you can."

"Did you think of how you felt about having to kill people?"

She was silent for a moment. "Well," she said, "yes." Sofía often gestured when she spoke, but now she clasped her hands.

"How did you feel the first time you were in a crossfire situation?"

"Is this sugar?" asked Sofía. She poured herself more coffee.

"You feel something in your stomach, and the acceleration of your pulse. I felt that I became red. Like a blush, but all over. How do you call that? *Adrenalina*. You feel the shot of adrenaline all through your body. Then you become tense. But you are clearheaded, immediately. I felt the acuteness of my senses, of my hearing, and, you know, an underflow. I didn't feel paralyzed because I knew that I would expect orders. I mean, you move in order and there is someone telling the others what to do. Unless he's hit. But if he's hit you know there is a second, and then a third. Like all armies in the world, you know. But more than the techniques of the military process, what matters is the inner attitude, to accept how you have arrived at your ideas, and that it is normal to believe in them."

She leaned forward. "There was a consensus about the armed struggle. We conquered the power, and now we have to defend it. The rest follows. You kill them or they kill you. And if you are consequent with those ideas and with yourself, then you have to go to the end, because that's the way a coherent person functions."

In the mountains, the Sandinistas' day ended at sundown. "We looked for a secure place, from which there could be a retreat, or a safe place for a better defense, a place with a protection like a wall or a hole or something so that we would not be completely in the open. We would prepare ourselves so that we would have at least a minimum advantage if there was combat. Then we ate. We talked and told each other stories. Also, we made an evaluation of our day's work and discussed problems, when there were any, of relations in our little group." Then they slept. "The best sleeps I had in my life were in Pantasma." They took turns standing guard. Sofia's guard was from three to six in the morning.

"What did you think about?"

"Usually you tend to remember things." She looked pensive. "Your personal problems. In a way you feel lonely. The nature is so vast and open, and you feel small in the middle. And besides, the mountains always give you a sense of solitude, you know. It's very quiet. It's difficult to get accustomed to it. You listen to the sounds of the night, the chirping of the crickets, the leaves, the wind through the leaves. But usually what I find strange and even frightening was all the sort of noises the trees can make when they are moved by the wind. So it gives you..."

She shuddered. We both laughed.

"An eerie feeling?"

"Yes. But sometimes the nights were very beautiful. It was like having a lamp. Then you realize that your eyes have become accustomed to this sort of light from the moon and the stars. Sometimes I couldn't believe it, it was so beautiful, you know." She smiled.

"You felt happy?"

"Yes, peaceful," she said.

Sofia had been hunched forward. Now, suddenly, she started shaking.

I turned off the wheezing air conditioner and opened the window. A waft of hot and dusty Managua air blew into the room, the rumble of motors. She relaxed in her chair. She unclenched her hands. She pushed her hair back. In the dying afternoon's light, she looked very soft.

"Do you think it's liberating for a woman to use a rifle?"

"Yes," she said. "In the first place, it gives you a sense of security—the security to know that you will defend yourself. But also, weaponry has always been a sanctuary for men and, let's say, a sort of privilege or a symbol of manhood, or strength, or whatever. And then you realize that you can use a weapon as well as anybody else. It's not hard to learn how to use. You can do it in half an hour, an hour. You learn to take it apart and clean it and put it back together blindfolded. It's not hard. you just practice and practice. Then there is a process that takes place, the identification of you with your weapon. You know it like you know your car or, I don't know, the things with which you paint yourself, your cosmetics. You are intimate with your weapon. Many people give them names."

"Did you keep it with you all the time?"

"Oh, yes," she said. "You sleep with it next to you, like this." She cradled an imaginary rifle next to her cheek.

"It was hard not to have it when I first came back. You feel that you miss something. It's like not having your handbag, you know. You always carry your bag, you never go out without it, you never forget it, and you're accustomed to the weight of it, and when you don't have it you feel that you are missing something. The first few days I was always looking where my weapon was, you know. It's very funny."

"Did you have to give it back?"

"Yes," she said. "I don't need it here."

She sighed and looked out the window for a bit. "I have to go back to Pantasma this week," she said. "To pick up my things. And I'd like to see my friends once more."

Could I come with her? I asked. Could I speak with her a few more times about what had led her to make the decision to be one of those who took up arms?

She'd think about it, she said. She would call me. But now she was already late for another appointment. She shook my hand and she left.

That night I called New York.

"What's new?" I asked.

"Not much. Marvin Gaye's father shot him."

"Oh," I said.

I'm not inventing, exaggerating, or gratuitously taking a cheap shot here. On April 2, 1984, I made several phone calls to New York from Managua, asked, "What's new?," and was told of Marvin Gaye's death over an insurance claim. I'd only been back in Nicaragua a few days, but already this other reality seemed... I don't even know how to describe how that reality seems in Nicaragua. Unreal? Monstrous? Unimaginable.

"I'm sorry," said Sofía when I spoke to her the next day. "But it would really be difficult to oblige you."

"I see," I said.

"It was really very romantic of me to think I could go to Pantasma to say good-bye to my friends," she said. "I am not well, and I have too much to do. I cannot continue the interviews."

"I understand," I said.

"I'm sorry," she said again. "I know what it's like to be a journalist in a hotel room. But, you know, there are many women like me. Many women who are professionals who have been involved in the military. If you want, I will get together for you a list of women you can interview."

"I'd appreciate it," I said. "I don't have much time left."

"I'll call you," she promised.

I did some looking on my own too, but without success. A few days went by. It was too hot to eat, too hot to sleep. One night I couldn't sleep at all: I'd become too anxious. So the next morning I did what any journalist in my position would have done. I went to the pool.

There, as I discovered, members of the press could often be found, print media on one side of the pool, TV on the other, lying on deck chairs, looking morose.

I lay down too, on the print side: they seemed the more morose.

It had to be possible, I brooded, to find another woman soldier in Nicaragua. Thirty percent of the revolutionary army had been women. Half of the civilian militia was made up of women. There were seven women's reserve battalions. Thousands of women were mobilized each year. And, judging from

my experience during my first trip, it was amazingly easy in
Nicaragua to get access to people and to information.

But the war had become worse. And, besides, it had immediately become apparent that being in Managua as a journalist was a different category of experience. On my first trip,
when I'd met people as an individual, I'd been treated with
warm Latin hospitality, a cheerful openness. But now, as a
member of the press, I encountered wariness, endless logistical obstructions, and—the reporter's nightmare—unre-
turned phone calls. I sat in my room dialing for hours—that
is, when I could get a line. The contacts I'd made on my first
trip did not call back. The Americans living in Nicaragua
whose numbers I'd been given did not call back. The car-
rental places did not call back. The army office did not call
back. None of the administrations called back. Nobody called
back. There was a war on. I was on hold in Managua.

As it turned out, I was not alone. At the pool, the reporters
griped endlessly.

"This is the worst place in Central America to work in. It's
even worse than El Salvador," I was soon informed by an old
hand. Everyone seemed to know this but me. In fact, there
was, around the pool, at the press conferences, and at the
various functions where reporters would troop *en masse,* an
old-boys'-club atmosphere among the press who had been in
the country since the revolution. The tribulations of newcom-
ers were viewed with amused detachment by those who felt
they owned a piece of the revolution, that they'd earned it.
Besides, these were hard-news reporters. They had no truck
for feature writers, whom they considered wimpy. To the dull
ache of depression and the hot throb of anxiety, I added the
stinging flourish of humiliation.

Yet I couldn't really blame them: they had their own trou-
bles. So I was grateful when someone exhibited mild interest.

"Having a hard time?"

"I can't get anyone to return my calls."

"Welcome to Managua."

It was the foreign journalists' only running joke. Not a very
good one, but there was a war on.

What was most frustrating was that, as I quickly realized, it was infinitely easier for representatives of the conservative American media to get their story. You had to spend only a couple of days in the country to realize what a joke it was to imagine that there was no free speech in Nicaragua. The opposition parties actually had press conferences. All you had to do was show up and you could meet as many people as you wanted who would talk to you endlessly about what they termed the Sandinistas' repressive policies. They'd invite you to their meetings, to their homes. And if you were too lazy to do even that, you could simply appear at the United States Embassy and line up for the guided State Department tour of Nicaragua. Many journalists do.

The others, for the most part, and to a degree dependent on the position of their publications in the media status hierarchy, chase frantically after their stories, stew a lot, pass petitions of protest among themselves, and, when they've really had it, go crash by the side of the pool, waiting to be paged for phone calls that never come.

"You won't get anywhere on the phone," the mildly friendly reporter advised. "Why don't you go around to these people's offices in person?"

"That's what I've been doing," I said. "But they promise you everything, and then they don't deliver."

"Welcome to Managua," he said.

I lay back in my deck chair and resumed my brooding.

Traipsing around Managua hadn't improved my morale any. In fact, I knew that part of my peculiar anxiety was the by-product of the city's angst-producing vistas. Managua is a dump. After the earthquake that destroyed the downtown area, the city was never rebuilt. As it happens, Somoza and his friends owned land in the outlying suburbs, and so it was those areas that were built up, American-style, suburban houses clustered around a mall. Worse than L.A., I thought. In what had once been the center of the city, the debris had not even been cleared until the revolution. Now it was tidier, but the capital of Nicaragua seemed like a city without a heart: in the old downtown areas some scattered buildings still stood, but most were carcasses of the old structures, surrounded by fields of rubble.

By the side of the pool, I sighed. I put on more suntan lotion. "Can I take this?" I wondered. "I can't take this."

Now the reporters were talking about piranha boats, Uzis, Composite Air wing flying, and OV-1 Mohawks. I couldn't understand a word they were saying.

At last they stopped talking. It was hot. Some of the reporters were sitting in the shallow end of the pool, and staring out, half submerged, at the unyieldingly blank horizon. Others lay, as I did, immobile on their chairs. If you shifted one of your limbs, you'd be burned by the deck chair's plastic covering. I knew I was being grilled by the sun, but I didn't have the courage to move. I hoped I wouldn't run out of suntan lotion, which would probably be impossible to find in Managua, or would cost too much from my dwindling funds. Deodorant went for the equivalent of fifteen U.S. dollars—when you could find it. But deodorant already seemed to me a ridiculous luxury in a place where you could often not find toothpaste, soap, toilet paper, milk, many medicines.

Some ninety miles away, in the port of Corinto, American mines prevented supply ships from docking in Nicaragua. One hundred and twenty-five miles away, in the Gulf of Fonseca, an American frigate sat, surveilling. One hundred and forty-five miles north, near the Honduran border, 15,000 troops of *contras* were massed, using American funds, supervised by the CIA. Ninety miles south, at the Costa Rican border, 3,000 troops of *contras* were massed, using American funds, supervised by the CIA. Two hundred and twenty miles away, in San Salvador, American "advisers" conferred with Salvadoran politicians about the upcoming election. A hundred and fifty miles away, in Tegucigalpa, Honduras, Defense Department representatives planned a $150-million escalation in U.S. military presence. Two hundred miles away, in San José, Costa Rica, high-level negotiations were being held regarding the Costa Rican debt to the United States, and what might be the trade-offs the neutral country would offer. In the Caribbean basin, 30,000 American military personnel were preparing to take part in an operation mildly entitled "Ocean Venture." In another operation, entitled "Big Pine II," 5,500 American army, navy, and air-force troops teamed up with several thousand Honduran soldiers for "exercises." Within a radius of several hundred miles, there were countless numbers—that is, unknown numbers—of American advisers, military training centers, tactical support units, combat vessels, radar stations, reconnaissance planes.

Sofía, at least, called back, with a list of about ten women. Poets, photographers, lawyers, professional women who had had some involvement with the military. She described each of them and I chose several to interview. When she offered to set the meetings up for me, I accepted gratefully. I knew by then what it would have meant to reach each one and set up the meetings myself.

But all the women she'd mentioned were in Managua now, and what I'd wanted was a woman at the front. To interview these women in their homes or in their offices wouldn't make as good a story, I felt. It's one thing to hear ideas expressed from behind a desk; another from behind a gun, with danger nearby. And maybe being at the front was something I needed to do for myself. I thought about this but I didn't know for sure. I added confusion to my panorama of dysfunctions.

"You're not going to get anywhere here," advised the mildly friendly journalist. "You should get out into the country."

"I can't find a car to rent," I explained.

"Welcome..."

"I know," I said.

Half a day's work by someone helpful, who knew the ropes, finally did produce an item resembling a car. "It's just been checked by the mechanic," I was assured by a sympathetic rental agent who correctly read my expression. But I was desperate. Cars are very difficult to get in Managua, as are parts and gas. There's a war on.

I decided to try a place called Estelí, halfway up to the northern border from Managua. I'd heard that there was a women's reserve battalion there, with eight hundred women soldiers. But in Estelí I was turned away. The reserve battalion had been disbanded; many of the women had been sent to the front, and the rest were awaiting orders. No, no one knew how to contact any of the women. For security reasons, each reported to a central location and was given her destination on the spot.

There was nothing to do but have lunch. A restaurant was found with the help of a little girl named Gioconda, maybe ten years old, who'd been playing barefoot in the street.

"Why do you have no shoes?" I asked Gioconda.

"Because I have no mother," she said.

"Did your mother die in the war?" I asked.

"No," she said. "In the house. The *guardias* came, with bayonets."

On the way back from Estelí, the car started spewing steam. I sat on the side of a ditch, waiting for the water to stop boiling in the radiator. It was about a hundred degrees, maybe more. On my last trip, the hills had been full of flowers. Now the countryside was brown and mean. I'd been in Nicaragua for a week and had spent all of the magazine's money and had no story. "What am I doing?" I asked myself. I no longer had an answer, only a tiny remnant of a remembered principle somewhere in the recesses of my clobbered psyche. I was ridiculous in New York, contemptible in Managua. I was depressed, confused, anxious, humiliated, dirty, tired, humorless, lonely, paranoid, and ashamed. And I'd only been there a week. Sofía Montenegro, who, like many of her compatriots, could have been settled quite comfortably in Miami, would undoubtedly spend her whole life in Nicaragua. So would Gioconda, who'd cried when we said good-bye.

That night, I called New York again, late.

"What's up?" I said.

"The Academy Awards are on. They were incredibly boring this year."

The next day was Sunday. I hadn't heard from Sofía, so I called her home.

"I'm sorry," she said. "I haven't been able to set up your meetings for you."

She sounded terrible. I could barely hear her.

"What's the matter?" I said. "Have you had a relapse?"

"Yes," she said, very faintly, and laughed. "Life in the tropics, you know."

"Are you in bed?"

"Yes," she said. "I haven't made your appointments."

"Have you seen a doctor?" I asked.

"I can't get one now. I will see a doctor tomorrow. I will call you."

"Don't worry about it," I said. "But when you feel better, there's something I would like to ask you."

"What do want to ask me?"

I hesitated. It seemed cruel even to keep her on the phone. I thought of her shivering in my room. But I said, "I was hoping you would reconsider, about our interviews. When you're feeling better, maybe you could think about this, and let me know." I paused, trying to think of persuasive arguments. But finally, I simply said: "It's not just another article for me."

"All right," she said, in that voice, but gently, to make it easier for me. "I'm not doing anything now. Why don't you come this afternoon?"

I found her house without too much difficulty. There are no addresses in Managua, but she'd given me a landmark: "From there, two blocks toward the lake, then two blocks east." It was a white house with columns, peaceful-looking, in a quiet neighborhood. She came to the door and kissed me on the cheek. Her cheek was damp with perspiration yet strangely cool. We walked into an airy room, filled with light wood and wicker. We sat in rocking chairs, and talked.

I'll never know for sure, unless I see her again, why Sofía

agreed to continue our interviews. I know it was difficult for her, for many reasons, to talk with me. Embarrassing.

Nicaraguans do not talk about their private lives with the press: personality journalism is unknown. In a country where every life is a novel, where there are three million tragedies, everyone tends to think his own story is humdrum. And to the Nicaraguans who are engaged, it is not the individual tales but the drama of the revolution that tells their common story.

And Sofía is modest. It was from someone else, for example, by chance, that I heard that she'd been a cofounder of her newspaper, *Barricada*. She had only mentioned vaguely that she'd been there at the start, right after the revolution. "There are many women like me," she told me several times. "I am of the average." It was important to her to make that understood.

Most likely, I think, she agreed to continue seeing me only on an impulse. Because she is what she wanted to become: a coherent person, accustomed to acting out the reasons of the heart.

Her father was a high-ranking officer in Somoza's National Guard, as were his brothers, as had been his father before him. Sofía's father fought against Sandino in the 1930s and eventually became a major, the commander of city garrisons. There were nine children, but Sofía was the only one who would become a Sandinista. Several are still in Nicaragua, not members of the FSLN but sympathetic. The others live in the United States. One of her brothers would become a notorious officer in the National Guard. He survived the revolution but was killed as he tried to escape during a jail transfer while he was awaiting trial. It was Sofía who brought her brother's corpse home to her mother. Perhaps this is what she thought about when she was the only one awake on the mountain, and had the eerie feeling.

The same year Sofía was born, 1954, there was an attempted putsch in Somoza's army. Afterward, the officers known to have been involved in the conspiracy were executed, and repression within the National Guard and in the country increased. Sofía's father was saved from execution perhaps only because his brothers were still powerful officers, but he was soon "retired." She still doesn't know precisely what her father's involvement in the rebellion had been. "He never wanted to talk about it," she says.

"Mine is a dramatic story, but it's not uncommon," she said. "Since you were born you were growing up with uniforms, guns, *guardias,* dictators, demonstrations, disappearances, the fear. It's all there, all the time. I'm thirty years old and I have only known war, one way or the other. Always, somebody in my family was involved in the war. So I'm a product of my surroundings. And for me it's only normal to get involved. I was always involved one way or the other."

Her mother was an attractive woman, forceful and pious. Sofía was brought up as a proper child, and taken to church each Sunday, where, among the men in uniforms, she and her brothers and sisters were made to sit demurely, in their pretty clothes, the girls wearing big hats.

When I asked her what she thought was the first step in her radicalization, she told me, after some reflection, that when she was about ten years old her father had given her a book by Voltaire.

In her teens, she was sent to the United States, where she spent two years as a high-school student in Florida.

"It opened my eyes," she said. "I learned what racism was."

"Did you feel discriminated against?" I asked.

"Not necessarily, because I'm not so dark. But I felt observed and foreign, alien."

So the Americanization process that was part of the status code of Nicaragua's bourgeoisie did not take, though Sofía went through the motions of obeisance to American culture: "It became an opportunity to observe a different vision of the world." She wore jeans, went to dances, dated, and necked at beach parties with the other kids.

"I always had the feeling that they were kids. They are probably kids still. Most of the time, you know, I found them boring. You couldn't talk to them. I was shocked that they didn't know history, or geography. They didn't even know where Nicaragua was: they were always confusing it with Nigeria. I felt different, apart, preoccupied with other things."

She became irritated in her history classes, where only United States history was studied. "There was one teacher who marked me. I realized that every time he spoke of whites killing Indians it was a battle, but when the Indians killed whites it was a massacre. And I raised my hand and I said, 'Why not a massacre or a battle from both sides?' And I remember he told me in a very arrogant way, 'If you don't like my class, you may as well leave it.' So I walked out."

It was in the Florida high-school classroom, then, that she performed her first gesture of political activism. But back in Nicaragua, her differences with her family now rankled. "It was my condition as a woman, which in this country was very sad. I saw no prospects for myself but what the tradition dictated, that I should be a housewife, a servant of my husband, with a very small scenario for my own life."

Defying her family's wishes, she became a secretary so she could put herself through university. She'd wanted to become an architect, but architecture classes, which were expensive, could only be taken in the daytime, when she had to work. She painted for a while, but then she decided to become a journalist. "I was past a certain point of personal involvement." Perhaps this is the point at which "personal involvement" became the organizing principle of Sofía's life.

The university was in turmoil; there was constant political discussion, talk of the FSLN guerrillas, demonstrations, Sofía's radicalization was completed. "It was fast. The *guardias* would come with a truck and park it in front of the university and just start picking up people you knew. Student leaders were put in jail. Your acquaintances, your friends disappeared, or were found dead in a ditch, tortured and mutilated and everything. Girls were picked up and returned raped by fifty *guardias* or something, out of their minds, totally nuts. And if there was too much upheaval in the streets, they came with machine guns and shot into the classrooms. They came with helicopters sometimes, to attack unarmed students. They were with tanks and we with stones." Sofía laughed. "So, of course, when you see one of your friends fall under a machine gun and you are standing there with a little stone in your hand, you say, 'Oh shit, they won't get me this way.'"

Sofía paused. "It's the same thing that's been happening in El Salvador," she said. "It's been happening for fifty years. So you become involved. I went from a very romantic and idealistic position to a radical position. It's a process. Your moderate opposition has a very short life, because the more you know, the more you are confronted with reality, the more you see that if all you do is talk you are talking a lot of bullshit. And besides, they suspect their own shadow. Everybody becomes an object of suspicion. You know that if some *guardia* looks at you a little too long and doesn't like your face, the next thing you know they are checking your house, your friends, and this and the other. You know that one day or the other they'll come and get you." Sofía snapped her fingers. "So you go."

She decided to join the FSLN, then still an underground party.

"But I had a little problem." She laughed. "And it was that my name, my last name, was very well known. Everybody knew in the university that I was the daughter of, and the sister of, and they didn't trust me."

"Was your name hated?"

"Yeah, sure." She laughed again, a little.

"How did you feel?"

"Horrible," she said softly. "It's horrible to feel social rejection for what your name represents."

"Were you resentful?"

"Well, I had hard times. I had to prove with my deeds that I was a trustable person."

So she joined another political organization, where the leaders knew her personally. "It was not exactly in accordance with my ideas, but it gave me a possibility to do something."

A year later, after her participation in the penultimate, 1978 insurrection, she was invited to join the FSLN. She was a courier, she kept a safe house in which "burned" guerrillas could hide, she transported people underground, she gathered information and passed it to the FSLN and to the foreign press. "I had access to some places since I was the sister of, and the daughter of..."

It was around this time, a year before the revolution triumphed, that Sofía's father died. He died, slowly, of amebic dysentery.

"My father was not the typical *guardia*," she told me. She looked pained. "I am probably talking of small differences that are not so clear to your eyes, but he was a clever, educated man, and an honest man. His story is the history of Nicaragua; it corresponds to the development of our situation; so I say it in that context. His political thinking evolved. I think that if he still lived now, he would not be totally in accordance with the revolution, but he would accept it."

"Did you love him very much?"

"Very much, very deeply. He was very sweet, and very polite, very uncommon for a *guardia*."

Sofía stood and went to a desk. She knelt, ransacked a drawer, and brought back two photographs. One was of her mother, at around Sofía's age, alluring, fashionable, determined. The photos must have been taken at the time of Sofía's birth, and the putsch. In the other, her handsome father looked at the camera with dreamy eyes.

Sofía studied the photographs too, over my shoulder. Then she went back to her rocking chair.

"He spent a long time dying," she said. "Almost a year. He died at the military hospital of the National Guard. The regime was going down. I remember that in the room next to him they brought a political prisoner, a woman. They couldn't afford that she die, so they were giving her some treatment in the officers' ward. I was already in the FSLN then, but I used to go visit him. Sometimes he would lose his mind, not exactly know where he was, but he had the consciousness that he was dying. And he complained privately all the time that Somoza was wrong. He couldn't take a stand publicly, because he couldn't take that risk. But I knew, in his last moments, I knew what his feeling of rejection of the regime was. In the end, he agonized for many days, and once, in one of these lapses of his mind, he started singing. He started singing with a very thin voice."

Sofía sang, rocking herself, to a melancholy melody.

Si Adelita se fuera con otro
Lu seguira por tierra y por mar
Y formar en un buque de guerra
Y por tierra en un tren militar.

"Do you know that song?" Sofía asked.

"No," I said.

"That song was sung in the 1910 revolution in Mexico, and that was the song that the troops of Sandino sang, and that's the last song my father sang."

Sofía still rocked.

"You now, on the first anniversary of the revolution we had a mass rally. And I was there as a journalist, in the middle of the crowd. It was full of people, and I was overjoyed, and there was this feeling.... And on the grandstand, there was a bunch of old men, the survivors of Sandino's troops. Old men, in straw hats. And then Mejía Godoy, the singer, he asked the whole crowd to sing, and he took his guitar and started singing."

She began again.

"*Si Adelita se fuera con otro...*" Sofía sang.

"And there were thousands of voices singing." She sang again. "At that moment those old men stood up and took their straw hats and went like this"—she waved an imaginary hat—"to the crowd, and all the crowd cheered and then went on singing. And I started shaking. If lightning had struck me I would have felt the same way, I think. Because in that group of old people there was an old man, with blue eyes and white hair like my father, with a certain look like him. He took his hat off and looked at me and smiled and moved the hat, and for a minute I thought it was my father. Then I ran out of the plaza like mad, and forgot about the assignment and the pictures and everything. I came home and cried and cried, because at that moment I realized that there'd been a message in the last song he sang, and that he'd survived. And I think that many people in the plaza felt the same way. I realized that my father would have blessed me, and approved. You may see it as a religious act, but that's the way I felt it. I felt he was saying, 'I couldn't do it, for many reasons, but I'm glad that you did.'"

It had grown dark in the room. Sofía turned on the lights.

"How do you think your old friends in Florida would react if they saw you carrying your gun?"

"I don't know. They'd probably think I'm mad. Or some sort of radical communist or terrorist or something. It's strange. I think that Americans won't change until they suffer in their own flesh and their own land the wars they impose upon others. And then they will see ... the horror."

Sofía paused. "I think that if you were in our place for a moment, or for a lifetime, you would do exactly what we do."

Sometimes Sofía would make me turn the tape recorder off. "I hate that thing," she'd say. And talk to me about people she'd known, who had died, about García Márquez and magic realism, about Central America. She knew I couldn't grasp it by myself: "For you," she'd say. "So you understand the *feeling*." Bit by bit, I put together the disparate things she told me with what I'd seen already and began to form an idea, my own no doubt, of the reality of a violent place under a hot sun, the jumble of poetry and rape, political rigor and the cold sweat of fear on warm brown skin, a kaleidoscope of church-going women and uniformed dictators and street musicians who cried while they played, of poverty and dignity and free-dom and deaths in the morning and rabid yellow-eyed dogs howling in the night, and laughing girl guerrillas.

I entered a kind of trance state.

In that mood, one night, I went with several Americans to a neighborhood called Ciudad Plástica, "Plastic City," one of Somoza's last architectural achievements. It's a dismal cluster of Florida-type fast-food places, where the remnants of Somoza society congregate to drink ice-cream sodas at orange Formica-topped tables.

There's a discotheque too, called Lobo Jack. It's rather posh for Managua, with upholstered banquettes, carpeting. On the dance floor, the kids were frenetic. We stood and watched for a while.

"You should see it when the Marines are here," said one of the Americans.

"The Marines come here?" I asked.

"Sure," he said. "From the embassy compound. They really whoop it up when they're here."

But that night there were only Nicaraguans on the dance floor. We stayed just a few minutes, but as we headed toward the door one of the men with us was clutched at by a Nicaraguan girl, about twenty-five, pretty, well dressed. "*¿Adónde va?*" she kept asking, stroking his face. She put her arms around him. "*¿Adónde va?*" With some difficulty, he disentangled himself and we walked out to our car. We drove away in silence.

"It's terrible," I said, "to think of those little Nicaraguan girls fucking those Marines."

"Why? What's the difference?" said one of the Americans. "If you want to get fucked, why does it matter who you fuck?"

"Are there those who love the conqueror?" I asked Sofía the next day.

"Yes," she said. "They think like Americans, they want to live like Americans live. That is why the Somozists could do that to their own people: they didn't feel Nicaraguan, they felt American. And they loved their masters. The sort of people who go to Ciudad Plástica, they are the product of their own class. But, you know, this is an open society, so they go there. We call them *plásticas,* "Plastic Girls." It's very sad. They are like little dolls. To tell you the truth, I used to have girlfriends who were what you would now call *plásticas.*"

"What happened to them?"

"Well, some of them left the country. Others still live here but they are housewives, people who just make their work, and they complain about everything, because of the shortages. I had a girlfriend I bumped into once, after many years of not seeing her, and she invited me to lunch. So I went and we talked. She asked me what I was doing, and I told her. And she said, 'You were always so dizzy with those ideas of yours, and one of these days you will get shot.' She said I looked quite diminished in my physical appearance."

"She didn't like the way you looked?"

"Yes, well," said Sofía, somewhat sheepishly, "I used to be a little bit sophisticated."

"You used to wear dresses?"

"Yeah," said Sofía. "I was chic."

Then she showed me another picture, this one framed. It was Sofía with plucked, arched eyebrows, very made up, in a low-cut dress, wearing a seductive expression. She put the framed photograph back on a little table, near a wicker bookcase that held the works of Lenin.

"I keep it there," she said. "To remind me."

"So, your lunch with your friend," I said.

"Yes, well, she was neatly dressed, and smelling good. And I said, 'And what are you doing?' So she told me she had a house, and this, that, and the other, and the house has a pool and so forth. At the time, we were in a really heavy military situation, and she started talking to me about her curtains. She spent almost an hour talking to me about how she couldn't find the right curtains, because of the shortage of material. That was her big worry. And I thought, 'What?! But are you kidding! You know where you are living, and you know where we are going, and you are talking to me about your fucking curtains when we are in a war?' And so I just decided that I wouldn't talk any more, just shut my mouth, and finish my lunch very politely, and give her a kiss of good-bye, and leave."

"She'd been a good friend of yours?"

"Yes, it hurt me. And I understood that if it hadn't been for my circumstances..."

"Did she have a husband and children?"

"Yes."

"Do you want to have children?"

"Well," Sofía said in a lighthearted tone, "I am always saying that after this"—she laughed—"emergency, I will have some time for myself and have a kid."

She pushed her hair back in a gesture I'd come to know.

"Are you tired?"

"Yeah, tired to the bones. Like everyone here. I have been tired for years."

"Yet you seem cheerful."

"I feel cheerful, because I like my job, what I am doing. I understand my world. I belong to it. I feel completely immersed in it, an actor of it. Even though my personal incidence might be small. Do you see? And I think most of the people feel like that."

"Are you lonely sometimes?"

"Yes, very much, sometimes. But I have made my choice to become a professional revolutionary."

One evening, a friend of Sofía's arrived at her house just as we were finishing an interview, and, to avoid asking personal questions in front of someone else, I decided to get quotes from her on some of the questions that trouble U.S. liberals about Nicaraguan policies: press censorship, Cuban and Soviet presence, attitude toward dissent. She gave me quite excellent answers, logical, persuasive answers. But we were both somewhat gloomy afterward. I, because I realized that it wasn't within the scope of any article I could write to spell these things out. And I think she was upset because she felt somehow betrayed that I could ask these questions after what I'd seen and heard. I don't know for sure.

Then we went to dinner, Sofía, her friend, and I. The conversation was desultorily political when she turned to me, her features set as I had not seen them before. "They call us terrorists," she said. "Do you know what terror is? It only functions up to a certain point, you know. It depends on the amount, the doses of terror that you are inoculated with, until there is a moment when there is so much terror that you can overpower it because you have nothing to lose. Absolutely nothing. Perhaps it would be a *descanso*. A rest. To face it finally and to make a final decision. And then terror doesn't function any more, because you don't give a shit any more. You are almost willing, you know, to get a final confrontation and get it over with. Because you are so tired of living like a rat. And when a whole population feels like that, a country is ripe for taking a decision. A decision to take up a weapon and say, 'Well, maybe they will kill me, but I will kill a couple of sons of bitches too.' Violence is the moment you are hungry and you have nothing to eat. That is violence. The violence against your body, your stomach. Violence is not to have any money, not to have a job. So your whole structure gets accustomed to receive violence. And at a certain moment to give it.

"People here are not fighting because some intellectual comes from the city to tell them that Lenin said this or that. They are fighting because some fucking soldier is raping his daughter and cutting his wife and ransacking his land. He's fighting for his life. About communism, they don't give a shit! It's ridiculous! They don't even know where Cuba is, what the Soviet Union is. The Soviet Union is something like a mythological place, if they have heard of it. You can sell that shit in your country but not here. It's absurd. Absolutely laughable. How can anybody believe that? Marx, Engels, that's for people like us. They don't know anything of that. But if you ask them if they know the Americans, they will tell you yes. They know what the CIA is. That, they know.

"In the United States, you think you have a democracy, and you think you are free, because you can criticize. But all you can do is talk. There is no action. Your democracy is candies in hell. They give you candies, but you are in hell. You don't even know your own history.

"Do you know," she said, "that when Reagan was elected, the *contras*, they celebrated. With champagne. And in El Salvador, the right danced in the street. They drank champagne there too. The death squad that day, they executed some people, and they put up a big board, how do you say, a banner, saying 'Viva Reagan.' Oh my God, it was terrible. In the middle of that war, they were drinking champagne like crazy. Do you know why American elections are so important for Latin Americans? Because you elect him and we suffer him.

"You are the only nation that has ever dropped an atomic bomb. You are the nation that has destroyed other cultures down to the earth without a sense of disgust or revolt. Other countries like Vietnam. And you did not stop the war. It was the struggle of the people under the bombs who stopped it. You protested, you went into the streets, only when the war was beginning to affect you.

"But you will be defeated here, just as you were in Vietnam. Because you don't understand our reality, that we are willing to die. That is our weapon: our moral strength. That, you don't understand."

It was tormenting to be addressed in the second person. In the United States we speak of "their" war, Reagan's war.

"Maybe," I said, "the generation that *was* revolted by the Vietnam war, that did protest, was too young and powerless then. Maybe now they would be more effective."

"Yeah," said Sofía. She relaxed and sighed. "I guess they could do a lot if they wished. If they really knew what is at stake." Then Sofía smiled at me, and changed the conversation.

Later I realized, when I remembered her sigh, that it was of resignation. Sofía was less naïve than I. Not more cynical, but less naïve.

I saw her in her house once more, and we talked through the Managua dusk again, smoked and talked.

I knew the odds were I wouldn't see her again. Chances were, she'd die. If there were a U.S. invasion, she would surely die, with thousands of other Nicaraguans, before she learned to love her masters.

And even if there were no invasion, chances were there

would still be a war next year, and she would probably be mobilized again. If she recovered from the dysentery.

But that wasn't what we spoke about.

"I used to call them the Amazons," she said of her girlfriends in Pantasma, "because we were so insecure. We were like the Three Musketeers, but like a joke, you know. You should have seen us. We were always walking like those cowboys—how do you say?—ladykillers! Like this... pretending we were John Wayne or something. And we would just go crazy laughing. But I laughed most when we went to the river to wash ourselves, because the river was full of stones, and we were always falling over. We looked so clumsy. So then we would call out to each other, 'Who will be the bravest? Who will kill the most *contras*?' But, you know, we were too scared to be funny all the time."

Still, she laughed.

"I hope I don't make a sad figure," she said to me later.

"No," I said.

"I wanted to be cheerful," she said. "I don't think this is about sadness."

"No, I understand, it's about hope," I said.

We both put out our cigarettes.

"We smoke like hell!" Sofía said.

I drove up to Pantasma anyway. Just, as Sofía would say, to "get the feeling." I knew that the fighting was bad up north, but as we threaded our way in a jeep on roads so steep that the men there plant corn on with ropes around their waists, there was only the sun-scorched mountains, the smoking volcanoes, the withered jungles, Spanish moss weeping heavy on diseased trees and, from time to time, a truck, a man on a brown horse, or an oxen-driven cart.

And in Pantasma, there was nothing more to see, only the same dull scars on the landscape. In the cantina where the journalist from Managua who had once been chic had been thrilled to get a drink and see her friends when she came down from the mountain, the shutters were half drawn.

There was only the owner, whipping his dog, and a pregnant peasant woman slowly lifting a Coke bottle to her lips. Outside on the porch, an idiot marched back and forth, using a stick for a rifle; he was standing guard against the second attack, which the inhabitants of Pantasma knew would come eventually.

In the evening, the inhabitants of the town would hold militia practice in earnest, after their reading lessons and their meals of beans and rice. And then some would stand guard while others slept. There would be only the sound of the dogs barking from time to time, but the people of Pantasma often stay awake to listen.

When we drove back that night, I saw fires on the mountains.

"Was it desolate?" asked Sofía on the phone the next day, my last day in Managua.

"Yes," I said.

She asked many questions. She became excited when she heard I'd met some of the local FSLN people. She knew they'd been in combat.

"What was her name, the woman?"

"Anna," I said.

"Anna! That's my friend," she said. "Was she skinny?"

"Yes," I said.

"Oh my God," said Sofía. "She used to be fat."

We were silent a bit.

"You know," said Sofía, "I was thinking about your reportage. And I was thinking of my girlfriends and what they are going through now, and so I would like you to make a low profile of my involvement."

"What aspect of it?"

"The aspect of my being a soldier. You see?"

"It's impossible to tell the story without it," I said. "And, you know, I'll have to simplify everything."

"Well, I would like it not to be overemphasized, my being a soldier for a moment."

Back in New York, I didn't answer my phone for a couple of days. But then I called a friend.

"How was it?" he asked.

"Rough."

He laughed. "I guess I won't have to hear any more of this moony stuff about how great Nicaragua is," he said.

"I want to tell you," Sofía had said, "about the earthquake. I don't know if this will interest you, but for many of us it was the first lesson. Lesson number one."

"All right," I'd said.

It was on the 22nd of December, 1972, at midnight. Have you seen the clock on the cathedral? It struck and it stopped at that hour. The whole world that I knew stopped at that hour. I'd been in the house with my family, I was the little girl of Mommy and Poppy, and we had a house of our own, and so forth, and we were sleeping. In fifteen seconds, everything was gone. We were in the street. It was the first time I ever really suffered hunger. Real hunger. Nothing to eat. Everything we had was destroyed. Out in the street, people were in their nightclothes. I recall that just as we went out, the whole block of houses in front of us just fell, like this, and we heard the screams of the people, and the whole world was shaking. I really thought it was the end of the world. And it was hot, terribly hot. And it was dark, dark, dark. You could barely see anything, just the whole thing moving. I'd gotten out with just my blanket, in my panties, and I was shaking and terrorized. It wasn't until dawn that I realized that I was almost naked and that our house was destroyed.

We spent a week on that very street, because we didn't know what to do, or how to get out of the city. That week, we had four hundred tremors. We looked for other people in the family, to find out who was alive and who was dead. The looting and robbery had started. There was no light, there was no water, there was no food. People would kill you for a piece of food. We spent a week without eating. Whatever little water was left was given to the children who had survived, but there wasn't enough. There was the lake, but it was contaminated, but after a few days there was no choice but to drink that dirty water, because you were so thirsty.

There were many people who had been crushed to death. And you couldn't bury them anywhere, because it was an asphalt city. There were thousands of corpses. The stench was horrible.

One of my brothers had dared to go into the house and he had gotten a shirt out for me, one of his shirts, a big shirt. I looked crazy, my hair all full of pebbles and mud. I looked like the Gorgon, with my long hair. I kept shaking. We all slept on the street. We slept together, on our street, for protection, while the children screamed and screamed. Because, you see, it was a middle-class neighborhood.

The thing is that the people in the poor neighborhoods, in the slums, they were not affected, because their houses were cardboard houses, and on the outskirts. So they took their revenge. They said it was the punishment of God and they felt entitled to take from the city what it had always denied them, and especially from the rich. So they came like locusts into the city and they would go to the rich neighborhoods and just grab things. You should have seen some of these images: a poor person carrying—I don't know—something that was useless in his house, like a color TV. Why the hell would they want a color TV? They had no electricity. No one they knew had electricity. Others were simply looking for food.

And that's when the *guardias* came, because the regime was frightened that this event would cause a terrible upheaval by the people against the dictatorship. So they sent the *guardias* in to prevent rioting, they said.

I saw them first when my brother and I walked across the city in the rubble to try to find my sister. They had some men against a wall, who had been looting. "Don't look! Run!" said my brother. So we ran. But then we looked back and we saw the *guardias* shoot the men and then take the bags of loot themselves.

Then they said they were going to close the city, to prevent an epidemic, they said. But there were still many people inside the houses, still alive, their relatives wouldn't leave without them. Yet you could not pull them out—they were trapped. So the *guardias*, they went from house to house. They would just come and pull out a gun and they would go, "Tick. Tick. Tick." Everywhere they saw a part of a human body moving, they would shoot. Because it was too much work, too much trouble to save anybody until international aid came.

People started forming groups to save their relatives, because they knew that if the *guardias* came, they would kill them. We moved about in the dark, it was grotesque, it was Dantesque. And then fires started all over the city, because they just started dynamiting the buildings, with whoever was left inside.

And so the exodus began. We were some of the last to leave. They said they would bomb the city and destroy what was left.

I miss the old city. I miss walking in the streets. People used to stroll a lot. And we had the very peculiar habit, like in all towns of Nicaragua, to sit out in front of our houses on rocking chairs, and have coffee or tea, and say hello to everyone who passes by.

Now it's become a city of cars. But, you know, I love it. In its poverty and its wounds, in its shit. In how ugly it is. Because it is ours. It's what we have, and also what we'll spend our life reconstructing. I love every little... You don't know. An American would say, "What has the revolution done?" Probably for them it's not much. It's just poor houses. But for us, we know that where there used to be a dirt road there's a paved road. Every little paved stone we put in the street means so much for us and for them. It's difficult to explain to someone who has everything.

But the old Managua is a city that still lives, in our memory. Many foreigners here laugh because we have no addresses. We say, "I'll meet you two blocks from where the Grand Hotel used to be." Even though there has not been a Grand Hotel for over a decade.

I'll tell you something. There is a little street here that was called El Arbolito, because in the middle of the paved street there was one single skinny little tree. So after the earthquake, the whole neighborhood disappeared, and the little tree also, but if you are going to visit someone in that neighborhood, they will tell you, "I live two blocks from where the *arbolito* was." But if you go there, you will see nothing. Because the *arbolito* exists only for us.

Now we are putting names on the streets, the names of our dead. Some foreign press laugh about it. But these martyrs are like the *arbolito*. They still live for us, all those who tried to change things. It's not because we have a cult for death, but precisely because we have a cult for life that we do it that way and not the other. I don't know if you get it. I tell you, it's hard to be a Nicaraguan.

CONVERSATIONS IN THE DARK

Everyone she knows seems so restless.

Anne meets Luke regularly for dinner, and sometimes they exchange confidences, because they're friends. The dinners are meant to be lighthearted, so the confidences are too. Old sex and drug stories, for example, that no one else wants to hear any more, now that everyone's keeping pretty tidy, or trying to, anyway. She's told him about her first LSD trip; he's told her about the two girls on the Sausalito houseboat in 1968 (just what you might expect). But, though she's asked several times, he won't tell her how he got the scar on his neck, an odd scar that descends from that very fragile hollow, just below the ear, runs alongside his jugular vein, then diagonally dissects the skin covering his larynx, and finally disappears, somewhere below his collarbone, under his T-shirt.

She'd known him for years before she brought it up, but finally her curiosity prompted her.

"Let's see. Which lie should I tell you?" he answered the first time she asked. "How about this? I was walking down the street, and there was Muhammad Ali, and he had the gall to give me this dirty look. So I said 'Look, buddy.'"

"Never mind," she said, laughing. "Forget I asked."

They meet once a week in a badly lit, ill-appointed, crummy Japanese restaurant in the West Fifties. They picked it because it's crummy, which amuses them, and because it's open late, which allows them to prolong their evenings, and because it's not usually crowded. She always arrives on time. He's always late. She's already had at least one hot sake by the time he arrives.

He tends to speak in longer clips than she does, especially at the beginning of the evening. Later, she becomes more loquacious, and then he usually tries to get a rise out of her, which amuses him. By now it's become a kind of game. He usually wins: she drinks sake; he drinks club soda.

At the beginning of the evening, she's cautious. Then she forgets. While he talks, she looks at his face, which she likes. Sometimes, when he turns his head a certain way, and the light catches it a certain way, she looks at his scar. She likes the scar, too; otherwise she wouldn't have mentioned it.

His natural expression is mischievous, but sometimes, if he's having trouble, with his work, for example, his features seem kind of out of place, which she also likes, except that she knows it means he's pretty unhappy. But it usually doesn't take long to get him to be in a better mood. Anyway, he doesn't talk too much about the things that make him unhappy. "Can't," she thinks. And she doesn't either, as a rule, though sometimes when she's had too many drinks she says something sad and forgets to make a joke about it, which irritates her the next day if she remembers it.

She got tricked, though, the other night. He was very late, and that evening the restaurant seemed particularly grim without him there. There were only two tables of diners, Japanese people carrying on opaque conversations. At the sushi bar, a couple of the more offensive types in the upwardly mobile line bantered with the chef, who wore a paper hat and a perpetual smirk. It depressed her to listen to their bantering. She would have gotten depressed just being there, if she hadn't been depressed already. Luke hadn't yet arrived, and she'd already had two hot sakes.

Leaning her arms on the Formica table, she drifted, from an idea to a recollection, back to an idea, to another recollection. "So chaotic," she would reprove herself whenever she became conscious of her mind's peripatetic course. "What does the chaos hide?" she asked herself.

That day, she had called a friend.

"Do you feel like going to a museum?" she'd asked.

"No," her friend had said. "I've decided never to go to another museum. I can't bear having to stand behind ten people to look at a painting."

"I know what you mean," Anne had said.

"I tried just last week. I went to the Met and there was this throng, you know, for the Van Gogh show. Poor Van Gogh. Do you know that only one of his paintings was sold while he lived? And here it was, like Bloomingdale's, exactly, a white sale, people craning their necks and elbowing each other for a sample of his poor mad, epileptic soul on those canvases. I thought of sneaking up to just spend a minute staring at an unfashionable old Fragonard or something, but it was too depressing to even cross the lobby."

Anne stayed silent.

"A bit heavy for this hour of the day, huh? Sorry. Don't know what's the matter with me lately. Do you want to go to a movie?"

"No. I don't know," Anne had said. "I guess not. Sorry."

"All right, I'll go to a museum with you. We'll go to the Frick. It's not so bad."

"No, you're right," Anne had said. "I just can't think of anything. I don't really want to go to the movies."

"No, me neither."

"Do you want to do anything?"

"Yeah," had said her friend. "But I don't know what."

"I know what you mean," Anne had said.

Finally, Luke loped in.

"Hey, baby!" he said. Which was a joke.

She smiled. She felt better now that he was here, but she knew she was too blue to carry on a successful pretense of anything else, so when he asked her how she was, she said, "Well, it hasn't exactly been a halcyon day, so it probably won't be one of my great nights. Sorry. I guess I don't feel so hot."

"Well, hey," he said, "no wonder. You need a drink." He pushed aside the two little white bottles already in front of her.

"Waiter! A hot sake."

He had a club soda, though, as usual. The waiter, she realized as she sipped the warm wine, wore a paper hat, like the sushi chef, and what seemed to be the house smirk.

"How's Michael?" he asked.

"Okay," she said. "Working."

"Joanna's worked late every single night this week," he said. "She's completely wiped out these days."

They ordered their food. He asked for another club soda. She had one too, and another sake.

Well, you get the picture, she had too many drinks.

Luke, though, didn't notice (or maybe he did), so he launched into one of his rather longer clips. She looked at his face. A nice face, she thought. A friend's face. She looked at his eyes, but he often turned his glance away from her while he talked. She looked at his scar, which the light now caught a certain way.

He paused.

"So, Luke," she said. "How did you get your scar?"

"Oh shit," he said.

"Come on," she said.

"Well, okay. When I was born, when I came out of the womb, my mother took one look at me..."

"Come on," she said.

He laughed and took a sip of his club soda.

Here's where she slipped.

"Look," she said. It was hot out, but, as in all cheap restaurants in New York, the air conditioner was on too high, so she wore a cotton jacket over her summer dress. She took off her jacket and held a bare arm out for him to inspect. Two-thirds of the way up between the inside of her elbow and her shoulder, there was a small, white, perfectly straight line.

"I'll trade you," she said.

"What is this? There's no tit for tat in these things," he said.

"Jesus," she said.

She laughed, and brought her arm back toward her body. She didn't put her jacket back on, because she'd had enough to drink so that she felt warm. She was tired suddenly. She put her elbow on the table and leaned her head on her hand. He looked at the little scar, still visible to him.

"I never would have noticed it," he said.

"No," she said, "it doesn't show much."

"Okay, okay," he said, "how'd you get it."

"Skip it," she said.

"No, tell me."

"Never mind," she minced, putting on a fake offended expression.

"Let's hear it. You know you're going to tell me anyway, now that you've started."

"All right, but it's a trade," she said.

"We'll see," he said.

"A boy did it," she said. But now she didn't feel very much, any more, like telling him about it, or making it funny. She was sorry she'd brought it up. Maybe she should have told a lie too. She tried to think of a lie, but she'd had too much sake. That was the trouble with sake.

"A boy did it?"

"Yeah, with a razor blade," said Anne. She stared at the scar for a moment. "He was holding a razor blade and he asked me if he could cut me there, so I said yes, so he did."

"That's sick," he said.

"Well, I don't know," she said.

"Long ago?"

"In high school."

"You certainly were a wild girl!" he said.

She looked up to see if he was ridiculing her, but he'd spoken affectionately, she saw. She looked away.

"It wasn't very wild," she said.

"Can I cut you there?" Rob had asked. Downstairs, Lily was playing a Chopin étude. He'd stroked the inside of her arm. He was holding the razor blade in his other hand.

She looked at him and at the razor blade and back at him.

"All right," she'd said.

She held out her arm. It was late in the winter, so her skin was very white. He had only caressed it with the blade, it seemed, but it had been deep enough to cut. The skin had parted. They both watched. For a moment, nothing happened. They could see several layers of flesh down, for a moment. Then blood had appeared inside the cut.

She remembered the day of the razor blade very well, even if she hadn't thought of it in years. But she thought of Rob sometimes. Sometimes more than others. She'd thought of him not too long ago. She'd been in a bar with two men she's known for years, and they were having one of these eighties conversations about relationships, and one of them had said to the other, to tease her:

"Anne always walks. She's always the one who leaves."

"That's not true," said Anne. "I was left once."

"Really?" asked the man who is her lover, interested. "You never told me that."

"Well, clearly, there's a lot we don't know about Anne," said the other man.

"Yeah, I was left once," said Anne. "Twice, now that I think of it, because once someone I really liked a lot stood me up for a date at the Fifty-ninth Street fountain. But that one doesn't really count, because it was a rock-'n'-roll musician. The other one was bad, though. When I was fifteen, someone walked out on me in a really bad way."

"I'll bet a lot of men have paid for that," said the other man.

"Yeah," said her lover mock-moodily, "I'll say."

"Well, coming from a phallic narcissist of the first order, I'll interpret your remark as a compliment," said Anne to the other man. "I'll bet you know a thing or two about punishment."

"Hey!" said the other man. "Let's not get personal."

"Exactly," said Anne.

"*No one ever breaks up with me,*" said the man who is her lover.

"*Really?*" Anne and the other man said at the same time.

"*No. They always rejected me out of hand before there was enough of a relationship to break up. Anyone who stays with me for any amount of time discovers my finer points, of course.*"

"*Of course,*" said Anne.

"*Any time I've had a long-term relationship I've been walked out on,*" said the other man.

"*That's funny,*" said Anne. "*I wouldn't have thought so.*"

"*Yeah,*" he said. "*After my Dr. Jekyll overwhelms my Mr. Hyde.*"

"*That's funny,*" said Anne.

She looked at Luke.

"Did it bleed a lot?" he asked.

"*I haven't slept with anybody else in almost a year,*" said Christine.

"*Really?*" said Anne.

"*The last one was Will,*" said Christine.

"*Oh, I haven't thought of him in ages,*" said Anne. "*I always liked him.*"

"*Terrible in bed.*"

"*Really?*"

"*Terrible. Too strung out.*"

"*That's funny.*"

"*I still have dinner with him sometimes, and I occasionally get tempted, but it's ridiculous.*"

"*I liked him a lot. That's really disappointing.*"

"*Don't even consider it!*" said Christine.

"*No, I wasn't. I mean, it's disappointing in the abstract.*"

"*You know who else is terrible?*"

"*Who?*"

"*Winston.*"

"*You went to bed with Winston?*"

"*I thought you knew.*"

"No."

"Well, at the time I probably figured it wasn't worth mentioning. I think Winston's principal erotic relationship is with his attaché case."

Anne laughed.

"I'm not going to bed with anybody else for a while anyway, because I've decided to get pregnant."

"Really?" said Anne.

"Yeah."

"You're really sure?"

"Yeah, I am."

"Does John want a baby?"

"I think so. I don't know if he's as sure about it as I am. I mean, I don't think he can imagine himself as a father. But he knows how I feel, so we've been trying."

"You have? You've actually started trying?"

"Yeah. It's weird."

"I bet."

"But it's the only thing I really want for sure."

"I wish I knew anything for sure," said Anne.

"Don't you think about it?" asked Christine.

"Yes, of course. But I don't know," said Anne. "I just can't decide."

"You should just do it. Just do it."

"I don't know," said Anne.

Last weekend, she'd gone up to Vermont, to visit her friend Peter. They drove into town on the Saturday for groceries. They were in a good mood. While he was in the supermarket, she ambled into the bookstore.

"You know what happened?" she said to Peter when he got back to the car.

"What?"

"The guy in the bookstore tried to pick me up!"

"You're kidding!"

"No. It was great. In New York, you practically never get hit on when you're past your twenties."

"You are telling me!" he exclaimed.

"Oh, I thought it was different for men," she said. "I always figure men have at least an extra decade."

"Not men with other men," he had said.

"Oh," she had said.

"Nobody's tried to pick me up in years. Years!"

His delivery had been funny. She laughed.

He started the car.

"Is there anything special you'd like to do now?" he asked.

"I don't know," she said. "I'm glad to be here. It almost doesn't matter, just as long as we drive by some more trees or something."

"I got some wine," he said. "Shall we drive over to the waterfall? It's very beautiful there."

"Yes," she said. "Yes, please."

At the waterfall, it was quiet and lovely. She sat among the tall grasses by the side of the river, and watched as Peter dived from the top of the falls. When he surfaced, he looked for her. She smiled and waved.

Anne and Rob were kneeling on his bed, naked, when he cut her with the razor blade. Did it bleed a lot? Maybe.

She remembers perfectly that the first time she met him he wore sneakers, chinos, a brown corduroy jacket, and a dark-gray cashmere scarf. He always wore the cashmere scarf.

It was at a chamber-music concert at the Donnell Library. They were introduced by someone they both knew from their high-school music department.

"Yes, I've seen you before," he told her.

She doubted it. She would have remembered.

"Yes," he said. "I took note of your physiognomy."

"Oh, you did, did you?" she said.

"Yes," he said. "I did."

The next day he spotted her sitting alone in study hall, strolled over, and sat down next to her.

"Hi," she said.

He put his books down on the floor and his feet on the back of the chair ahead of him. He surveyed her for a moment.

"I like your hair," he said. "I like long hair." Then he took his scarf off and tied it around her neck, over her hair. She drew her hair up from under the scarf and then let it fall again, but she didn't take off the scarf.

"So you like long hair?" she said.

"That's right," he said. "And long thighs too. You don't mind if I have arrested opinions on such matters, do you? I have very arrested opinions on everything. Let's see, what else do you need to know?"

Then, in prompt succession, he told her that his instrument was the French horn, which was the hardest brass to play, though of course, he was proficient at the keyboard; that his two best friends at school were oboe players (he named them, and did she know them—no? where had she been?); that his favorite writer was Sartre (and didn't she think of that play every time she saw the "No Exit" sign in the cafeteria—no? he certainly did, every single time, it drove him crazy); that he was the best student in the advanced composition class; and he asked if she was a virgin.

"That's right," she said.

"Well, we'll soon remedy that," he declared.

"Not a chance," she said.

"We'll see," he said.

With perfect timing, the end-of-the-period bell sounded. He unknotted the scarf and drew it back toward him. Then he stroked her cheek with a bit of the soft cashmere.

"It smells nice, your scarf," said Anne.

"Did it bleed a lot?" asked Luke.

She looked at her arm. "I don't remember," she said.

"You don't remember? How can you not remember?"

Lately it seemed as though all of her friends were either having affairs or talking about affairs. Even people with perfectly adequate lovers or spouses were talking about affairs, as in "Of course, affairs are ridiculous."

"Yes," she'd say. This time she wasn't leaving, she'd decided. Everyone she knew seemed so restless.

Not long ago she'd had a telephone conversation with a friend whose marriage seemed in trouble.

"*These things pass,*" she'd said.

"*What drives me crazy is never to make love with anyone else,*" he'd said. "*I never realized how much my identity was bound up in making love with a lot of women.*"

He sighed loudly, for comic effect.

"*Here's my theory,*" said Anne.

"*Let's hear it,*" he said. "*I could use a theory.*"

"*I think it has to do with our generation. Sex is just a metaphor.*"

"*You always think everything is a metaphor,*" he said. "*I think sex is sex.*"

"*Well, of course, but it's also a metaphor. Or, okay, it has other analogs, all right? But anyway, in the sixties it just seemed so normal to us to be promiscuous, you know?*"

"*So far it's not a theory,*" he said. "*It's a frustrating memory.*"

"*Well, and so now we're all in these monogamous relationships, or trying to be. But meanwhile, all our formative training was designed to teach us how to function in precisely the opposite situation. So even when we get into a relationship with somebody we really want to stay with, after the initial couple of years our old conditioning slams back into gear. So we're torn, in a way.*"

"*It's still not a theory,*" he said. "*It's a sad fact, and affects people of any age, under the ancient title heading 'The Quest for Adventure Versus the Quest for Security.'*"

"*It doesn't only have to do with sex,*" said Anne.

"*But mainly,*" said her friend. "*Or so it seems to me these days.*"

"*Well, I don't know,*" said Anne. "*I think not. Just think of … For example, speaking of the quest for adventure, just think of how, on a terrific spring day like this in, oh, say, 1965, you'd get into a car with a couple of friends and just take off. I mean, not a pitiful afternoon drive or just another weekend in the Hamptons. There'd be a few of you sitting under a tree passing a joint or something, and someone would say, 'Uh, hmmm, maybe we should drive cross country.'*"

He laughed.

"It's true," he said. "And you'd actually do it."

"Or you'd get halfway there, anyway. But talk about adventures...."

"I think you're right. Actually, now that I realize it's not just sex, I'm even more depressed. The trouble is, I'm so depressed that sex would help. A lot."

"What?"

"A lot."

"Sex would help a lot?"

"No, a lot of sex would help. With a lot of different women."

"You know what I think is going to happen to people of our generation?"

"What? Is this part of your theory?"

"Yes. I think one of three things is going to happen. One: we'll stay put with whomever we've decided to make a commitment to, but revert to our old habits and start having lots of affairs, and therefore probably feel guilty and torn. Or two: somehow figure out how to stay faithful and have a pleasant but boring half century ahead of us. Or three: leave the person we're with, and live alone in miserable, intolerable isolation."

"Hey, wait a minute!" he said. "Why can't it be something between one and two?"

"That doesn't fit into my theory," said Anne.

"If I could only make love to somebody else, just once. Just once."

His tone was so plaintive she laughed again. "It's too much trouble," she said, "for just once."

"Why?" he asked. "For example, why couldn't you and I, if we felt like it, just go somewhere and make love? And then we'd feel much better."

"No," she said, "we wouldn't."

"Just once," he said.

"There'd be trouble afterward."

"Afterward? Why?" he asked. "Why couldn't we just do it for twenty or thirty years?"

"Okay, here's another theory," she said.

"What?" he said.

"It's spring," she said. "Everybody goes through this in the spring. You'll feel better in the fall."

"The fall! I have to wait until fall to feel better?"

"It's not that long," she said. "Time goes by more quickly when you're in your thirties."

"Yeah," he said, "because we're that much closer to death."

"Right," she said.

It's true, she and her friend Elizabeth agreed, when you need a thrill, if you leave out sex and drugs there's not much left.

"Memories," said Elizabeth.

"Fantasies," said Anne.

"Food," said Elizabeth. "What about food?"

"Hey, I didn't say anything about sedation. We were talking about thrills," said Anne.

"I'm five pounds overweight," said Elizabeth.

"Not me."

"Did you diet?"

"No, I've been nervous."

"I have to start running again."

"I wish there was a new form of exercise."

"I wish I could just take slices out of my midriff."

"I wish I could get a nice, hot nutritious bowl of Beta-endorphins," said Anne.

"Work," Elizabeth had said.

"What?"

"Work can give you some thrills."

"It's true," said Anne, "but you really have to work so hard for it."

"Yeah, that's true," said Elizabeth.

"You have to pay a lot for a little thrill."

"That's true," said Elizabeth.

"Besides, it's not a new thrill."

"No."

"Do you know that Mae West line?"

"What Mae West line?"

"From Klondike Annie. She's trying to decide between two

men, one of whom she's already had a thing with. Anyway, she's trying to decide and she says, 'Caught between two evils, I generally like to take the one I never tried.'"

Anne had imitated Mae West's voice. Elizabeth laughed.

"Well, I don't know," said Anne.

"I'd like to go on a camel ride," Elizabeth said, "in Africa."

"That should be easy to arrange..." said Anne.

"No, I'm serious," said Elizabeth. "I've been checking it out. North Africa, like Morocco or Tunisia. You can travel around by camel."

"You're kidding," said Anne.

"No, really. I keep trying to decide what to do with my vacation. Doesn't it sound great, if you think about it?"

"It's true, actually, it's a good idea. Are you really going to do it?"

"No," Elizabeth said. "Don't have the money."

"Oh," said Anne.

"So," said Elizabeth, "that's it, I guess."

"You know," said Anne, "I think there are places around New York where you can go horseback riding. Do you want to do that sometimes?"

"That's a great idea," said Elizabeth.

"I'd love to do that," said Anne.

"Me too," said Elizabeth. "It's better than nothing."

"Let's do it. Next week."

"Okay, and then we'll go out to dinner and celebrate," said Elizabeth.

"Celebrate what?"

"I don't know," said Elizabeth. "Life?"

"Okay," said Anne.

"Do you miss Joanna now that she's working at night so much?" she asked Luke.

"It's terrible," he said. "I feel like I never see her any more. Plus I'm sick of staying home by myself."

"Why don't you go out?"

"I do, some nights. But it's too exhausting every night," he said. "I don't know how you do it."

"I'm tired all the time," she said.

"Why don't you stop?" he asked.

"I don't know," she said. "Lots of reasons."

Lily would knock on the door. "Hey, you guys, I'm lonely. That's enough for today."

Every day after school, when she didn't have a piano lesson, Anne rode back with Rob on the subway to his house in Forest Hills. His parents were seldom around in the late afternoon, so Anne and Rob and his sister, Lily, two years younger than Anne, three years younger than Rob, had the house to themselves.

Lily, who went to school in the neighborhood, was always home by the time they arrived, lying on the living-room couch, one denim-encased leg flung over the back of the couch. For a long time, Anne wondered how Lily got her pants on so tight; one day she asked Lily and the younger girl showed her how she lay down flat on the floor and wriggled her skinny hips into her jeans.

"Finally!" Lily would announce when they arrived. "And it's about time."

"We're busy," Rob would state, hurling his bookbag, and then Anne's, toward an accustomed corner of the living room. "We have business to transact upstairs."

"I bet," said Lily.

"Hi, Lily," Anne said. She liked Lily.

"No small talk," Rob peremptorily declared. "We're in a hurry."

"But I have nothing to do," pleaded Lily.

"Why aren't you practicing, young woman?" Rob queried in a professorial voice. He flung his coat and Anne's in the direction of the bookbags, took her hand, and headed toward the staircase.

"Piss," said Lily, and picked up her copy of *The New Yorker* again.

"And don't bother us except if they come home," Rob called down from the second-floor landing.

"Fuck you!" Lily yelled from the living room.

Anne leaned over the banister. "We won't be long," she promised.

"Oh, sure," Lily called back.

Rob kept striding toward his room, still holding Anne's hand.

"My transference relationship with my analyst is reaching catastrophic proportions," said Dorothy to Anne.

"Why?" asked Anne.

"Well, he's become the man of my life."

"Isn't that supposed to happen?"

"Do you realize what that means, about my life!"

"For heaven's sake!" said Michael's mother.

There was a pause. Under the tablecloth, Anne nudged Michael's knee with her own. His glance swung abruptly back to his mother.

"So," he said. "What else is new?"

Rob undressed himself, and her. His sneakers, her sandals, his chinos, her pleated skirt, his black crew-neck sweater, her black crew-neck sweater. He dropped each item on the floor by the night table. She liked to keep her underpants on, unless he insisted. Sometimes he retrieved his scarf from the bottom of the clothes pile, to take to bed with them.

"Let's have intercourse," he'd say as soon as they lay down. He always used that word. He'd take off her barrette.

"Absolutely not," she'd say.

"We'll see," he'd say.

"Forget it," she'd say.

"God," he'd say, "how primitive."

But they did everything else they could think of, on his narrow bed, with fingers, lips, tongues.

"Has anybody ever licked you here?" he'd ask, his mouth on the back of her knee. "Have you ever been licked right here on this very spot?"

"No," she'd say. "It tickles."

He'd set the alarm clock on his night table, because they often forgot the hour while he pressed his pelvis against hers. Sometimes he ejaculated by accident. "Oh shit," he'd say. He preferred to be ready.

He liked best to have her make him come with her hand, but her arm often tired.

"Unbelievable, all these years of wasted piano lessons," he'd say.

"I'm telling you, you don't do enough octave scales. You can forget Beethoven with those lousy wrists."

So usually he'd masturbate, while she watched. He used his mother's face creams, hand lotions. They were expensive and subtly fragrant (like the scarf, she now realized, which, in bed, he sometimes tied around her neck, her waist, one ankle), and he'd come in creamy greens and blues.

She watched, not knowing why she liked it. Sometimes he looked at her. Sometimes he closed his eyes.

"How can I take this every day? I can't take it," Paul said to Anne late one night last week as they were walking, on upper Broadway, back to his co-op apartment for a drink. On the traffic island of his block, a ragged cluster of homeless people sat or lay on the benches. He gestured toward them:

"Do you think I should have them up for dinner?"

"No," she said. "It's not your fault."

"You think it's not my fault?"

"No," she said. "It isn't," she repeated, because she really wanted to make him feel better. "It's not your fault."

"You know, the other day I saw a drunk lying on the street. He was only half on the curb, his legs were sprawled out on the street. Then a car came up and wanted to park right there. You know, it's hard to find parking spaces around here."

"Yeah," said Anne.

"So the car honked. But the drunk was out cold. So the car kept honking. And the drunk didn't move. Maybe he woke up, but he didn't move. After all, it was his home. The car kept honking, though, because, you know, it's hard to find a parking space. I could really empathize with both of them."

"It's not your fault," said Anne.

"Have you heard of this new magazine, Missing?"

"No," she said.

"It's a magazine for parents whose children have disappeared."

"God," she said.

"I know," he said.
"Well," she said. *"I don't know."*

She lay, between Rob and the wall, leaning on her elbow. Sometimes, when he looked at her, she smiled.

She liked it because it was forbidden. She didn't get much out of it sexually; she wasn't really awakened that way yet. But she learned that if you love someone, you want to see him come.

"Now," he'd say, and he'd ejaculate straight up, to see how high it could go. His semen splattered on his abdomen, the sheet between them, her hip bone.

Invariably, within minutes, he had an erection again. All he had to do was put his hand between her thighs, or even kiss her shoulder. He had an eternal erection, it seemed.

The alarm clock had rung ten, then fifteen, then, in another instant, twenty minutes ago. Each minute was now dangerous.

"It's late," she'd say. "We'd better get dressed."

"Wait," he'd say. "Wait just a minute, okay? There was something I wanted to tell you."

"What?"

"Uh, wait. I'll tell you in just a minute."

So she would put her arms around him again.

"Are you tired?" asked Luke.

"A little," she said. "Do you want to have dessert?"

"I've decided I'm giving up sex," Anne's friend Miriam had told her the other day.

"Why?" Anne asked.

"I'm too fat," said Miriam.

"Yeah, really," said Anne.

"I've decided I'm giving up sex," Anne's friend Alexander had told her the other day.

"Why?" Anne asked.

"I can't stand any more having to tell my lovers the story of all my other lovers."

"Yeah, really," said Anne.

"You know what I mean? You get into bed with someone and you have to go through the whole story of your entire sex life from prepubescence on. I simply can't go through it any more. It's too boring. It's too long. It's too boring. It's not worth it."

On the corner of Fifty-seventh Street and Madison, Anne ran into a friend she hadn't seen in a long time.

"What are you doing this far uptown?" she asked, "at this hour? Why aren't you working?"

"I haven't done any drawing in months," he said.

"Really? Are you frantic?"

"No," he answered. "My therapist says it's not surprising that I'm not working, since art is a form of expressive release, but these days I am getting my expressive release in therapy, only it's verbal."

"So I have this really ridiculous problem," said Gary when their main course arrived. "I don't know what to do, it's really upsetting."

"What?" she asked.

"Do you want to hear it?"

"Yes," she said.

"You know I've been having this relationship with this man, Keith," he said.

"Yeah," she said.

"Well, he's gotten a grant, and he's gone to Europe."

"Will he be away long?"

"A year. But here's the thing. There was a going-away party for him, and at the party I met the man who'd been his lover before we got together. And it was, oh, it's ridiculous, it was one of those attractions, you know, those strange attractions that are impossible to...I don't know. Do you know what I mean?"

"Impossible to resist or impossible to succumb to?" asked Anne.

"Well, I guess...both."

"Yes," said Anne. "I know what you mean."

"I don't know what to do. That's all I think about."

"Have you seen him since?" she asked.

"Yeah," he said. "Ostensibly for a casual drink. But it was, it was...ridiculous."

"What are you going to do?" asked Anne.

"I don't know. What do you think I should do? Is this a ridiculous problem?" He laughed.

"No, I don't think it's ridiculous," she said.

"So, what do you think I should do?"

"Keith is going to be away a year?" she asked.

"Yes," he said.

"A year is a long time," she said.

"That's what I think," he said so promptly they both laughed.

"Who knows what'll happen in a year?"

"Exactly," he said. "That's what I think. Anything can happen in a year."

"Absolutely anything," she said.

"Do you think this is a ridiculous problem?"

Sometimes Lily would come and bang on the door.

"Haven't you had enough?" she yelled.

"No!" Rob retorted. "Scram. Beat it."

"It's disgusting. You've been in there three hours, for crying out loud."

"We'll be out soon," Anne called out.

"I have nothing to do," pleaded Lily.

"Go improve your mind," said Rob. "Believe me, you're in dire need."

"What?"

Rob didn't answer.

"I can't hear you," called out Lily.

"Go flex your budding intellect, I said," Rob yelled. "But do it elsewhere."

"How?" asked Lily, trying the knob. But Rob never forgot to lock the door.

"Will you beat it, please? I'm not talking to you any more."

"Just tell me one thing," they'd hear from right behind the door. She was probably leaning her head against it.

Rob released an exasperated sigh but didn't answer.

"What do you think is the best way to flex my intellect in the hour left before dinner?"

Anne started laughing.

"Christ," Rob muttered for Anne's benefit, and put his cheek on her belly so he could feel it spasm while she laughed.

"Sometimes I feel like a pathetic bachelor," said David.

"A pathetic bachelor?" she repeated. "What are you talking about? Do you know how many married men fantasize about exactly the life you have!"

"I like the life I have. I see some of my friends turn into homebodies and I think, 'Oh, I couldn't do that, I could never do that.' No, I know my life is great."

"You don't sound very convincing."

"Well, everyone else is in couples."

"Everyone in couples is complaining," she assured him.

"I guess I have the life I want," he said. "It's just that sometimes..."

"Different prices," she said.

"Oh, I don't know what's wrong with me lately," he said. "I think it's my job. It's just not challenging me enough any more. I think I need a new job."

"Yeah, maybe," she said.

"Or a vacation," he said. "Or maybe it's my apartment. I really should fix it up, but I'm so sick of that place. You don't know of any apartments, do you?"

"No," she said. "Haven't heard of any."

"I don't know what it is," said Roger, "I just can't find a woman I want to live with. I can barely find a woman I want to have dinner with!"

"Maybe you should discuss this with your mental-health professional," said Anne.

"That's all we talk about," he said. "I think it's just that I don't meet the right women. You don't know any women I'd like, do you?"

"No," said Anne. "I can't think of anyone offhand."

If Rob didn't answer her, Lily would stand a while in the hall anyway. Then they'd hear her customary exclamation.

"Piss," she'd yell, as she stomped away.

"We'd better get dressed," Anne said. "We really have to now."

"Wait, just a minute," he'd murmur, into her belly. "Just a minute."

"How are you doing?" Anne asked Philip when he called her to have lunch.

"Oh, depressed."

"About work?"

"No, life."

"Anything special?" she asked.

"No," he said, "I guess not."

"Maybe you won't feel as bad," she said, "if you don't take it personally. The culture, you know, is depressing."

"Yeah," he said. "Hard times."

"Maybe you need a new job," Anne said.

"Yeah," he said. "I just don't know what to do."

"It almost doesn't matter what you do. You just need to get out of this rut. Almost any risk would do."

"That's easy for you to say, but you know there's the house, and Patty and Lawrence."

"How is Lawrence?" Anne asked.

"Oh, he's great. He's learning how to read."

"That must be exciting," said Anne.

"Yeah," said Philip. "It really is."

She always got dressed and went downstairs first, so that he could wait until his erection went away. Otherwise, when he walked into the living room Lily would invariably declare, "A hard-on *again!* Really, Rob. Barfo."

Usually, it was around that time that Rob's parents came in from the city.

"Well, look who's here," his dad said as he passed through the living room to get to the den.

"What are you devils up to?" his mother said, taking off her coat.

"Hello," said Anne.

"We're little angels," said Lily.

"We're working on a new theory of relativity," said Rob.

Somewhere else in the house, a maid prepared dinner, and the parents had gin gimlets, while the three of them lounged in the living room. In the raised, carpeted southern end of the room, there was a Bechstein, and sometimes Rob and Lily played Brahms four-hand pieces, or an arrangement of a Liszt rhapsody, while Anne turned pages. Sometimes Rob read through a piece of music none of them knew. He was a terrific sight-reader and, for example, could read through a Chopin polonaise at the correct tempo, which left Anne tremendously impressed and Lily impatient to try it in her turn. Sometimes all three of them would sit at the keyboard and struggle through the score of some symphony. Anne always wound up sitting in the middle.

"It's so unfair," she'd say. "I always get all the weird clefs."

"It's good for you," said Rob. "You're not rigorous enough."

"Shut up and let's play," said Lily. "I plan not to make a single mistake."

But he always managed to make the girls break up before they'd gotten through a page or two of the scores. He played his entire bass part one interval higher, or the hook line of "Where Are You, Little Star?" right at the beginning of the recapitulation of a Bach concerto theme.

"Keep going! Don't stop!" Lily would warn Anne, but both girls had already started laughing.

"I'm sorry about this week," said Elizabeth to Anne. They were walking down Lexington Avenue together. "Maybe we could go next week. Do you think the stable will be open Memorial Day weekend?"

"I'll call," Anne promised.

They passed an ice-cream store.

"Let's get some," said Elizabeth.

"Not for me, thanks. You go ahead."

While Elizabeth was in the store, Anne waited outside, looking up at the sky. It was that time of day when the sun appears for a moment and then disappears again behind the buildings. But the sky was still very blue. Elizabeth came out with a double-scoop cone. They resumed walking.

"This is great," said Elizabeth.

"What kind?" said Anne.

"Swiss almond vanilla. Do you want some?"

"No, thanks."

"Have some," said Elizabeth.

It had already begun to melt. Anne tilted her head sideways to lick the ice cream near the cone, where it was starting to drip. Suddenly sunshine struck her cheekbone. She looked up, her mouth still on the ice cream, and saw her friend smiling at her.

Then they resumed walking.

"Michael!"

"What?" he answers from the bedroom.

"I can't believe you threw your gum into the toilet again."

"It didn't flush?"

"No. I've already told you it doesn't flush."

"I thought it flushed."

"No, it doesn't flush, and I have to remove it with my hand."

"Sorry," he said.

"I already told you once."

Then they ambled back to the couches on the other side of the room and played whatever game Rob managed to invent that day. When they found one they liked, they'd play it for a week or so. For example, Rob made Lily memorize the street names from the subway station on Queens Boulevard to their house. The names were alphabetical. "Austin, Burns," Rob and Lily would start chanting together, which always made Anne laugh. "Clyde, Dartmouth, Exeter, Fleet..." But the streets ended at the letter "O," for Olcott.

"Pulchritude," said Rob. The trick was to continue with a word that at least one of the other two didn't know.

"Patellate," said Lily.

"Patellate?" asked Anne.

"That's okay," said Rob.

"Phalanx," said Anne.

"Phalanx! We know phalanx," said Rob.

They both looked at Lily.

"No, I don't know phalanx," she admitted.

"Disgraceful," Rob declared.

"You go," said both girls.

"Pawky," said Rob.

"Pawky!" the girls exclaimed together.

"Look it up," he said. He always won, and contemptuously denied Lily's accusations that he memorized words from the dictionary.

"I have to get out of town for a while," said Luke,

"Where are you going?"

"Haven't decided yet," he said.

"Hello?"

"Hi."

"Hi. How's it going?"

"Can't work."

"Spring fever?"

"No."

"What's wrong?"

"I don't know. Maybe it's this call I got today from my manager."

"What did he say?"

"He asked if my songs would all be done this quarter."

"This quarter?"

"Yeah, I'm a bookkeeping entry, this quarter."

They ate cashews by the handful while waiting for dinner.

"Did you practice today?" Lily's mother would call out from the den.

"Yes," Lily would call back, whether she had or not.

Anne would look at Rob, and if he turned toward her she smiled at him, and he slipped his index finger between the arch of her foot and her sandal.

═══════

She looked at Luke.

"What's the matter?" he asked.

"Oh, nothing," she said. "I'm sort of a wash-out tonight."

"You're never a wash-out! I swear."

"You're a pal," she said.

"So I sit around and wonder," she told a friend in her living room, "what the answer is to 'What does the chaos hide?'"

He smiled.

"More chaos?" he suggested.

"That's funny," she said. "But it's probably something really banal. You know, like object-loss or something."

Anne is in the ladies' room, in the stall. In front of the mirror, four women stand talking.

"I'm so bored with this job, I think I'll use the time to have an office affair."

"With who?"

"Has to be either Bill or Randall."

"Oh, please."

"Randall is out of the question."

"Bill's worse."

"It's a toss-up."

"What about Norman?"

They all laugh.

"You think they talk this way about us?"

"No."

"I don't have time to read the paper this morning," says Anne. "Anything I absolutely have to know before lunch?"

"These scientists have all these new theories about chaos."

"Oh, really?"

"Yeah," he continues when he sees she's really interested. "It has something to do with thermodynamics."

"Like what?"

"Well, I don't understand exactly. But there's this great term."

"What?"

"I forgot."

She puts two packs of cigarettes in her pocketbook.

"I know," he says.

"What?"

"Strange attractors."

"Strange attractors?"

"Yeah, strange attractors are these organizing particles. They used to think it was chaos but now they think there's a molecular organization. I don't know, it's very complicated and I don't really understand it."

"'Strange attractors' is a great term," she says. "It's funny, just the other night someone was talking to me about strange attractions."

"Who?"

"Oh, it was part of a long conversation."

She leans over to make the strap on her shoe one notch tighter, makes a decision, and stands.

"I'll be back early," she says. "Let's have dinner together, just the two of us."

"All right," he says.

"We have to have a talk."

"Oh, no," he says. "Is this going to be about the chewing gum in the toilet?"

She laughs. "Okay," she says. "Skip it."

Luke is staring down at his club soda. He's not usually silent this long.

"I'm glad to see you," she says.

"Me too," he says. "Am I acting strange?"

"No," she says. "Not at all. Why do you think you're acting strange?"

"I don't know. I guess I didn't have such a great day myself."

"It's too bad you don't drink," she says.

"All right," he says. "I'll have a sake."

"No," she says. "I think it's good that you don't drink."

"No, I'm not going to have a drink," said Anne's friend Linda.
They were having lunch. "I've got a joint I'm going to smoke
on my way back to the office."

"How can you work after you smoke?"

"How can I work if I don't? I still smoke every afternoon.
I thought you knew that," said Linda. "Right after lunch.
Gets me through the rest of the day, you know?"

"Doesn't it make you feel weird?"

"No. I like it. It does bother my sinuses sometimes, but I
don't intend to stop. It's the only vice I've got left and I refuse
to give it up."

"God," said Anne, "you must have a stronger psychological
constitution than I do."

"No, I'm just more bored."

"Impossible," said Anne.

"Are you really that bored?" asked Linda.

"Sometimes," said Anne. "It depends. I don't know. This
week my work is driving me insane. So maybe I'm talking
about the tedium of constant exasperation. Maybe I'm frustrated, not bored."

"I'm both."

"Are you?"

"Yeah. I don't know what to do. Maybe I should have an
affair."

"You know, you're about the tenth person who's mentioned
affairs to me in the last couple of weeks!" said Anne.

"You see a lot of people," said Linda.

"What is it?"

"It's spring," said Linda.

"Well, that was my theory, but I don't know. I mean, lately
it's really incredible. Or am I imagining it?"

"No," said Linda. "Nobody knows what to do with themselves."

"Do you have affairs?" asked Anne.

"No," said Linda. "It's too complicated. I mean, because of
being middle-aged."

"Middle-aged?" Anne laughed.

"Well, you know," said Linda. "I mean, I'm not a little nineteen-year-old any more, whom a man can just pick up at a dinner. It's complicated, it's elaborate. You have to spend a lot of time with someone. You have to have lunches. You have to get to know each other. You have to fall in love. It's too complicated."

"You think it's complicated to fall in love?" Anne asked. "I think you mean that it creates complications. Not the same thing."

"No, I think falling in love gets more and more complicated. Well, for me it is. I only meet someone once a year or once every two years I could even theoretically fall in love with. And it gets worse as time goes by. I mean, there are fewer and fewer people. But even then I can never position myself properly. Even if I meet someone who might interest me, he won't make a move unless I give a cue, just because I'm a married woman. And I'm perverse about giving cues. And who wants to give cues anyway, since the whole point is to have someone pursue you. I mean, to feel desired, not just to have one more thing to arrange, to organize, to plan, to calculate. Then I might as well just put in extra time at the office. What I want is something else."

"Well, yeah," said Anne. "But then you are talking about falling in love after all."

"Maybe. Oh, you know, I'm not too clear on all this. Can't sort it out."

"You know, now that I think of it," said Anne, "nobody even talks about falling in love. People talk about affairs."

"Simpler, for people who can't sort things out," declared Linda. "Lately I've been thinking about an affair really seriously. I don't know why, for sure. Though it's not as though I could leave Timothy. Sometimes he enrages me, of course, and there are things about our relationship that drive me crazy, but I figure it would be the same with anybody."

"Well, yes," says Anne. "I think, after a while, I don't know. I mean, I don't know how much it depends on the person you're with."

"No, I chose him. I don't think I'd be better off with someone else. I mean, I don't want to leave Timothy, at all. And the funny thing is, we even have good sex. In fact, it's often great sex, considering the ridiculous number of years we've been together. And he's ... well, he is my family. I mean, much more than my own family was. And we have a child. Well, we are a family. I guess we are. Which means a lot to me. But I look at myself in the mirror in the morning, when I come out of the shower, I look at myself naked and I think, 'I can't believe this is it.' I mean, I can't believe I'll never experience my own body again or someone else's in, you know, a new way, and that soon it'll be too late. Sometimes I think just about kissing someone else, just someone else's mouth, my mouth on someone else's mouth. And lately I think about this more, I mean it.... I, it hurts, almost, you know? Maybe especially lately, because there is this man I think about in a way. Well, that's what makes me want to cry in the morning, in the bathroom in front of the mirror. But I know I'll probably let this go by too.... I can't even figure out how to do it. The logistics, I mean. How and when can I ever have an affair? I can't ever spend an evening out without Timothy. He has a fit. Anyway, I guess I can't handle it, any of it, the cues, the logistics, any of it. So I'll just let this go by. Although, you know, I tell myself that, but then, whenever I run into this man, I..." Linda sighed. "It's bad."

"You know," said Anne, "it goes away if you don't do anything."

"But that's terrible," said Linda. "It's terrible that it goes away."

Anne smiled at her friend. "Well, just think of it this ⌐ she said. "Just another three or four decades to go a⌐ of this stuff will bother you a bit."

"Oh God," said Linda. "By then I'll be rea⌐ heart transplants."

"Hey, don't knock baboon hearts. Yo⌐ one someday."

"I wish I had no heart at all," said⌐

"Do you want to hear a joke?"

"No. Don't try to make me feel better. I don't want to feel better."

"What do you want to do?"

"The truth is," said Linda. "I'd do it, but I don't know how to handle the practical problems."

"You really think it's the practical problems?"

"Yes, I really do."

"Maybe it's because you're ambivalent."

"Well, of course, I'm ambivalent. I'm not free. I mean, practically speaking."

"I don't know if it's a practical issue."

"That's where you're wrong. You don't know. You're funny, you know. You're naïve, because you don't live the way I do. There are practical problems," said Linda. "I go home and have dinner with my husband and my child. What is the answer to that practical problem?"

"Well, I see what you mean," said Anne. "But there must be practical solutions?"

"What?"

"What about during the day?" said Anne.

"Timothy calls my office six times a day."

"Can't you have your secretary say you're in a meeting?"

"He'd get suspicious."

"At lunch?" said Anne.

"Too sleazy," said Linda.

"Well, I don't know," said Anne. "A weekend sometime? Or is that too sleazy too?"

"I don't know," said Linda. "It would depend on how it
          feel. I can't tell in advance, whether it would be

          ge it, you mean?"

          'd have to be lies, and so forth. But, no, what
                    the possible disappointment. Then I start
                              that's stupid. It means so little, after

          Anne.

                    sider the lunchtime thing after all,"

said Linda. "The thing is, we'd have to go to a hotel."

"Maybe what's operative is the hotel you pick."

"What do you think?"

"The Carlyle?" suggested Anne. Both women laughed.

"The Carlyle!" exclaimed Linda. "That's absurd."

"I think they have the nicest upholstery. Crewel, believe it or not. I stayed there once."

"But it's so far uptown."

"Worth it. The last thing you want is shabby armchairs around the room."

"Actually, maybe it's not so bad that it's uptown, so I don't bump into Timothy midtown," said Linda. "Crewel, huh?"

"Yeah," said Anne. "How sleazy can it be, in all that chintz and crewel?"

"Do you think men think this way?" said Linda. "No, I think they're much more romantic than we are."

"How's it going at work?" said Anne to Timothy.

She'd arrived at their house early for dinner. Linda had called to say she had to stay at the office an extra hour and to go ahead and have drinks without her. The child had been put to bed. Timothy and Anne had already had several drinks.

"Work? I don't know. Lately I can't concentrate. All I think about is sex!"

Anne laughed.

"Of course, there's nothing I can do about it. I mean, I couldn't think of having an affair or anything. It would kill Linda."

"You don't ever consider it?"

"No, I don't think about affairs, I think about sex. Sex is different from affairs. I'd be too guilty to have an affair, but it's true, sometimes all I think about is sex. Sometimes I don't think about it for a long time and all of a sudden there's someone and I think, 'I wonder what she's like, naked.' And I think, 'Oh, I'd like to touch that.' It comes in waves, you know. Sometimes it doesn't occur to me at all, and sometimes that's all I think of. It's sort of bad, lately."

"It's spring," said Anne.

"Springish," he said. "Almost summer now. It's springish and we're youngish."

"That's terrible," she said, laughing.

"Would you like some coke?"

"No, thanks," she said.

They heard the front door slam.

"Hi!" Linda called out. "It's me. Are you starving? I'm sorry, I couldn't help it."

She'd meet Rob after school by the gate that surrounded an adjoining park. When they were alone, he nuzzled her neck while she leaned against the fence, until someone interrupted them. One of his friends particularly liked Anne, which amused and irritated Rob. An oboist.

"A simple instrument," he once opined.

"Sure," said the friend. "Sure, Rob. Give us the lowdown on the difficulties of the French horn."

Anne laughed.

Rob took off his scarf and tied it around her neck.

"Cunt," he said.

She laughed.

But one day when she walked toward him at the gate, he was standing with his back to her, staring out at the winter-desolated park.

"Hi," she said. It was bitter cold, and her breath came out steamy.

He didn't answer. She hooked her finger on his belt.

"Hi," she said again.

He turned around. He looked over her head. She looked at him, but couldn't read him.

"I've made a decision," he said.

"What?" she asked.

"We have to have intercourse," he said.

"Oh, come on," she said, smiling.

"I'm not kidding," he said, very matter-of-fact.

She looked at him for a moment.

"All right," she said.

The subway ride was the worst part. It was such a long ride. *Oh God,* she thought, *I can't believe I'm going to do this. I can't do this.* He wouldn't even talk to her. He wrote in a little notebook he always carried, with his Rapidograph. "The Number Two nib is the only one to get," he had informed her long ago. She tried looking over his shoulder at what he was writing—naturally, she tremendously admired his handwriting—but then he switched seats and sat across from her, and went on writing.

"Are you angry with me?" she asked.

"We'll see," he said, and went on writing.

The train was upholstered in plastic that imitated cane. Anne stared at the plastic webbing. *Oh God,* she thought, *I can't believe I'm going to do this.*

The house was empty when they arrived. She followed him up the stairs. He didn't even hold her hand.

But in bed, he was a little nicer. He took off her barrette. He settled her hair on the pillow the way he liked it.

He looked at her, and she looked back.

"I wish you'd smile," he said. "I like it when you smile."

She smiled.

He rolled on top of her. But when he tried to come inside her, she shifted up slightly, involuntarily.

"Please," he said.

"Okay," she said.

He tried again but, tight with youth and panic, she was, as it turned out, impenetrable.

"Relax," he pleaded.

"I'm trying," she said.

"Relax," he whispered. "Please."

She shifted a little. She really tried to relax.

"Please, please, please, please, please," he whispered right next to her ear. It made her giggle.

"Please," he whispered again. She held her breath while he pushed.

"Relax!" he exclaimed out loud. "Oh my God, why can't this girl relax? What have I done to deserve this? Oh shit!"

She started laughing.

His erection, his unending, endlessly hard sixteen-year-old's erection had failed him. His penis buckled against her.

She wriggled under him with laughter.

"Oh shit," he said. He slid off of her and sat on the side of the bed, his head in his hands. "Oh shit," he kept saying.

She leaned back against the pillow and put her hand on her mouth.

"Rob?" she said.

"Oh shit," was all he said.

There was a knock on the door.

"Hey, you guys!" Lily yelled. "Hey, I'm lonely."

"Are you going to vote?" Luke asks Anne.

"Oh, yeah," she says. "Absolutely. Aren't you?"

"Yes, though talk about futile gestures...."

"I think gestures are better than nothing."

"Do you want to have an early dinner?" Anne asks on the phone.

"No! No!" he says. "A late dinner. As late as possible, to delay my return to my nocturnal prison."

"Don't want to go home lately?" Anne asks.

"I can't sleep! I don't want to go back to that cage. I can't sleep! You can't imagine what a horror it's turned my life into."

"Have you tried Dalmane?"

"I've tried everything!"

"How long has this been going on?"

"Weeks. Weeks? Centuries!"

"Maybe you should go to one of those stress doctors—you know, those people who teach you relaxation techniques."

"I tried. I went."

"And what happened?"

"Oh, he drove me wild. First of all, he tried to make me relax in the office. Which made me hysterical. *Then he told me about these various self-hypnosis techniques and everything. You know, conjuring up supposedly pleasant, soothing images, like imagining a balloon floating in a blue sky or something. Absurd! If I see a balloon, it's* bleeding! *If I see a balloon, it has a death skull on it!"*

"You're infuriating."

"I'm infuriating?"

"I love you but you're infuriating."

"I have to go home."

"Why?"

"Because I'm infuriating."

"We never have sex at night any more," says Miriam.

"Too tired?" asks Anne.

"No. We watch TV."

"What do you watch?" asks Dorothy.

"I can't stand it any more. I can't stand working on this any more."

"You've been having a bad time of it lately," says Anne.

"I think there should be an AA that would be Artists Anonymous."

"You mean a place where you could go to get help working?" she asks.

"No, just the opposite. A place where you could go to be cured of the compulsion to create art. You know, you'd have someone to call, just like alcoholics do who want a drink, and your AA pal would say, 'Don't do it! Don't wreck your life with this stuff.'"

"Look at this photograph. Do you think I'm starting to look like my father?"

"Not very much, no. Why?"

"My mother told me I'm starting to look like my father. Like around the chin, she says. My mother's been driving me crazy lately. Now she's in analysis."

"Oh God," says Anne.

"She calls me up, crying, and says that our relationship has always been a tissue of lies."

"A tissue of lies?"

"Yeah. I'll tell you, it's the last straw to have your mother in analysis. But, then, there's always something else that feels like a last straw."

"Sometimes," says Anne, "I think we're all sitting on a
haystack of last straws."
"A tissue of lies, I have to hear!"

It wasn't long before Rob told her one afternoon outside school
that he'd rather not bring her home with him that day, because
Vanessa was coming over.

"Vanessa, from my composition class," he said. "We have some
stuff we have to work on."

And that was it, for good. Just like that.

Vanessa, who was a year older, already—as Anne knew from
the school grapevine, which was very explicit about such matters—
owned a diaphragm, was very pretty, had longer hair, very silky.
And it was Anne's darkest suspicion that she was a better pianist.
Probably just whips through both volumes of the Beethoven son-
atas, thought Anne with some bitterness.

Is this funny? I'm trying to make it funny, but, oh, how she loved
him. How she loved him. How she loved him. How she loved him.

After school she now wanted no activity but to go home and
lie on her bed, face down. The twice-weekly piano lessons that
interrupted her schedule were a torment.

And, of course, one day when she'd been staring at herself in
the dresser mirror for a while, she went and got some scissors
and cut her hair off. She didn't even take off the barrette, only
grabbed hold of it and cut her hair off just above it.

And he never called her again. Only spoke to her briefly, when
they met outside school. Though, of course, she never let on that
it hurt so much. Never let on once.

"What are you up to?" he'd ask.

"This and that," she'd say, and toss her head back if her hair had
fallen on her face so that he could see she was smiling. She became
good at composing that smile.

"I feel like there are all these different voices I hear," Marc
said to Anne. "There's this passion that in a way I want to
relinquish myself to."
She said nothing. It was very late, and her eyes smarted,
so she closed them. He wouldn't even be talking about this if

it weren't so late, she thought. It wasn't like him.

"There's the voice of this passion, but then there are these voices of caution I hear."

They were at the Algonquin, having a drink. They'd been turned away from the main bar in the lobby, because Marc wasn't wearing a tie, so they'd gone into the Blue Bar.

"I've never been in here," Marc had said.

"I like it," Anne had replied, "because it's so tiny. Kind of comforting, in a way."

"It's pretty dark."

"I like that. I like conversations in the dark."

Now it was almost closing time.

"Last call!" announced the bartender.

"Do you want another drink?" asked Marc.

"No," said Anne. "Doesn't your voice of passion talk louder?"

"I don't know. The voices of caution talk longer."

He'd been staring at his paper coaster. He looked up.

"Are you okay?" he said.

Anne opened her eyes. "Yeah," she said. "Are you?"

"I'm sort of hungry. I think I didn't get enough to eat."

"I'm sorry," she said. "It's true, I wolfed all the peanuts."

The worst of the pain went away after a few months. And then, of course, it was another boy who caused her to have that peculiar sensation, most peculiar because it's the only sensation that is experienced with the knowledge that it will never recur, the tearing of that costly membrane. It was Rob's friend, the oboe player, who'd always liked her so much. It was easier with him: he lived in Manhattan. They were often alone, because his parents went away a lot. No one ever knocked on the door.

And, anyway, he really loved her. It was done bit by bit, or, rather, inch by inch, almost unintended, until the very last moment. Afterward, she washed the sheet at the kitchen sink. He leaned against the stove and watched her. "Are you sorry?" he asked. "No," she said, though she didn't know whether she was or not. "Do you want me to help you with that?" he asked. "No," she said. She could tell, he really loved her. She was quite in love with him too, actually. It was several months before she left him.

Rob graduated that spring. She didn't run into him again until several years later, at a party. She thought he seemed provincial.

When she was in college, she saw Lily from time to time. Lily, now fifteen, had dropped out of the Queens high school she found intolerable and would come up to Anne's campus at first for weekends, then for longer periods, to hang around with some people Anne knew only a little. So they didn't run into each other very often. When Anne learned Lily was taking heroin, she was so upset that she called Lily's mother and told her she thought Lily was hanging out with a bad crowd and should be brought home.

"A bad crowd?" repeated Lily's mother. It was already an obsolete term. There were already no more bad crowds.

"Yeah," said Anne. "Take my word for it, make her come home."

"I see," said Lily's mother. "Well, I'll try."

"I'm sorry," Anne said to Lily. But Lily never forgave her.

In later years, when she thought of Rob, she wondered what had happened to Lily.

That day, Lily had been downstairs, practicing a Chopin étude, the one in C minor. She kept making mistakes, though.

"B natural, for Christ's sake," Rob had addressed the carpet, and Anne had laughed.

They were kneeling on his bed. He was showing her the objects in his night-table drawer. Regular boy's things, mostly, but also some reeds and a pack of razor blades. He'd decided to learn the oboe that month. "I know I can do it in a month," he had declared. So he had borrowed a friend's extra instrument. But he had no reed knife, so he used razor blades to trim his reeds. There was a brand-new pack in the night-table drawer.

He picked it up, and slid out a blade. He touched the inside of her arm.

"Can I cut you there?" he asked.

It was late afternoon, late winter. Downstairs, Lily, dutiful, began the étude again.

"All right," she'd said.

When it had started bleeding, he leaned over and put his mouth on the wound.

Then he kissed her, so she could taste her blood on his tongue.

She'd had so much sake that it didn't seem strange to her, twenty years later, in the Japanese restaurant, to be back in the penumbra of that room in the house far away, where on the bed the two kids kneeled naked against each other with blood on both their tongues.

Lily stopped playing.

"You look tired," says Luke to Anne. "You want to go?"

"Yes," she says. "I'd better."

"Do you want to get together next week?"

"I thought you were going to go out of town."

"I'm not sure," he said.

"Oh," she said.

"I don't know lately what to do with myself."

"I think everybody's feeling that way lately," she said. "I hear all this, you know, chatter, about that. Everyone I know seems so restless. That's all they seem to talk about."

"What do people say?"

"They say they want a new job, or a camel ride in Africa, or an affair."

"Affairs are ridiculous," he says.

"Yes," she says.

"If what they want is freedom."

"What?"

"Freedom," he repeats, louder. "Hello? You've had too many sakes."

"No, I know what you mean. But I think people talk about affairs because they're analogs."

"Analogs?"

"Yeah," she says.

"What are you talking about?"

"Freedom," she says, somewhat indignant that he doesn't get it.

"Freedom versus love, you mean? Fun versus love? Fun versus safety? What?"

"Freedom versus whatever," she says.

"I think you're talking about love," he says.

"No, it's this chaos," she says. "All this chaos."

"But that's why you're talking about love."

"No," she says. "You know, meaning."

"Well, that's not a new problem," he says, but gently. He's humoring her now, she can tell.

"Does all this chaos hide passion? Or lack of passion?" says Anne.

"I always know you've reached your sake saturation point when you start hitting these rhetorical stratospheres," announces Luke.

"Does all this sound incredibly hokey to you?" she asks.

"No," he says. "Or if it does, I don't mind."

"Okay, partly it's about love."

"Yeah, I think so," he says. "It's pretty schematic: love versus freedom."

"No, it's not that schematic. Because, for example, there's one kind of love versus another kind, you know? But, anyway, all this has to do with a lot of other things too. Not everyone's talking about love, anyway. They talk about a lot of things. Some people have all the love they want, and they still have this terrible restlessness."

"Nobody has all the love they want," says Luke.

"Well, yes, but what I'm saying is... Oh, you know what I mean. You're just being contrary."

"Okay," he said. "I'll stop."

"I think," she said, "that a lot of what I'm talking about has to do with the sixties."

"That's just because that was when we had our youth," he says. "Everybody feels that way about the era in which they had youth."

"No," she insists. "It was different. It's different to have grown up in the sixties."

"Sixties what?" he says. "Style? Ideas? Politics?"

"Everything is politics," she says.

"You're starting to talk in conceptual fragments," he points out.

"It is," she insists. She knows she's being fuzzy.

"Speaking of the sixties, I saw *Apocalypse Now* again last night."

"Again?"

"Fourth time."

"It certainly is the ultimate sixties movie," she says.

"Yeah," he said. "The sixties. Wow!" Which is a joke. She laughs.

"I don't know," she says. "About the heart of darkness. Was that it? Or is this it?"

"'Whip the horse's eyes,'" he intones.

She laughs.

"That's funny," she says.

"I know," he says. "I don't even know why."

"What is it?"

"It's from this obscure Jim Morrison song."

"Oh God," she laughs. "It's true, a lot of it was just silly," she says. "But did you hear about that poll?"

"What poll?"

"The one about how two-thirds of the people who are eighteen to twenty-two are voting for Reagan?"

"Yeah, I heard about it," he says. "Let's not talk about it. We're both too depressed already. You need to go home."

"I can't believe it," she says. "It means that if people our age, if we turn out to be deadbeats..."

"*If!*" he says.

"...there won't even be anyone to take our place."

"I don't want to talk about them."

"I don't know," she says.

"And as far as we're concerned, we're deadbeats already. Why do you think we need all these analogs, as you put it?"

"No," she persists. "Maybe it's a good sign."

"It's a sign of nothing. Only confusion."

"Maybe confusion's not such a bad thing. I mean, there are worse things than confusion. Maybe what all these people are saying is..." She paused. "...is..."

"Lost the old train of thought, eh?"

"No. It's just hard to articulate. I just hear all these people talking, you know, about something. . . ."

"I think you see too many people," he tells her. "You spend too much time on the phone, you go out too much."

"Yeah," she says. "It's true. I just can't bear to spend a single evening at home. Too lonely. It's really sick, I guess."

"So why do you do it?" he says.

"I like to talk with my friends," she says. "They make me less lonely. And, also, it keeps something in place for me."

"What?" he asks.

"I don't know how to explain it," she says. "What am I talking about?"

"It doesn't matter. Don't worry about it, I don't know what I'm talking about either."

"I guess I'm just tired," she says.

"I don't really think we're deadbeats," he says. "I don't know why I said that. You're right, I was just being argumentative, I guess. In fact, I'm pretty sick of being told we're deadbeats."

"Yeah, me too!" she says. "I mean, as long as we're still confused, it means something can still happen."

"Good," he says. "I'm glad we got that settled."

"It's freezing in here," she says.

"Okay," he says as she puts her jacket back on. "Let's get the bill. God, that waiter really has a smirk on him, doesn't he?"

"Yeah," says Anne. "And you know what? It's a house smirk. Check out the sushi chef and the line-up over there."

Luke turns to examine the characters at the sushi bar. He laughs.

She smiles at him.

"So, Luke," she says, "what about it?"

"What?"

"Your scar."

"Jesus!"

"Well," she says. "Okay."